What people are saying about

Word Witchery

I was blown away by Katie's unique and rich style of writing in her poetry. I have never seen that before! Brilliant, simply Brilliant! Words are indeed spells, poetry is magic, and Katie's *Word Witchery* masterfully weaves together information that combines magic, spells, incantations, and historical information. A must-read for anyone seeking to harness the power of words and manifest their desires.
Shawn Robbins, author/co-author of *Wiccapedia, The Witch's Way* and *The Crystal Witch* with Leanna Greenaway

This is a wonderful reminder of the magic of words, from ancient love poetry and global traditions to a wide range of modern rituals. Katie celebrates female poets through the centuries and provides practical exercises to help us connect to that same fire of inspiration. *Word Witchery* is an invigorating look at the power of poetry and magical texts to bring transformation and healing.
Stephen Ball, author of *Playing Card Divination: Every Card Tells a Story* and *Elemental Divination: A Dice Oracle*

Wow! I was Captivated! *Word Witchery* is a truly inspiring, spell-binding, well-researched and timely book dedicated to the sacred feminine, the creative spirit of women, muses, priestesses, goddesses, and poetesses. Coming from a line of magical, creative women, Katie Ness masterfully explores the link between poetry and magic, between words and the sacred feminine, in the form of prayers, psalms, hymns, incantations, spells, rituals, mantras, and blessings. Profoundly researched

and brilliantly written by a writer who clearly understands the power of words. Katie gifts us a glimpse into the life of mystical women writers, often lost or forgotten, and includes pathways for readers to create their own magic via the weavings of poetry and magical writing. This book is a must-read for everybody interested in the sacred feminine, channeled and expressed through the magic of words.
Christa Mackinnon, Psychologist & shamanic teacher, founder of the Modern Medicine Woman Training and best-selling Hay House author of *Shamanism* and *Shamanism & Spirituality in Therapeutic Practice*

It was from sadness that Katie was inspired to connect with loved ones no longer with us by writing poems, prayers, spells, and invocations. Her use of poetry and word craft was the magical thread that tethered these loved ones to her. In her quest for knowledge, she discovers how innate it is in us to utilise the power of words to invoke a magical outcome. We've been weaving with words since antiquity from geometric symbols on cave walls, evidence of the beginning of language and human intelligence to pottery and golden charms inscribed with poetic incantations showcasing belief in the power of words to connect with the divine.

Within the book is a strong emphasis on the sacred feminine and the lost voices of women poetry-mystics and word witches throughout history in an attempt to honour their lives and works and bring balance back into our world that still leans towards patriarchal inclination. Here Katie reminds us of and celebrates the feminine that has been almost lost to obscurity.
Word Witchery is a fascinating, well-written guide rediscovering ancient voices whose lives and work have been fragmented, forgotten or lost. With the inclusion of practical rituals and spells for readers to incorporate into their own magical practice

or healing journey such as creating an altar, devotions to goddesses, tarot poetry, love spells, healing rituals, protection and banishing spells, abundance and prosperity magic, art-craft and talisman making and much more.
Scott Irvine, author of *Ishtar & Ereshkigal* and *The Magic of Serpents*

Word Witchery by Katie Ness gracefully weaves the practical and mystical worlds seamlessly together. This potent book explores the language of the soul, to help us all feel, hear and trust our innate intuitive wisdom on a deeper level. I am mesmerised by its depth of history, wisdom and spirit. I believe *Word Witchery* will live on as a field guide for the modern goddess.
Melanie Salvatore-August, Wellness teacher and author of *Kitchen Yoga* and *Fierce Kindness*

Word Witchery is a thoroughly researched compendium of spells, incantations, poems, and ideas. It is both inspired and inspiring.
Dr Rupert White, Editor of The Enquiring Eye: Journal of the Museum of Witchcraft and Magic

Insightful and fabulous. It's a 'wow' from me! The more I read, the more I wanted to delve deeper. It is articulate, thought-provoking, written with passion and from the heart — magickal! It is thoroughly researched across cultures and countries and times, and a practical guide to enhance your personal practises. A must-have on every witch's bookshelf.
Laura O'Rourke, Editor-in-Chief of Witches Magazine

With her gentle voice, Katie invites us to the poetic realm of word magic. She is a muse that inspires many and this book is a daughter born of her enchanting soul. The following chapters are intertwined with wisdom of many mythologies, rich in

spellcraft, adorned with personal experience of word witchery. Beautiful. Charming. Empowering.
Johana Reuter, Editor at Femme Occulte

Katie's opus is a mystical call to arms – an encouragement to explore the unseen spaces and seek out the unheard voices of this world, through forests of symbols that remind us just how much magic words can wield.
Chiara Amendola, Editor-in-Chief at Occulture Magazine

A wonderful book that encourages and inspires the reader to weave their own golden threads of creativity into powerful words and poetry that is truly magical.
Hannah Semple, poet and Editor-in-Chief at Pagan Dawn Magazine

In *Word Witchery*, poet and priestess Katie Ness celebrates the power and magic of words from ancient past to modern paganism. The first part delves into the history of how language is connected to magic. The second contains spells and rituals, including Goddess invocations, poems for esbats and sabbats, healing rites, and charms for protection or to attract what you wish to manifest. There are instructions for bibliomancy, or divination with books, as well as guided visualisations to let words take you on spiritual journeys. My favourite chapter is 'The Lost Voices of the Feminine Divine', which explores female esoteric writers and poets since ancient times. This book is a well-researched study of the magical power of words, a grimoire of beautifully phrased spells and rituals, and offers oodles of inspiration for literary creativity.
Lucya Starza, author of Pagan Portals titles about *Candle Magic, Poppets and Magical Dolls, Guided Visualisations*, and Scrying, and the gothic novel *Erosion*

Word Witchery by Katie Ness is both an inspiring exploration of the magical nature of words and a how-to book for developing your own relationship with that magical nature through the medium of poetry. From ancient magical texts to goddesses whose domain is sacred words to ancient Word Witches, Ness provides plenty of fodder to feed the creative fires that she stokes with rituals and spells built around magical words. Whether you're itching to create your own enchanting poetry or simply interested in the multi-faceted history of magical word-crafting, this book will captivate you.
Laura Perry, author of *Pantheon - The Minoans* and *Deathwalking: Helping Them Cross the Bridge*

Reclaiming and re-membering our Mother-Tongue, Katie weaves a powerful spell with the magic of her words; a guide to lead us home.
Siobhan Mac Mahon, Word Witch and TEDx Talk – Reclaiming the Wisdom of the Feminine

Word Witchery

Walking the Path of the Poetry Priestess

Word Witchery

Walking the Path of the Poetry Priestess

Katie Ness

London, UK
Washington, DC, USA

First published by Moon Books, 2025
Moon Books is an imprint of Collective Ink Ltd.,
Unit 11, Shepperton House, 89 Shepperton Road, London, N1 3DF
office@collectiveinkbooks.com
www.collectiveinkbooks.com
www.moon-books.net

For distributor details and how to order please visit the 'Ordering' section on our website.

ISBN: 978 1 80341 706 6
978 1 80341 902 2 (ebook)
Library of Congress Control Number: 2024940795

A CIP catalogue record for this book is available from the British Library.

Design: Lapiz Digital Services

UK: Printed and bound by CPI Group (UK) Ltd, Croydon, CR0 4YY
Printed in North America by CPI GPS partners

Contents

Although only breath, words which I command are immortal.

– Sappho

For my Grandmother and Aunt Carol, your words and magic live on and breathe through me, may no one ever again in any lifetime silence your voices!

For all the Word Witches I have Known/ Will Know/ Know – Keep on Weaving, Seeking, Chanting and Dreaming.

Foreword

Return to the land/of your belonging/dig up the bones
of the forgotten/follow the old dreaming paths.
The truth has been trapped/in a sarcophagus of soil and silence,
but there is a new story/more beautiful than anything
you could possibly imagine/and the time has come
for it to be heard.

Somewhere deep inside us we still remember a time when we could commune with nature, when we spoke the language of trees, when we – 'breathed in rhythm with the Earth/moving beneath our feet/ moaning in her ecstasy/a psalm written/in the body of our souls'. We are remembering snatches of this eternal song of our belonging. They filter through our dreams, come to us in ritual, in women's circles, out walking in nature, in odd moments like *'a remembering of something lost/and to be found'* and, no, we are not mad or weird or strange we are simply reclaiming and remembering our sacred interconnection with nature, with this Earth we call home. All indigenous cultures know, honour and celebrate this interwoven connection between us and nature, between us and the otherworld.

We are beginning to wake up to all that has been lost, forgotten and banished, overturned in the name of progress and the rational. For centuries we have been living under restrictive and patriarchal narratives which have been reductive of anything outside of their ken; ridiculing and condemning all other more intuitive, creative ways of seeing as superstitions or crazy or, in the worst cases, as dangerous or evil. So much has been lost and destroyed both within ourselves and outside of ourselves on our precious, devastated Earth. We have become disconnected from our belonging, forgotten that we are participants in the great cosmic mystery and guardians of this precious planet.

And yet – and yet there is hope, I believe, for we are beginning to remember. We are beginning to trust our intuitive knowing – that the Earth herself and all her living trees, plants and creatures are animate; alive with their own energy and wisdom, imbued with spirit. Remembering that our world is interwoven with all the other worlds, woven through with myth and magic, that we are a part of this great fabric of life, sharing the planet with all of creation, seen and unseen. We are once again learning how to communicate with this great living body of earth. Reclaiming the devotional and magical power of sound and words to reconnect us the great mystery that is our birthright. We had simply forgotten the language of this call and response, this beautiful reciprocity between us and all of nature.

This timely book is part of this vital revival and remembering. Now, here in this important book we have a wonderful exploration and celebration of the power and magic of words, sounds, incantations and prayers; how they have always been used to bring us closer to the truth of ourselves and to the great mystery of this Earth. Katie writes 'The goddess has always walked with me, like a shimmer, reminding me of the healing powers of poetry, writing and words and their deep-rooted sacred past as magical and devotional expressions'.

In ancient Ireland these *'magical and devotional expressions'* were called *Imbas Forosnai* (in Irish) meaning inspired illumination, the kind that the ancient poets in Ireland would receive after going into ritual; words inspired by the Divine, words imbued with wisdom and healing for the community. I came across this expression a couple of years ago when I returned to live in Ireland after 35 years living in the UK. Now, at last I had words in my own indigenous language which described what I had always intuited and felt when I wrote and performed my poetry – in an understanding that was of the body rather than of the mind – that the spoken word carries a special power of its own, that it can invoke something mysterious and intangible. It is as if the audience and poet enter a liminal, magical space together in which something is transmitted that defies logical or rational understanding; magic if you like, a spell. As Katie says 'Words are magic and that's why it's called spelling'.

Katie speaks to this beautifully in this book, leading us through the importance of the first sounds we hear in the womb, through the power of chanting the ancient Vedic sound Om, through the oldest known Semitic spell and the ancient poetry magic of many traditions including the Celtic and the mediaeval Welsh Bards. This book affirms that intuitive knowing and draws together many strands of our 'remembering' for that is what we are doing, those of us who are called on this path, we are re-membering *'piecing together the broken remnants of our tale'*. Now, more than ever, we need this forgotten tale, we need a new story, a vision for a way forward for humanity. We are not separate from the Earth and Katie speaks to this, reminding us of the mysterious and sacred energy still present at sacred sites, as if the land itself holds a memory. Speaking of a profound visit she made to the site of the Goddess Minerva, Katie says 'I felt there needs to be a remembering and a revival of pilgrimages and offerings to her at this site'

Since returning to Ireland, I have visited many ancient sacred sites and holy wells, places that are still very much still alive and visited. Trees growing beside the wells are adorned with rags and beads and scraps of cloth – offerings to the spirits of the well or left as thanks to the saints and deities for healing or guidance received. And on days when my mind is not too busy, I can, if I'm lucky and open, sense a presence in these places; a reciprocity between me and the spirits of the land.

Poetry is the language of the soul and it is often in times of great distress that it bubbles up.

Katie writes 'deep in grief. I began to write! My grief sent me on a quest to learn the link between poetry and magic, between words and the sacred feminine'. I too began my journey of writing poetry at a time of my life when I was deep in grief, lost to myself and to the world. The poems became like a bread-crumbed trail out of a very dark woods; each one briefly illuminating the path. Slowly I began to understand that the poems were both dis-spelling the patriarchal narratives that had colonised and very nearly destroyed my mind since I was very young and beginning to tell – to remember and unearth – an ancient story of belonging. A belonging to myself and my own body and a belonging to the Earth and her rhythms – The story of the Sacred Feminine.

In her chapter honouring lost women's voices, Katie brings these women to life again and gives them back their voices, encouraging and inspiring us to give voice to the truth of ourselves, to remember the ancient and eternal wisdom that has both gone before us and is within us longing to be born for both us and for the healing of our world. Katie speaks of people, 'witch sisters' and friends who have encouraged and inspired her along the way and we all need those precious others who see and encourage our light to shine.

I believe that Katie has created just such a friend for her readers in this book. Katie's book is a rich addition to the landscape of our remembering, our piecing together of a forgotten way of being. In the rich section of the book dedicated to ritual – and with plenty of ideas for creating our own ritual poems – Katie gifts us with the wisdom of her many years walking the priestess and poet path. Here we find sensual and beautiful practices that honour the body and the soul, practices that can bring us back into the truth and beauty at the core of our being. In these intense and difficult times, as we go through humanities collective and powerful shadow, we are reminded of the power of the Sacred Feminine to transmute the darkness into light, to birth a new world, to rise *'from the depths of our greatest fear/burning every illusion into ash/until all that is left is love'.*

Katie's journey has led to the birthing of this book, this gift to each of us, this wise and loving companion on our own journey as we too struggle to give birth to a new world, each in our own way. A world where we celebrate the truth of our interwoven belonging with all of life and remember our place within the unfolding story of the cosmos.

Fragment
Listen,
the whole world
is calling out to you,
pouring its crazy music
through the holy temple
of your own body.
Listen,
you know the tune -
rise up
set out
you know the way
home.

Siobhan Mac Mahon, Word Witch, Poetess and TEDx Speaker *'Reclaiming the Wisdom of the Feminine'*. May 2024.

Note: words in italics are extracts from Siobhan Mac Mahon's poems.

"The roar of joy that set the world in motion is reverberating in your body. The body becomes light as the sky, and you, one with the Great Musician, Who is even now singing us into existence

— The Radiance Sutras

Part I

"Poems are charms to be said rather than read. They need to be repeated like mantras before they can realise their full potency."

— Germaine Greer

My Path as a Word Witch

I'm nervously staring at a blank screen. Imposter syndrome hit me like a train. I say, *"How do I start the book?"* and my fiancé replies *"Start with Minerva... Start with the goddess, she'll guide you."*.

It's the full snow moon of February and I am standing in front of Minerva's Shrine in Chester, UK. Two months prior I lost a loved one to a stroke. Gone in an instant. He was only 66 years old. A tidal wave of grief enveloped me and an overflow of poetry poured out of me, like the Ace of Cups from the tarot. Tears and love and invocation surged. In an attempt to connect with him from the other side I wrote poem prayers and spells, they were my magical threads that tethered him to me with love, like a direct phone line to the otherworlds. I've done this before, I remember. I remember being five years old and losing my grandmother, the woman whom I had inherited a love of poetry and storytelling from, had suddenly vanished to spirit at the age of only 58 years old. Even at the tender age of five, I knew exactly what to do! I wrote her letters and poetry, folded them up and placed them behind a picture frame of her in her favourite dove blue coat, like posting mail through a letter box – the picture frame became a doorway to the realm she now resides in.

Grandmother Monica, was an Irish woman from Kilkenny, who married my Grandfather Cerealis, a half English Romanichal and French man whose ancestry dates back to the 1500s central and South East of France. My genomes stretch further back in my mitochondrial DNA to Sardinia, Cyprus and the Levant. The old magic of the Celtic Bards, French Troubadours and ancient near eastern mystical poetic hymns collide and sing in my blood. But I'm sure it does for all of us in different ways; when we look a little to the past, we learn more about ourselves.

Surrounded by hedge and river and houses and dog walkers I stood before Minerva's shrine chanting poetic incantations to her with my rune drum. I called upon her energy whilst I contemplated my ancestors and connected to spirit. A soft reverence in my voice coiling with the heartbeat of the drum in the bite of February's air.

Minerva's shrine is two thousand years old and it is the only known monument of its kind in all of Western Europe still in its original location. Protruding from the ground like a giant old tooth by the river bank, it looks more like a dishevelled witch's cottage, overgrown with wild flowers and small crooked trees along the fringe of its roof. Minerva is the Roman goddess of wisdom, art and talent. The etymology of her name means *'She who knows'* or *'She who remembers'*. It was common for poets and artists to petition her for inspiration and wisdom. To ignore her, you'd have your talent revoked. Known as a muse goddess, there's an expression called *Invita Minerva* in which if you want to channel creativity you have to invite her in and honour *her* knowing. At the time I was by her shrine I didn't know this about her, I was simply, as a pagan witch, priestess and history geek, visiting a sacred place in Britain and giving my respects because sadly this site is neglected in comparison to other magical locations across the UK and I felt called to visit her, perhaps she felt lonely and forgotten? I felt there needs to be a remembering and a revival of pilgrimages and offerings to her at this site.

Looking up at Minerva's weather-worn shrine, I pause, take a breath and suddenly blurt out *"I think I want to write a book .... A book about poetry as magic in relation to ancient women's forgotten voices and the goddess!"*

My partner replies *"I think Minerva has gifted you that spark of inspiration, that sounds like a wonderful idea!"*.

I thanked Minerva by leaving flower petals and a ribbon by her now weathered plaque.

Much of my creative expression, especially with words, comes from what the ancient Irish coin *Inspired Illumination.* It is like I am doused with inspiration from a divine force, a muse or genius and I know exactly what the finished piece will look like even before I've started it. This ability isn't something I can switch on or off, it is beyond my control and sometimes the ideas and imagery appear to me at the most awkward times – when I'm washing the dishes or brushing my teeth! Oftentimes, it comes to me when I'm around water, usually in a shower or bath when I can't grab a pen or pencil! But then, this makes sense because, although a Libra, my birth date 11th October is governed by the moon (the tides of the Balsamic waning moon to be precise!) and I have a lot of Scorpio in my chart. Water is my strongest element; it is my portal into the gloaming from where my creative inspiration flows from. So, to me, language and words are potent and fluid like water; threads weaving from the pool of resplendent light which flows through the tapestry of the collective unconscious and eventually permeates into our psyches.

I come from a line of creative magical women. My Grandmother was an Irish word witch and tap dancer, a natural storyteller who instilled in me a love of reading books and prayers, and when she was a young woman, she was a professional dancer for Blackpool Tower's ballroom. Her eldest daughter, my Aunt Carol was a playwright and poet (her life was very tragic and she only managed to publish one poem in her short life, in a book entitled *Top Poets of 1968*), she also divined with the crystal ball. My great Grandmother Florence read tea leaves for her neighbours and was known to cast spells and write poetry. According to our family lore, she was an English Romanichal (Rromani) who spoke Angloromani and would teach my Grandfather customs that were passed down the family. My Grandfather told me stories of her and the superstitions she practised, I felt pulled to these frequencies with curiosity and awe. Everything these women are, lives on in me. I am a practising witch, initiated priestess, poet, dancer and artist.

When I was a little girl in the summer months I'd spend all day, every day in my local rose gardens, in my favourite red dress, communing with the spirits of nature and writing poetry, spells and journaling. I remember making rose petal anointing water. I remember collecting twigs, stones and shells for my altar or making mud pies for the goblins and finding 'fairy dens'. I used the base of an old water fountain bowl as a cauldron. I've kept diaries and grimoires since I was 13, it was at this age I started learning about Tarot, dream work and the chakras. At age 15 I began stapling paper together to form my first haphazard book of poems whilst watching the film *Practical Magic* repeatedly. I excelled in Literature, Art and Religious Studies at school and college. At university I gained a degree in Fine Art with an emphasis on video projections involving poetry, sacred feminine and the subtle majesty of nature within and around us.

Whilst at university I stumbled upon Greek Cypriot students who welcomed me into their world for over four years and for four summers I was blessed to spend time in their country, visiting sacred sites and connecting to the energies of Aphrodite. She became a patron goddess of mine (it is even in both my western chart as a Libra and in my Vedic chart I am governed by Venus). I often revisit my dear friends Despina and Evangelos and have so much love for Cyprus, its people, their culture, songs, folk poems, ancient history and language. It is my home away from home and it cultivated an interest in hymn-like poetry from antiquity. The lyric poetry of Sappho to honour Aphrodite, the poetry-hymns of Enheduanna of Sumeria, the mystical bhakti poetry of Mirabai and Lal Ded and more.

A dear friend in my 20's encouraged that magical creative spark even more, I bloomed because of her fire, we grew close as 'witch sisters' for a time casting spells in the rain, cackling over herbal tea, co-directing a magical dream- like split screen art video piece together with a poetic monologue as the soundscape. To have a kindred spirit like that in one's life is a true gift and I am grateful for that friendship from my young adult past. A celestial firebird darting across my brooding quiet sky like a lick of flame red paint. At the same time a friend of my father named Phil helped me print out my first (unpublished) illustrated poetry collection, entitled *Fragments of Light.*

By 2014 I was beginning to be published in a variety of wellness sites, writing about yoga, wellbeing, reiki, the chakras and women's circles. But something was missing, for a spell I lost connection to my pagan and poetic roots. In 2017 I embarked on a year-long journey to be initiated as a pagan priestess which nourished my intuition, my connection to the sabbats and my Celtic ancestry from both my parent's ancestry (my dad's being predominantly Scottish and my mother's, Irish), opened me up to call in poetic incantations once more. I flew to Bali in 2019 to attend another priestess training, this time with a spiritual teacher Sharada Devi of the *Be Woman Project,* it is through her I took a deep dive into the energies of the sacred feminine and the teachings of Vedanta and Sanskrit invocation, particularly working with Saraswati – the Hindu goddess of writing, language, poetry and manifestation through the power of words, the voice and puja ceremonies. To be a part of a temple of women and to have a devotional practice to the gods – that liminal space of the other worlds gave me permission to come proudly out of the broom closet as a priestess and hedgewitch! Within the verdant jungles and sensuous thunderstorms of Ubud Bali, I said a heartfelt prayer poem, stepped into the temple with my sisters and danced in honour of the goddess. It was one of the most enchanting times in my life.

But it wasn't until the tail end of 2020 when I survived an ectopic pregnancy that the magic of poetry came flooding back to me full force and desired to expand out like the vibration of a bird's call in the dead of winter. Bedridden, unable to dance or practice yoga asana, deep in grief. I began to write! Poem after poem after poem. I was channelling something bigger than me. It was the first time Hekate walked with me – a guide during my grief. I was inspired to write poetic hymns to her, then Rhiannon appeared to me in a dream, a gentle mothering presence supporting me through brutal pregnancy loss. I wrote a psalm to her too. I was exceedingly unwell after the lifesaving operation, but regardless of how weak I felt, I plucked up the courage to submit my poetry to literary sites, I had nothing to lose for I had almost lost my life anyway. After over 100 rejections, I finally had three poems published and it snowballed from there. My grief sent me on a quest to learn the link between poetry and magic, between words and the sacred feminine. For thousands of years, we've written and performed poetry in the form of prayers, psalms, eulogies, hymns, incantations, spells, invocation, ritual, canticles, mantra and blessings and as a budding folklore & occult historian I find this incredibly fascinating!

Back on the February-damp mound where Minerva's shrine stands. I'm here with her. I'm alive. I am full of gratitude. I have two poetry books to my name published and an assortment of articles about poetry for ritual, goddesses and witchy topics with incredible occult & folk magazines, I am on the verge of studying for a Master's degree to further research and explore our innate desire to converse with the borderlands of life and death and where the spirits walk, through poetry and traditional craft like pottery, symbols on lace, Petra glyphs, mosaics and burials and I am learning to play the lyre so I may perform my poem-spells like the ancient priestesses once did. The goddess has always walked with me, like a shimmer, reminding me of the healing powers of poetry, writing and words and their deep-rooted sacred past as magical and devotional expressions.

This book you are holding in your hands is what was birthed through me from love and loss. It has been my anchor and guiding light; I hope you enjoy it. I have split it into two parts: Part one focuses on the history of our connection to language, words and poetry – magic. I've tried to keep things in digestible chunks so it's accessible and easy to find golden nuggets you find interesting. The second part is what I've named 'Welcome to the Temple' where you can find spells and rituals created by me (and witchy sisters) if you wish to incorporate them in your own practice or perhaps as therapeutic writing/poetry activities. None of the rituals are set in stone, adapt how you desire.

I also mainly focus on the sacred feminine and lost voices of women poetry-mystics from antiquity up to early 19th century as this is my passion, I have tried my best to research as many poetesses from as many cultures around the world as possible, which was difficult due to not being as well documented or their work destroyed but I wanted to be as culturally diverse as I possibly could so you may get to know them a little, perhaps writing about them and saying their names breathes life back into their forgotten spirits and imbues them with power once again.

I wanted part of this book to make space in our world to rediscover such incredible voices whose lives and work have been fragmented, forgotten or lost. And I wanted to create a space for those identifying as women (or who work with the sacred feminine) for their voices to be heard and encourage them to ritualise their life and heart-songs through the activities in the book and shine light on the women poets and writers who came before them, to inspire them to create their own magical writing.

Awakening the Tongue

Our Ancient Union between Words and Magic

I've always felt you have to name a thing before it comes to life, like a witch's spell. –Vanessa Ives, *Penny Dreadful*

Linguistic expression has enabled humans to summon their own enchantment, incantations, rituals, sigils, protections and blessings since time immemorial. Before musical instruments, before dancing and painting, there was the word and simple symbols.

Paleoanthropologist Genevieve von Petzinger spent years cataloguing Neolithic symbols written on cave walls by ancient humans. These symbols can be found across numerous caves in Europe and are dated to be around 30,000 years old. The symbols she found ranged from dots, lines, triangles, squares and zigzags to more complex forms like ladder shapes, hand stencils, something called a tectiform that looks a bit like a post with a roof, and feather shapes called penniform. These symbols also travelled: they aren't only found in caves, but also etched into deer teeth strung together in an ancient necklace. Homo naledi buried their dead and carved symbols on cave walls at least 100,000 years before modern humans which give evidence of funeral rites and markings to remember loved ones.

Clearly meaningful to their creators, these geometric signs are one of the first indicators of our human ancestors' intelligence and capacity for symbolic meaning and language. Perhaps these ancient humans wrote protective sigils, spells or runes? Or is this the beginning of words and language? Or shapes representing a person's name in the burial mound? Or perhaps they are simply artistic signatures left by the artist? Regardless, these abstract signs represent our innate desire to communicate with each other through votive, devotional and mnemonic means.

Göbekli Tepe, Turkey, is considered to be approximately 12 thousand years old and to date, the oldest temple complex in the world. Built during a time when the rest of humanity were still hunter-gatherers, archaeologists are deciphering the unusual markings and symbols carved into the stone among the humanoid monoliths and animal forms. It has been made apparent that the T shape is the word 'God' and the H shape inside a semicircle is the word 'Gate', it has been proposed that this place is a portal or gate to commune with a supreme being and thus these symbols are now considered the first symbolic form of writing (in reference to spiritual belief) in the world.

In a Channel4 documentary, historian Bettany Hughes shows us fascinating petroglyphs, inscriptions and symbols on a rock face of the Ḥismā Plateau in the west of Tabuk in northern Saudi Arabia. This place is home to Arabic inscriptions carved by the Thamud and other ancient tribes dating back more than 2,600 years. Acting like a message board for a trade route between these pre-Islamic tribes, inscribed in the rock are prayers and blessings among crude drawings of camels and other animals.

Hughes then takes us to Gobustan reserve in Azerbaijan to show UNESCO protected Petra glyphs called the '7 beauties' which are possibly female deities, priestesses or references the Pleiades close to tribal signs engraved on the rock called 'Tanga' with other surrounding inscriptions. The local archaeologist explains this was not only a trade route for the silk road commerce, but has been a sacred site for 40 thousand years. Hughes finds more inscribed prayers on the rock face at the bay of Grama, off the coast of Albania, written in ancient Greek by sailors petitioning the Dioscuri (Caster and Pollux) for safe seafaring along the tempestuous Ionian waters. A complex in Albania called the Apollonia, and dating from 7th century BCE, was much revered throughout the mediterranean as a culture centre of learning, trade, art, poetry and libraries. It was a place so renowned for its beauty and housing one of the biggest libraries in the Roman world that a temple was built close by which was tended to by priestesses, they kept the flame of inspiration burning. Coins have been excavated from the site, depicting these priestesses dancing around streams of flame. All these inscriptions and symbols are a rare glimpse into past lives, allowing us to bear witness to ancient civilisations communicating with each other, they show us what has mattered to us as humans. We have been writing as a form of mnemonic story-telling, blessings or for supernatural intent for a very long time.

Harappan is an undeciphered script from the Indus valley and it is approximately eight thousand years old, it is currently believed to be one of the oldest written languages in the world to date. What's interesting about this written language is that the symbols carved into the tablets appear to be an assortment of rune-like letters next to shapes that look like hieroglyphs which include the cross, the swastika and even circular symbols similar to ancient pictish petroglyphs and all the tablets include bovine creatures.

Rongorongo, which means *"to recite, to declaim, to chant out"* is another indecipherable glyphic language of the polynesian people of the remote island of Rapa Nui (Easter island). According to a 19th century missionary, these inscriptions on wooden tablets were seen in every family home as perhaps house blessings and claimed they numbered in the hundreds. However, when Europeans returned a few years later to collect them, only a couple dozen could be found. Four of the tablets have been carbon dated to about 200 years old. Although the wood is not that old, it is believed the proto-writing is much older and could be the last surviving remnants of this now extinct language. The script is made up of 120 pictures consisting of animals, plants and other natural and celestial elements. It is so interesting to me that a number of these lost languages are influenced by earthly and heavenly entities.

Trobrianders of Papua New Guinea belief declare that there are words that are primordial in origin which create a specific mystical reverberation when the practitioner breathes life into them.

In Eisenberg (221 CE) a votive tablet has been found that supports evidence that Nemetona is also a goddess of war as well as sacred groves. She is frequently conflated with the God Mars and Goddess Victory (or described as Victoria Nemetona). Therefore, as a goddess of both war and peace (in the form of sanctuaries and groves), she is actually a liminal goddess of life and death and protectress of boundaries (making sure battles don't bombard into sacred places).

On three hilltops of Slieve na Calliagh Ireland, there are a mass of cairns (womb-tombs) dating back to 3600 BCE, most of these monuments have been destroyed, however, remains of a kerbstone and interior slab are found which are engraved with signs. As with most chambers, cairns and barrows, these places were not merely graves, they were considered portals to the spirit world, these writings were a way to communicate and ritualise the abode. Remnants of quartz pebble have been found, showing these sanctuaries were once covered with this stone material and would have sparkled, particularly during solar alignments.

In the Beginning There was the Word

In the womb we hear vibrations and sounds from our watery world, as we are being birthed, we hear the first sounds of our mother's words and cries – this energy is the act of creation, bringing life forward, the mother manifesting the child into being and then she utters our name – naming something gives it power, a simple incantation cast with symbolic syllables. And upon our death, medical research has proven that the last sense to deteriorate is hearing, so it is innate to us to fill our ears with story-telling, poetry, well wishes, loving words and laughter.

In the beginning was the Word, and the Word was with God, and the Word was God. John 1:1 New Testament Scriptures

If we consider this quote that God (or an omnipresent force) created the world with the frequency of words, it alludes to the understanding that worlds were (and are) created through the utilisation of cymatic sound waves made manifest as syllables and words. We can observe these waves in nature, with each vibration associated with a correlating geometric shape that unfurls and expands like a mandala.

The ancient Greeks called this frequency *Pneuma* which means 'air in motion' or breath or the cosmic spirit. The Greek philosopher Plotinus describes pneuma as a feminine entity that vibrates through and within us as psyche.

Let every soul, then, first realise this: that she made all living beings herself, breathing life into them, those that the earth feeds and those that are nourished by the sea, and the divine stars in the sky; she made the sun itself, and this great heaven, and drives it round herself... Let her behold the great soul, since she herself is another soul. Let only her encompassing body and the body's raging sea be quiet, and the sea and air quiet, and the heaven itself at peace. Into this heaven at rest, let her imagine psyche as if flowing in from outside, pouring in and entering it everywhere and illuminating it: as the rays of the sun light up a dark cloud, and make it shine and give it a golden look, so psyche flowing into the body of heaven gives it life and gives it immortality and awaken what lies at rest. (Plotinus, Enneads 5.1.2)

Everything that exists is energy and resonance so as we speak words, our vocal cords in the larynx create vibrations. These sounds are pure energy and these frequencies can be directed. When we are conscious of this, we gain awareness that we can harness and wield our worlds with words in the same dynamic as God (lifeforce). Through our words we create our reality.

This energy is known by many names by many cultures across the globe, *Qi* in China, *Ki* (Reiki) in Japan, *nilchi'i* in Navajo, *prana* in Hindu philosophy and *Nwyfre* to the Celtic druids. Rendering this intrinsic spirit through intention, breath and vocal vibration we begin to birth our worlds through words.

In ancient Vedic scriptures the syllable 'Om' is considered a magical sound to utter and was incorporated at the beginning and end of fire rituals and sacrifice of which is no longer practised. However, Om is still embraced today within meditation and puja ceremonies as a vibrational fire cleansing of the subtle body and mind – ultimately connecting us to the old ways of sun worship and to our own inner flame (sun) in our navel of which all other organs and chakras swirl around it like the planets – It stokes and churns our internal *Agni* (Agni is a Sanskrit word for 'fire' and represents both our inner fire energy within our digestive system/solar plexus and is the name of the god of fire. Our internal Agni churns our prana) to encourage an inner sacrifice of the ego and what does not serve us, so that we can regain liberation from our karmic constraints and be close to the source – Our *hOMe.* Uttering the sound of Om is a sonic spell and is considered to symbolise the Goddess of Speech called Saraswati who is patroness of words, language, music, learning and the mother of the Vedas.

Om is considered, metaphorically as a cosmic egg from which the potential of all frequencies and words manifest in the *wOMb* of the divine mother – the one who births life with her sacred words (Sarswati), the one who invokes growth and abundance (Laksmi), the mother who protects all her children as they walk through life (Durga) and the destroyer goddess who wields time and ends our Om (our vibration) when our time is up (Kali), to be reborn again as the next potential reverberation made manifest.

The Vedas, (from which Om resides) are ancient Hindu sacred poems written in Sanskrit. They contain mystical messages, charms, spells and incantations in the form of epic poetry and devotional chants known as 'Mantra'. The etymology of the word 'mantra' is 'To Think' – meaning 'sacred text used as a charm or incantation to manifest thoughts'.

OM moves the prana [spirit] or the cosmic vital force. In man, OM expresses prana or the vital breath. In every breath, man utters it, repeats it unintentionally and inevitably. Every vibration in the body and in the universe emerges from OM, sustains in OM, and returns to OM.

Every humming emerges from OM, sustains in OM and returns to OM. A child cries, "OM, OM;" musicians hum, "OM, OM;" bees buzz, "OM, OM" the ocean roars, "OM, OM. –Ford Johnson, *Confessions of a God Seeker: A Journey to Higher Consciousness*

The Druidic version of Om is *Hu* and linked to a deity named Hesus (potentially an early Christian druid hybrid of Jesus) whose attributes are associated with the great oak and also the sun disc. Hu is as an epithet of this deity, in reference to the masculine omniscience and An is the sound representing the feminine, and these syllables have been known to be used frequently in the chanting and words of the Bards.

Interestingly, the Egyptian minor god, HU, is the power of the spoken word. He personifies the authority of utterance and in Mandarin Hu translates to 'call', to 'cry out', to 'breath out', to 'exhale'. Exhaling out the frequency of your divine words.

Aristotle tells us that the first Oracle, a Priestess at Delphi, bore the name Phēmonoē which means *She who speaks the mind of God*. Chilōn, the Sage of Sparta, made a pilgrimage to ask her: "What is the most important thing for a human being to learn?" And Phēmonoē chanted: ΓΝΩΘΙ ΣΕΑΥΤΟΝ – KNOW THYSELF. (translation: gnōthi Seauton).

To know thyself is to be conscious of one's words and actions, to simultaneously go within to your psyche and expand it out to the collective pneuma – to inhale and exhale your vibration resonating with the greater Om or Hu or Qi. We do this with poetry, singing, chanting, storytelling, writing, sigils, incantation and invocation – any way that this energy can move through us and we can harness and direct it with intention and awareness, thus enabling us to weave, alchemise and transmute our human experiences like love and pain via our words.

And it is said that words are spells, that's why they call it 'spelling'. The word 'Magic' has roots in old Persian 'Magush' meaning 'to have power'. In other words, we spell out the power of the world-soul with our words. The world-soul can speak through us and the signature of all things.

The Latin word *grimoire* means "book of spells." So, to spell a sentence is to sentence someone to your spell. We all perform magic whether we are conscious of it or not. Whenever we speak, we *are* casting spells.

Consider this: When we add an ***S*** in front of the word ***Word*** it becomes ***Sword***. We now see that symbolically this means words can become weapons, words can cut deeply. When you add an ***L*** in the middle of ***Word*** it creates ***WORLD***. And like the World tarot card, this word is always in motion, an energy of whirling and wholeness as a huge cosmic cyclical force of energy and represents cosmic consciousness; the potential of perfect union with the One Power of the universe.

All of these words sound similar because they are connected. Be careful with your words, they can become swords or worlds. They can harm or heal.

If there is one chant in the universe; It is to Create –Chris Griscom

From the historical archives and archeological artefacts, we know there was once a sacred connection between chanting wordcraft or poetry and the gods, whether you were a wife singing a joyful folk blessing as you baked bread sending good health into your food, a mother humming soothing lullabies to your babies for protection from disease or a high priestess invoking a goddess with a poetic hymn in the temple space for good harvest, fertility and rain. It all had the same resonance.

You can see flickers of this resonance for poetry in later historical artefacts such as the lyrical knives at the Victoria & Albert Museum, London. These rare 16th century Italian knives are engraved with poetic melodies and musical notes. One such knife reads: *"The blessing of the table. May the three-in-one bless that which we are about to eat."* And the other side reads: *"The saying of grace. We give thanks to you God for your generosity."* An art historian and musicologist researching the knives have found the rest of the set in the USA, Belgium, France and other parts of the world and has managed to recreate what the benediction and grace would have sounded like with an operatic choir. In short, these musical knives were used to encourage chanting prayers and blessings at a renaissance banquet.

In our increasingly capitalist and consumerist world it is quite difficult to quantify and explain why craft and storytelling matters, why it's a devotional practice imbued with meaning and love. However, if you consider the COVID pandemic of 2020, it was a frightening time, it was a time of immense global trauma and tragedy – we thought our world as we know it was going to end. After we took inventory of our basic needs, what else did we do? We started to get creative! We shared poetry, funny dance videos, songs, online theatre productions and plays and more. This is a time of great crisis and yet humans have this intrinsic need to express ourselves and communicate creatively as a way to cope, process and even remember – a sort of modern oral folktale tradition via songs, stories and poems. There was even an increase in an interest in paganism, folklore and the occult which is a common occurrence when you see a great transitional period in a community. In times when humans feel their most vulnerable and disempowered, we turn to beautiful activities to help us try and make sense of what we're facing.

> *...Even back in palaeolithic times, a really tough time of survival from wild animals and extreme weather, people are still finding the time to make beautiful things, like a jadeite hand axe, a lion headed human, drawing symbols on cave walls, we are hardwired to express ourselves through stories to help us through the tough times and bring us closer together as a community.* –Bettany Hughes, History Hit

In the mediaeval period manuscript creators were called *'Limners'* from the Latin *'Lumen'* which means *'Light'*. This essentially made them bringers of light and when we consider that the word *'muse'* means to reflect, ponder and absorb thought from a genius (helpful spirit) and that the word *inspiration* is derived from ancient Greek to mean *'breathe in spirit'*, we notice that we as word witches – as humans – are vessels of the muse, we breathe in divine spirit to bring light into this world via our magical creative expression. Our writing and poetry act as a bridge between the otherworlds and our own.

Excavating Magical Poetica

I worship in my heart, the Goddess. Whose body is awash in ambrosia, beautiful like lightning, who, going from her abode to Shiva's royal palace, opens the lotuses of the lovely axial channel –Bhairav-Stotra

In this chapter are a collection of digestible nuggets I've excavated to show that we've been utilising poetry as a way to invoke or manifest an outcome in a magical way since the dawn of civilisation which came out of the fertile crescent in what is now modern day Near East. These are incredibly fascinating historical artefacts and archeological finds of poem-spells inscribed on objects, poetic hymns to deity marked on clay tablets – used for sacred ceremony, fragments of fragile pieces of poetic charms and writings on papyrus and parchment as well as petroglyphic symbols and writings on rock faces of deserts and mountains.

The Ancient Near East

Lady coloured like the stars of heaven, holding a lapis-lazuli tables! Dragon emerging in glory at the festival…in wisdom by the Great Mountain! Good woman, chief scribe of An, record-keeper of Enlil, wise sage of the gods!" –Extract of a Hymn to Nisaba translated by Jeremy Black, *The Literature of Ancient Sumer*

The oldest known spell is ancient semitic and was spoken by the Canaanites in the third millennium BCE. It is 5000 years old and it was borrowed by the Egyptians to keep snakes away from the tombs of their kings because they believed Semitic magic to be very powerful. The epic poem-incantation 'The

Exaltation of Inanna' written by the Sumerian high priestess, Enheduanna, was written and performed around 2300 BCE to petition Inanna, an ancestor of Aphrodite, and considered the Queen of Heaven.

Many Sumerian clay tablets have been found across sites located in modern day Iraq, a variety of which are hymns invoking goddesses such as Inanna, described in Enheduanna's poetic hymns as Queen of Heaven and *"Lady of the Countless Instruments of Power"*. Enheduanna petitions Inanna for empowerment and courage. Nisaba, goddess of writing and literature has numerous poems devoted to her. One such hymn (c. 3rd millennium BCE) is a poem praising Nisaba which was once accompanied by music; this clay hymn, among others, was discovered in her sanctuaries which were often attached to libraries and scribal houses. Nisaba, (much like the later Roman goddess Minerva or the Celtic goddess Brigid) was considered the spark of inspiration that allowed any scribe or poet to create any written work. She is represented as a woman holding the lapis lazuli tablet of the heavens and a gold stylus.

Best known as the pyramid text, the Cannibal Hymn is funerary in nature and heavily uses metaphor, used only for funeral rites of royalty. In this hymn the dead king is encouraged to butcher the gods, cook them and eat them so that he can absorb their powers to assist him in resurrection and divine status after death. On a funerary stela inscribed on the tomb of Wahankh II Intef of Thebes (c.2070-2020 BCE) are two poetic hymns dedicated to Ra and Hathor. Ra in this hymn is invoked as the setting sun and Hathor is addressed as the goddess of the western sky and music. With the direction of the West being associated with the setting sun – therefore the land of the dead, we know this is a funerary devotional poem. Two harpist songs from 1353-1336 BCE are carved on tomb-chapel walls of the ancient New Kingdom of Egypt. The first is engraved with four musicians and a blind harpist and the other is written with accompanying scenes of a banquet. Both are funerary with a traditional view of death as 'a good fate'.

An ancient Egyptian burial chamber was excavated in 1885 and it was found to be a tomb of a *Kher-heb* magician-priest. Inside the tomb is what archaeologists now call the Ramesseum magician's box. Within the box are fragments of four ivory magical wands carved with images of protective demons and sigils, medical/magical texts on papyri, a cobra wand made of copper alloy and a doll-like figure of a lion-headed woman with articulated arms, holding a serpent in each hand possibly, Weret Hekau, who was the goddess of magic and the supernatural. She was also placed on ivory knives as a charm to protect pregnant and nursing mothers from the underworld. The texts contain different spells ranging from medical care, the protection of children, and charms for daily life. There are also copies of hymns and for the coronation of King Senusret I, suggesting this magician also served as a high priest in a local temple and he may have specialised in aiding both pregnant women and children, as many items pertain to birth magic practices.

The oldest love poem in the world entitled *"Bridegroom, Spend the Night in Our House till Dawn"* is by an anonymous female poet from ancient Sumeria. The tablet was unearthed at Nippur, in lower Mesopotamia (modern day Iraq). Inscribed in cuneiform on a clay tablet the poem is both erotic and spiritual in nature. The erotic poem is addressed to King Shu-Sin and it is thought that the poem may be connected to a "sacred marriage" between the King and a priestess of Inanna. In erotic language of the monologue, the priestess expresses her ardent desires and longings for Shu-Sin, drawing heavily on imagery related to honey and sweetness. Historians believe this poem to be ritualistic in nature, and was part of a sacred rite, in which the King would symbolically marry the goddess Inanna, mate with her, and ensure fertility and prosperity for the coming year. A priestess would probably represent Inanna, the Sumerian goddess of fertility, and the king Shu-Sin would represent Dumuzi, the God of shepherds, on the eve of their union. This poem was also probably sung during fertility feasts.

Performed by the incredible musician and classicist Bettina Joy de Guzman on YouTube (link in my bibliography) you can hear what a hymn-spell to Hathor would have sounded like. This hymn is labelled 'spell 186' from the ancient Egyptian book of the dead, written on the *Ani Papyrus*. Bettina breathes life into this incantation, giving us a glimpse into how such a spell would be performed by priestesses for sacred ceremony long ago. She sings:

> *Hwt-Hr nbt Imentet, im weret nebt Ta sert iret Ra, immet, Ht-f Hrd nefert m wiya n HH St Htp n ir mAat m Xnnut n Hstiw tA st r ir nSmt wrt r DA pa mAat*
>
> which translates to *Hathor, lady of the West, you of the starboard side, lady of the sacred land; Eye of Ra in his forehead, beautiful of face in the bark of millions (of years) seat of rest for the doer of righteousness, ferryboat of the favoured ones; whose (place it is) to provide the great bark to take the righteous across.*

Bettina sings authentic ancient poetry and composes with historical instruments using traditional rhythms and interpretations. To me she is a modern-day priestess or chantress, bridging the ancient world with ours through poetry, hymns and songs, some of them were almost lost in the sands of time.

An ancient Egyptian poem called the *Magical Lullaby*, popularly known as the 'charm for the protection of a child' is an inscription from the 16th or 17th century BCE. This poem illustrates the ancient Egyptians personal religiosity and spiritual practice as this was a spell sung to ward ghosts away from sleeping children. *Heka* (Egyptian magic) was a common feature of daily life; both in medical and religious practices in ancient Egypt. The Magical Lullaby is an example of an everyday lullaby-spell mothers would use as a way to wish for protection over their children as they sleep. The mother sang about the items that she possessed in order to harm the spirits of the dead. She carried lettuce to 'prick' the ghosts, garlic to 'bring them harm', and honey which was considered 'poison to the dead.' Many other poetic spells, charms and rituals were performed by the ancient Egyptians for love, ward off evil, fertility, tomb sigils, appease the gods and petition for good harvest and more. Language and the written word were considered sacred by the ancient Egyptians, they believed it to be a magical gift given to them by Tehuti (Thoth) God of thought. They also believed that the alchemical process of language being transformed into writing was governed and protected by Seshat, whose name means 'Female Scribe', she is the goddess of writing, record keeping, wisdom, books and archiving memories of the dead.

> *Follow your heart while you are alive. Put perfume on your head, clothe yourself with fine linen. Make holiday and don't tire of it!* –Harpist Poem, Ancient Egypt 1400 BCE

On display at the British Museum is a 6th century late Sasanian ceramic incantation bowl. These bowls are quite plentiful archeological finds across excavation sites around the Levant which suggests this was a common practice of protective sympathetic folk magic of that time. The incantation is inscribed in a spiral fashion around the entire interior of the bowl and reads:

> *By the strength of the word of the living and established Gods. By the name of the holy angels…Bound and clasped and sealed from his heart and from his mouth, and may their eyes*

> *be blinded, may their ears stop up, may their feet not walk after him, bound and sealed are the curses and the oath, (both) new and ancient. Again, bound and sealed and clasped and sealed are their mouths; they are pressed by the name pressed, trampled, stirred are all the sicknesses so that they may not harm him.*

Another incantation bowl in the ancient Iraq collection at the British Museum is inscribed in Mandaic with a protection spell-poem against Lilith demons (before she was considered Adam's wife, she was a wind spirit turned night demon and she wasn't just one being, there were many Liliths!), It is dated to be from 500–800 BCE.

A 13th century Ewer jug from Kashan, Iran, also on display at the British Museum includes a Persian love poem inscribed and interwoven with a knot pattern and interspersed with lotus flowers (Lotus is a very potent symbol of magic and passion, considered an aphrodisiac to the ancient near and middle East) suggesting the poet hopes that the one he desires is bound to him and thinks of him every time she refreshes herself – how very erotic!

Ancient India

> *She who shines everywhere sings, you who hold the mysteries in your hand – Of will, knowledge and action – Reveal to me this path of illuminated knowing. I long to merge with you and be filled with your nourishing essence.* –The Vijnana Bhairava Tantra (The Radiance Sutras).

In ancient Sanskrit poems such as the Devi Gita, the Mahābhārata or the Maṇipravāḷam Poem you find evidence of devotional erotic poetry, heavenly nymphs addressing sexual issues, how to brew a love potion, binding vows and prayers to the divine. The Mahābhārata even chants *"The race of womankind is the seat of desire"* and Mantras are a form of poetic-spell to chant repetitively for abundance, purification, protection and blessings. Bhakti yogis chant devotional poetic mantras to connect with and become a devotee to a deity. Sanskrit is considered a sacred, magical language, no swear words exist in the Devanāgarī script, and each mantra is said to house specific syllables carefully threaded together to create a precise divine frequency for a particular outcome.

The Vedas are a collection of 2nd century BCE poems and hymns, the most well-known are *The Ramayana* and *The Mahabharata, the Upanishads* and *the Bhagavad Gita.* All of which are composed of archaic Sanskrit and teach of enlightenment, dharma, karma and connecting to deities through melodic chanting mantra, Bhajan, kirtan and ritual. From these texts we see the birth of yoga philosophy and the yoga sutras.

The Ancient Mediterranean

> *I sing of Artemis, whose shafts are of gold, who cheers on the hounds, the pure maiden, shooter of stags, who delights in archery, own sister to Apollo with the golden sword…to the rich land of Delphi, there to order the lovely dance of the Muses and Graces. There she hangs up her curved bow and her arrows, and heads and leads the dances, gracefully arrayed, while all they utter their heavenly voice.*
>
> *The Homeric Hymns and Homerica* with an English Translation by Hugh G. Evelyn-White. Homeric Hymns. Cambridge, MA., Harvard University Press; London, William Heinemann Ltd. 1914.

The oldest surviving complete melodic poem incantation is the Seikilos epitaph from the 1st or 2nd century CE. It is a funerary poem inscribed on a tombstone. It is Hellenistic Ionian and recorded with notation to accompany it with musical instruments. It was common practice to perform sacred poems with instruments, particularly the lyre during rites of passage rituals.

Across the ancient Mediterranean thirty tablets of text engraved on very thin strips of gold were discovered. They are dated to the late 5th century BCE and the 2nd century CE. These tablets are called the *Hipponion texts* and were found in burials, with the oldest coming from a burial of an ancient woman in Southern Italy. Upon translating the text, historians found them to be votive in nature, in particular they are associated with the mystery cult of Dionysus and Persephone plus with instructions to the deceased about how to function in the underworld in order to lead a fruitful afterlife. Most of the texts vary from single words, to prose and hexametral poems invoking the gods. The longest text describes the hexameter of meeting Hades, finding the pool of memory and then to seek Persephone who will give you permission to drink from the pool and enable you to go on your great sacred way.

Residing in the ancient Cyprus collection of the British Museum is a 600-400 BCE silver bird-headed spoon dedicated to Aphrodite as 'Golgia' (title as Great Goddess of Cyprus). The bird is most likely a dove because doves are attributed to Aphrodite and during this time writing was often used for religious purposes. The Cypro-Syllabic inscription on the spoon is in metres, hinting at the existence of hymns and poems now lost. This spoon was possibly a gift to the Great Goddess as part of a ritual to her. Archaeologists excavating the Amathus tombs in Cyprus also unearthed spells written on clay tablets, one of which is a sex curse and translates to *"May your penis hurt every time you make love."* And in the ancient site of Kourion, twelfth century BCE Cyprus, a protective poem petitioning Christ as part of a mosaic floor has been found almost intact – an early reference to Christianity coming to the island and perhaps the homeowner wanted to bless their home?

On display at the Louvre is a 4th century BCE Greek nude female curse doll bound and pierced with thirteen pins which was discovered in a terracotta vase with a lead tablet bearing a binding spell (Katadesmos) in Egypt. The tablet petitions multiple chthonic gods such as Kore (Persephone), Hades, Pluto, Ereshkigal, Anubis and divine demons.

> *I entrust this binding spell to you chthonic gods (παρακατατίθεμαι ὑμῖν τοῦτον τὸν κατάδεσμον θεο[ῖ]ς καταχθονίοις), Pluto and Kore Persephone Ereschigal and Adonis also called Barbaritha and Hermes chthonian Thoth Phokensepseu Erektathoti Misonktaik and Anoubis the powerful Pseriphtha, who holds the keys of Hades, and to you chthonic divine demons, the boys and girls prematurely dead I conjure all the demons (ὁρκίζω πάντας τοὺς δαίμονας) in this place to assist this demon Antinous. I conjure you, Antinous spirit of the dead, in the name of the Terrible and Fearsome, the name at whose sound the earth opens up, the name at whose sound the demons tremble in fear, the name at whose sound rivers and rocks burst asunder. I conjure you, Antinous spirit of the dead (ὁρκίζω σε, νεκύδαιμον Ἀντίνοε), she should be loving me, desiring me, telling me what she thinks. If you do this, I will release you (ἀπολύσω σε).*

The anonymous creator of this doll and tablet appears to have gotten inspiration and instruction from *The Greek Magical Papyri*, explaining how to make a wax or clay figurine for a binding spell:

> *...and make her with her arms behind her back and down on her knees. And take thirteen copper needles and stick 1 in the brain while saying, "I am piercing your brain, [name]"; and stick 2 in the ears and 2 in the eyes and 1 in the mouth and 2 in the midriff and 1 in the hands and 2 in the pudenda and 2*

> *in the soles, saying each time, "I am piercing such and such a member of her, [name], so that she may remember no one but me, [name], alone. And take a lead tablet and write the same spell and recite it. And tie the lead leaf to the figure with a thread from the loom after making 365 knots while saying as you have learned, "ABRASAX, hold her fast!". You then place it, as the sun is setting, beside the grave of one who has died untimely or violently, placing beside it also seasonal flowers. The spell to be written and recited is: "I entrust this binding spell to you, chthonic gods (παρακατατίθεμαι ὑμῖν τοῦτον τὸν κατάδεϲμον θεοῖϲ χθονίοιϲ) ...*

Polyphonic poetic chanting from Albania and Greece is an oral tradition that dates back to the Illyrians (Iron Age) to pass wisdom and folk canticles down the generations and was said to have inspired the myth of the sirens. And one blessing commonly said by Albanians to guests in the home is *"Blessed are your feet for bringing you here."* Which I find an incredibly simple and sweet invocation of kindness and love.

In Nea Paphos archeological site in Cyprus the Palindrome amulet was found by archaeologists in 2011. A palindrome is a sequence of letters or text that reads the same backwards as forwards. The word is formed from πᾰλίν-δϱομος in the Ancient Greek, which means 'coming back'. Palindromes were created and used since ancient times, right up to the Middle Ages and were often used as talismans with words intentionally chosen to have magical or sacred properties. Palindrome poetry still exists today, for example, in Russia. The longest known poetic palindrome was written by Velimir Khlebnikov (Razin, a poem).

Speaking of Palindromes, it seems the *Templar Magic Square* or *Sator Square* may have finally been deciphered.

The Templar Magic Square Palindrome is an intriguing object and hasn't been deciphered for two thousand years, until potentially now. It is a stone square with Latin letters engraved to form five words which are: SATOR, AREPO, TENET, OPERA, ROTAS. Or can be read as: ROTAS, OPERA, TENET, AREPO, SATOR. People in the mediaeval times thought it had magical properties and would inscribe it in manuscripts, wood, stone and even bread. It's also been found on houses for protection and even on a human skull. Sator translates to 'Creator' (or grower), Tenet means 'to hold' or 'to sustain', Opera means 'labour' or 'effort' and Rotas means 'to rotate' or 'circulation' but nobody knew what Arepo meant because it isn't a Latin word. The first attempts to study and decode this palindrome started in the 1800s and questioned why this was written in the first place? What was it for?

A direct translation could mean: 'The sower Arepo works the wheels with care' or 'As you sow, so shall you reap' or 'The creator preserves his work'. However, a new translation has come about from a scientist called Bob Greenyer working at the *Martin Fleischmann Memorial Project* and is doing research on this magical square and its connection to low energy nuclear reactions.

Greenyer's research is showing that under the right conditions, elements can go through something called the Fractal Toroidal Moment which is basically a whirlwind vortex. This process is the very definition of alchemy where particles are being ripped out of their source and transmuted into something else elsewhere, the markings also look like the yin and yang symbol. With the process of moving water and turbulence plus the use of sound frequencies, it can create mini vortexes – you can create and destroy matter and change chemicals. You might be wondering why Greenyer believes this has anything to do with this ancient square with an obscure magical wording?

In Pompeii where this square originated, Greenyer discovered there was a huge immigrant community of Jewish people during that time. Jewish people (even though most of this is written in Latin), read from right to left, rather than left to right. So, with this logic we should read it as ROTAS, OPERA, TENET, AREPO, SATOR instead. Semitic magic and alchemy were very much revered even by the ancient Egyptians, their magic was known to be heavy with symbols, ancient principles and that cross between science and mysticism. Greenyer proposes that this was written by an ancient Jewish alchemist who moved to Pompeii and created this square in Latin *but* encoded a secret knowledge about ancient scientific techniques. Greenyer theorises that 'AREPO' potentially could be shorthand for 'A–REP–O' meaning '**A**lpha ***REPEAT*** **O**mega', basically meaning "Alpha repeats to Omega eternally". So, with this new concept, the translation now reads *"The Divine Creator from Alpha repeatedly to Omega, comprehends and works with whirlwinds."* This deciphering is a map or equation related to Greenyer's current scientific research and could be the beginning of incredible technological advancement working with processes that create vortexes which move and change particles. Such technology could create cleaner air, change chemicals like carbon dioxide into oxygen, medical breakthroughs to combat disease and more. This magical square is literally the epitome of wielding our world with words! It is so fascinating to me that ancient wisdom keepers had so much knowledge and understood the connection between magic (or the divine) and science and learned to wield those energies together. Sadly, much of this knowledge is either lost, fragmented or coded in a way we don't fully understand, not yet anyway!

These palindromes were quite common across the ancient world because they were transportable and didn't take up much room, they may have originated from a longer spell, and later condensed into this simpler method to engrave on amulets and talismans.

Another example of a word charm, is this ancient Hebraic Incantation, which comes in the form of diminishing a fever demon. Unlike ABRACADABRA it isn't meant to be written down but to be chanted out loud with the final letter hissed like a healing, protective snake.

Ochinotinos
Chinotinos
Hinotinos
Inotinos
Notinos
Otinos
Tinos
Inos
Nos
Os
S

According to anthropologist Paolo Mantegazza, Sardinia is the *'land of the muses'*. Paolo noted that the Sardegnian shepherds excelled in the art of erotic love poems whilst the women sang poem-spells during wool plucking and weaving sessions, chanting magical words into the textiles they spun. Today Sardegna is renowned for its improvisational spoken word poets who perform *Bolu Poetry* in the style of *"Canto a chitarra"* or *"Cantu a tenore"*. It is a form of choral chanting, both meant to breathe life and power into the words they incant. These poets are not just performance poets, but also wisdom keepers of Sardinia's ancient past, their connection to their land and cultural heritage.

Some historians trace the Sardinian fervour for poetry to the Bronze Age period of the Nuragic civilization, when the island served as a nexus of exchange throughout the Mediterranean. A 3,000-year-old Nuragic bronzetti statue, for example, wore an ornate cape, with intricate designs, a speaking stick gripped in one hand, bells on his ankles, suggesting him to be the tribe's *Sa Cantonàlzu*—the shaman poet and storyteller.

The necropolis of *Is Loccis-Santus* based in Sardinia has an intriguing petroglyph inside, that palaeographic and linguistic analysis reveals is the word *'Bidente'* which comes from the Sardinian Nuragic name *'Bipenne'*. This is the name and symbol of an ancient astral divinity whom the water priestesses at holy wells and water temples like the *Pozzo Sacro di Santa Cristina* would have performed evening rituals and prayers to. On a clear evening, the water's surface was used as a huge mirror map so they could track the heavens and therefore communicate with *'Bipenne'* and other deities.

Duenos vase, a kernos (which is a round vase made up of three identical bowls joined together) was found in Rome, in 1880. It has been dated to the second half of the 6th century BC and deciphered as a curse written by a woman named Toteria who was exceptionally angry to be rejected by her lover. Originally thought to be Latin inscriptions. Linguist Bartolomeo Porcheddu, professor of the Sardinian language laboratory at the Cagliari University, has re-analysed the vase and discovered the curse to be in Sardinian. It reads: *"She who sends me prays to the gods that no virgin is to be your companion if you do not want to be satisfied by Toteria."* To which the potter, who wanted to remain out of the diatribe and to keep his distance from the curse, added: *"A good man made me, and because of me in the hands of that good man do not return evil."* In other words, he said: *"don't shoot the messenger!"*

Professor Bartolomeo goes on to say that *"this vase is considered a 'talking object' that reproduces a trine that is in conjunction between Jupiter and Saturn with respect to the sun and the earth that manifests itself in the night sky. When these two planets are at a 120° distance on the celestial sphere, they draw an equilateral triangle just like the Dueno Vase. In ancient times, this conjunction was considered a gift from heaven."* In other words the vase represented the celestial beings that Toteria was petitioning to activate the curse. The vase is an offering to Jupiter and Saturn as a prayer or wish.

Nordic and European

In the poetic Edda, a giantess named *Gunnlöð* is written as the guardian of the elixir of knowledge and poetry. This wisdom and magic is kept hidden deep in her mountain cavern. And a 14th century Norse curse-poem is inscribed on a rune-staff asking trolls, giants, elves and valkyries to strip the individual of their power and afflict them with illness until they yield to desires and uncontrollable lust for the person inflicting the curse. Interestingly, in regards to Norse poetry, only a few fragments written by female skálds (poets) have survived with the longest only being eight stanzas long. From the Netherlands, a Frisian weaver's sword made of yew inscribed with a runic poem was found and has been deciphered as a love spell. This spell was carved with charmed wood and woven with intentional words so it has a magical charge.

Celtic and Medieval Britain

> *Merlin, Merlin! Where are you going? So early in the day with your black dogs! I have come here in search of the red egg; the red egg of the serpent, on the shore of the hollow stone.* c13th Century Celtic Poem, Anonymous

The obscure world of Celtic poetry and writing goes back over 1,500 years and there are specific themes that weave throughout, like poetry that is magical or incantatory in nature, writing honouring the gods, epic fantastical love songs and votive chants to the natural world and seasons. Later in the Middle Ages, many poems conjure a similar magical charge – the mysticism of words with unusual alchemical drawings found in parchment manuscripts across mediaeval Europe right up to the 17th century.

The Celtic Druidic path involves training and initiation to becoming a bard or Filid (Shaman poets), not only to preserve traditional Celtic literature and incantations for ritual and magic but to also act as conduits to the liminal, channelling *Awen*, through the creation of their own devotional poetry. Bards in mediaeval Wales were sometimes described as 'Carpenters of songs'. There was even a special posture for spell making: standing on one leg, with one arm outstretched and one eye closed, perhaps to concentrate the force of the spell, but the power lay mainly in the spoken words. The strength of a spell lay in the spoken formula, usually introducing the name of a god or spirit in order to procure they're intervention, through the power inherent in the name – similar to mantras invoking gods of ancient India.

Rune poetry dates back to approximately the 10th century and it was practised by the Norse, Icelandic and Scandinavian people and rune poems can even be found in old English. The oldest known rune poem is Anglo Saxon, it speaks of the mysticism of nature, the stars, death and even God. The use of a divination instrument to create poetry is extremely fascinating.

Within the *Æcerbot* old English manuscript dated from the 7th century there is a reference to an ancient goddess of pre-Roman England called Erce. The text is Anglo Saxon, poetic in nature with magical intention. It includes instructions on how to make offerings, ritual and prayer to invoke her. The entire *Æcerbot* is a metrical charm that details lengthy prescriptions for ritual performances, particularly to invoke the energy of mother earth and fertility goddesses for good, bountiful harvest or remedy fields. There is a plethora of Anglo-Saxon metrical charms such as the Wid Dweorh poetry charm, a charm for staunching blood, the Heliand and Genesis poems and poetic charms for farming, bees and herbs. Charms were sets of instructions generally written to magically resolve a situation or disease. These charms involve some sort of physical action, including making a medical potion, repeating a certain set of words, or writing a specific set of words on an object.

Another Anglo-Saxon manuscript, called the *Lacnunga,* includes an abundance of herb charms and medical remedies, one of which is a birth charm decorated with serpents as an invocation to Mugwort and as part of a larger charm called 'The Nine Herbs' The Nigon Wyrta Galdor healing spell.

Women of Medieval England would wear a votive girdle around their stomachs during pregnancy and childbirth. These girdles had amulet scrolls tied to them and inscribed with protection blessings petitioning St Margaret who is the patron saint of childbirth.

From Northumbria, England, an early 8th century Anglo-Saxon box called 'Franks Casket' was found. Made from whalebone, it is densely carved with imagery and Runic inscriptions. On one of its sides, you can see the three 'Wyrd Sisters', to their left is a Valkyrie with a raven beside a warrior's grave-barrow. The rune inscription frames the whole piece as a mourning poem. This depiction shows evidence of wise women being at the forefront of rites and ceremonies devoted to birthing and death. It was common practice for local wise women to anoint and shroud the deceased and perform funerary rituals accompanied by hymns and songs to prepare them for the afterlife.

In the Vatican library there is a manuscript, copied in the 13th century, which contains a series of *piyyutim* – Jewish liturgical poems. One particular poem is a curse called 'Put a curse on my enemy'. The manuscript, including the poem-curse was written by Rabbi Elijah of Norwich, England. According to historical sources, there was a synagogue in Norwich that was burned down during the expulsion of the Jews in October 1290. A stone column, glazed pottery and this manuscript miraculously survived.

A manuscript of old English poems from around 960 CE contains two female-voiced elegies called *'the wife's lament'* and

'Wulf and Eadwacer'. The historian, Mary Wellesley, considers these poems to be written by women because of the use of feminine grammatical endings. Alongside these poems are some emotional riddles that describe pain, loss and being separated from a loved one.

The *Book of Nunnaminster* archived at the British Library is a dainty 9th century Anglo-Saxon manuscript of a prayerbook. It was written in the kingdom of Mercia (The Midlands of the UK) but what is unusual about this text is that not only is it made of gospel extracts, it contains a variety of prayer-incantations such as a prayer against poison, an Irish breastplate prayer to protect the body during battle, blessings for body parts include the skull, tongue, teeth, fat, and organs. It contains prayers in Latin with feminine grammatical word endings which historians propose this book was made by and for women.

The *Exeter Book* is a large codex of old English poems said to have been produced in the late 10th century AD. The book, archived at the British Library contains epic poems of saints' lives, gnomic poetry, wisdom poetry, heroic poems, elegiac verse and riddle poetry. The elegies primarily explore the themes of alienation, loss, the passage of time, desolation, and death, and deal with subjects including the sorrows of exile, the ruination of the past, and the long separation of lovers. Through them we encounter lonely seafarers, banished wanderers, and mournful lovers whilst the riddles explore religious and mundane topics. Interestingly some riddles have double hidden meanings, at surface level their subject matter appears to be entirely innocent or spiritual in tone, yet the subtle language has hints of bawdy connotation!

The history of ancient and mediaeval poetry-spells and epic poetry in devotion to the gods or for magical intervention and healing is an abundant tapestry – from the ancient Greek *Iliad*, the *Odyssey* and Hesiod's *Theogony*, the *Epic of Gilgamesh* from ancient Mesopotamia, the *Bhagavad Gita* from ancient India, the hymns of *Avesta* from ancient Persia and the *Mabinogion* of ancient Welsh scripture, these words speak to us across time, a sirens call from our past reminding us to connect with and channel occult and magical energies from the liminal. Our ancestors knew that poetry and utilising specific words or syllables had power, it is a symbolic language full of intention and meaning, vessels that carry lyrical messages – the warp and the weft, woven with elemental power connecting us to deities, the dreadful and the divine.

Words Are Spells
That's Why They Call It *Spelling*

If words are spells, then a poem is an amalgamation of magical words, set with intention to invoke or manifest a specific outcome. Language and words are fluid, like a water serpent – slipping through nooks and crannies, meanings get lost over time but they recreate themselves like new skin, like new rain becoming an ocean. Poetry and spell casting exist in the liminal realms, they are gatekeepers to portals within our subconscious mind, space, time and the aether; heightened ways to harness and manifest our seeds of potential. Poetry is the instrument of language from which thoughts manifest, spell casting is the direction of intention, calling forth forces beyond ourselves such as deities, ancestors or nature spirits. And ritual is bridging the two energies together to perform ceremonies, to summon our own enchantment and create sacred spaces with mind, body, voice, soul and spirit.

"The tongue is a witch!" according to George Webbe, an Anglican Minister in 1619 New England. There is truth in this statement for our words are our thoughts made manifest, words are the root of the root and the bud of the bud of magic. Words have the power to heal or to harm, to ruin or transform, to hinder or empower.

With some words we can create anagrams like the palindrome amulet and spell. The words we use can have a hidden meaning. Death is an anagram of *'hated'* because hating someone kills love. Evil becomes *'live'* because evil is the antithesis of all life. Earth is an anagram for *'heart'* and makes us consider mother earth being our intrinsic heartbeat that imbues all living things with life and (my favourite) God is *Dog*! Dogs embody pure unconditional love and although their lives are shorter than ours, they teach us so much of kindness, to be alive in the present moment and being joyful.

Let's have a brief look at the etymology of some powerful words!

The Origins of the word 'Witch': Etymologist Anatoly Liberman traces it to a proto-Germanic root, *wit-ja,* which is related to *wise* and *wisdom.* Witchcraft is essentially 'Craft of the Wise'. Another suggestion is Old English *wigle* meaning "divination," and *wig, wih* "idol."-essentially someone who uses divination to invoke deity. it could also be descended from a Proto-Germanic *wikkjaz* meaning 'necromancer' (one who wakes the dead).

The Norse word ***blotgydia*** means 'priestess of sacrifice' and the word ***blót*** refers to blood sacrifice of which the English word *'Blessing'* derives from and descends from the Anglo-Saxon *bloedsian* which means *'to make holy (with blood)'.*

The Origins of the word Magic: The Old Persian *magu* is derived from the Proto-Indo-European meg-**magh* (meaning: be able). The Persian term may have led to the Old Sinitic **M$^{\gamma}$ag* (mage or shaman). The Old Persian form seems to have permeated ancient Semitic languages as the Talmudic Hebrew *magosh,* the Aramaic *umgusha* (magician), and the Chaldean *maghdim* (wisdom); from the first century BCE onwards, Syrian *magusai* gained notoriety as magicians and soothsayers. The word 'Magi' also comes from the same old Persian root as *'magush'* – representing one who is of priestly cast and practises magic, 'to be able, have power'. The word magic in French is magique, in *Latin* magicus, and Greek *magikos.*

The name **Heka** is actually the old Egyptian word for magic and describes the supernatural force that Ancient Egyptians believed created and permeated the universe. The word Heka translates as "using the Ka." In Ancient Egyptian religion, Ka refers to the divine spirit that protects a person which is similar to prana, Qi, Ki and Pneuma of which we wield and commune with through wordcraft and vocal invocation. Heka is the Egyptian god of magic, Hek*ate* has the feminine grammatical ending to her name which implies she is the feminine aspect of magic – the goddess of magic and thresholds.

The root word for **Scripture** is *skrībh* which is pro-Indo-European meaning to cut, separate or sift. This was from a time before the use of paper or papyrus and people would cut or carve words (scripts) into wood or stone. It is nice to consider magical writing's earlier connection to the earthly material.

Weird is from the Old English word *wyrd* meaning 'destiny' or 'fate'; and is of Germanic origin. The adjective (late Middle English) originally meant 'having the power to control destiny'. The weird sisters (or wayward sisters) are three characters in Macbeth who practise witchcraft. They knew the *wyrd* or *fate* of others. They held a striking resemblance to the three fates or the three faces of Hekate in classic mythology.

Abracadabra is a magical formulation from Late Greek Abraxas, cabalistic or gnostic name for the supreme god, and thus a word of power. It was written out in a triangle shape and worn around the neck to ward off sickness and dark forces. Another magical word, from mid-15c. writing, was *ananizapta. Abra'* is the Aramaic equivalent of the Hebrew *'avra,'* meaning, **'I will create.** ' While *'cadabra'* is the Aramaic equivalent of the Hebrew *'kedoobar,'* meaning 'as was spoken.' Together the phrase means, 'I will create as has been spoken'.

Etymology of the word **'Poem'**. Is from middle French ***'poème'***, from Latin *poēma,* from Ancient Greek ποίημα (*poíēma*), from ποιέω (poiéō) and it means *"I make"*.

In Middle English, **spell** meant *"to mean"* or *"to signify,"* which probably developed from Anglo-French *espelier,* itself from Middle High German *spellen,* meaning *"to relate" or "to talk."* This spell, in modern English, then came to mean *"to read slowly (letter by letter)."*

So, we discover that the root meaning of 'Spell' is to relate to others and the cosmos through intentional communication. And, poem is shown to mean 'I make' and Magic has roots in 'to have power'. Here we see the energies of poetry and magic collide, they are two sides of the same coin. Poetry is a magical instrument, we wield through speech and writing as intentional acts to have power and manifest – we *will* what we *create* of which has been *spoken.*

What Does It Mean to Be a Poet?

And the Word became flesh and dwelt among us
–John, 1:14

The Arabic word for Poet is ***Sha'ir*** which means 'a person, especially a poet, endowed with unique perception or insight'. It is also suggested that the ancient Chinese word for 'poetry' **shī 诗** means *'Word Temple'*.

Kavya is a Sanskrit word for 'Poet' and it means 'Poetry in Motion' or 'Laden with the sentiment, having foresight with the qualities of a sage.' and in Indo-Iranian, the term 'Poet' is *Kavi* which means 'Visionary'.

The Lithuanian word *"Kerai"* which means *"magic"* and Middle Irish word *"creth"* which means *"poetry"* both originate from the sanskrit word *"Kriti"* which translates to *"do, make"*.

The Latin word *'Fata'* originates from *'Fari'* which means *'to speak with prophecy'* and in ancient Rome the *Fatae* was an oracular goddess of destiny who spoke the divine word. The *Parcae* were another form of Roman fates that presided over births and deaths. Tombstones depict them writing scrolls of destiny with funerary inscriptions decreeing their chanting at the time of a person's birth.

The old Irish word for 'Poet' is ***'Fili'***, pronounced 'Fee-lee' which means 'seer'. The word "file" is thought to derive from the Proto-Celtic **widluios,* meaning "seer, one who sees'. This suggests that the filí were originally prophetic poets, who foretold the future in the form of verse or riddle, rather than simply poets. Ancient Ireland revered its bards, who commanded status, power, respect, celebrity, and fear.

Another old Irish word ***Dán*** has origins in proto-Indo-European and means 'Skill', 'Gift' or 'Poem'. It basically means fated or to have a calling, to channel and communicate with cosmic forces via our talents such as singing, poetry and other abilities. The first-millennial Celts believed their poets could literally kill with magical satire. According to folk tradition, the poets conjured up invectives that blistered the skin of foes and sent rival poets (or stingy patrons) to their graves. Early Irish law even criminalised satirical "crimes of the tongue".

The word ***Awen*** is old Welsh which means 'flowing' and loosely translates to 'poetic inspiration'. The belief that when we open ourselves up to divine inspiration, Awen flows through and around us. Druids believe when we sing or chant or perform poetry, we are connecting to the Awen.

Awenyddion is a mediaeval Welsh title given to those deemed magician-poets. It is described as the power of poetic insight or soothsaying. They spoke magical and prophetic verses whilst in a mantic sleep.

The goddess Saraswati's name stems from the Sanskrit root ***"saras"***, which means "that which is fluid." or 'to flow like the river' or 'pooling water' and translates to 'speech'. She is considered the Hindu goddess of poetry, language, words, knowledge, the Vedas (epic poems), learning, wisdom and the arts. Her energy parallels Awen, describing poetry-craft as flowing like water as we connect with divine inspiration.

In Greek ***Helice*** means 'Willow' and in Greek mythology Helice was Zeus's nurse, she was associated with water. Her priestesses used willow in their water magic and witchcraft. The willow muse was called Heliconian and was sacred to poets and as we've discussed earlier, the energy of water in various cultures is associated with the flow of intuition and the flow of poetry to bring prophecy. It makes sense considering so many poets write about nature and the sea.

The belief that the flow of water inspired the flow of writing has been a practice of the ancient Hindus to the Druids. According to the author and researcher, Max Dashu, in her book *'Witches and Pagans: Women in European Folk religion 700–1100'* there were ancient Germanic priestesses who practised water gazing to intuit inspiration and messages from the gods, which was a custom that carried on into mediaeval Spain and France.

The Poet as a Conduit of Magic: Poetry *Is* Magic

Do you remember those moments as a child, those times we embraced our creativity? When we spoke the fluent magic of the sea, soil and stars? I remember speaking secret languages with my sister, writing love letters to a crush, poetry as prayer to a grandmother who had passed away, mud pies and rain dancing and living room forts and *the floor is lava!*

I picked rose petals from a neighbour's garden to make magical rose water, I made wands and dolls with sticks, stapled poetry pamphlets together, told stories, created dance routines, crafted paper fortune tellers with secret sigils and predictions inside each fold, left notes for people to find in my local library and more. It is intrinsic in all of us to create, play, speak and conjure words with joy and find magic in the everyday.

Tiny hands making tiny palm prints as our first painted sigil, tiny feet splashing puddles – a joyful rain dance! Happy Birthday chants and blowing out the candles were our first incantations. We recognised that reality is fluid, it is poetry in motion, we were bridges between worlds with our writing, drawing, dancing, singing and daydreaming.

I remember moments as a little girl, sitting in my red dress writing poetry under a willow tree or with the rose bushes and talking to the spirits of nature. Communicating with that very real invisible force undulating through everything with devotion and beauty. I have always loved roses and willows.

Poetry is prayer, it is ritual, it is spellcasting. Poetry is the language of the human heart and soul communing with the divine within and without. We recognise now that poetry and magic are not separate – we live, we breathe, we hum, we write, we speak, we chant, we cast spells.

As a Word Witch/Poetry Priestess I envisioned this book to be a doorway, to weave two worlds together – between the realms of devotional poetry incantations by forgotten poetesses of antiquity and with modern day word witchery to invoke, to cast, to love, to grieve, to manifest and to heal our voices through poetry as magic. This book is a devotion to the sacred feminine channelled through word-magic and ritual. It is a prayer to the creative spirit in the hearts of women, muses and goddesses for thousands of years. This is for everyone who identifies with and/or works with the sacred feminine in their personal witchcraft practice.

Come, roam with me in the rose garden, lounge by the river, sit a while under the willow, find your interior sanctuary where truth, beauty, lushness and magic coexist within the borderlands.

Let your word-magic unfurl, flow and flower. Avowed to autonomy, embracing empowerment, we seek the robustness of roots through the practicum of poetry; and in the signature of all things – our truest magic blooms.

With this book you may wish to keep a journal to hand for the poetry activities in later chapters.

Invita Minerva: Opening the Circle with Minerva

Create a small altar to Minerva with items you feel represent her. Some examples are:

- Honey, Olives, Pear, Myrtle, Mulberry (jam).
- Blue, gold, red and White candles.
- Piece of clay or stone.
- Small golden bowl of water.
- Dragons Blood or Orange blossom incense.
- Your poetry and art.
- Your favourite books.
- Your trophies and certificates you've achieved.
- Owl feathers, or even Crow feathers (birds known for their intelligence).
- Crystals for wisdom: Sapphire, Ruby, Clear Quartz, Lapis Lazuli.
- Craft items like wool, sewing supplies, candle making, embroidery etc.
- If you don't have a statue of her, you can find an image that you feel represents her such as the Queen of Swords tarot card for example.
- Include an item that represents your personal power and another item to represent your intuition.
- Place an object on your altar that represents love, connects you to your heart-door which opens up and out to the wider world.

Take a moment to be with your altar, connect with your surroundings. Invite the elements in, perhaps a candle for fire, glass of water or tea for water, a feather for air and a stone or dirt for earth.

Pick up some of your items one at a time and hold them to your heart with your eyes closed and offer them up to Minerva with your palms open. Call out her name. Petition her to guide you with your inspiration, with your poetry-craft, ask her for an abundance of wisdom, clarity and creative expression.

Hail Minerva!
she who knows,
She who remembers.
Muse Goddess of insight
I invite you here with love
Witness my poetry, my art
My creativity
I offer it all to you.
Maiden of skills and craft,
Gift me with prowess as I invoke inspiration
Goddess who knows the way,
the Owl-Eyed lady
Show me the way with my hands
Show me the way with my voice
Show me the way with my mind
Minerva, enliven me with your wisdom
Oh Goddess of One-Thousand Crafts!

This poem-spell is optional, feel free to use it or make your own. Making your own will feel more personal but this one I made is here as a guide. Keep a journal with you to note down what comes up for you as you invite Minerva's presence. Take slow deep breaths down into your belly as you take yourself on a visual journey with Minerva. Consider how she appears to you, does she give you a message? Jolt of inspiration? A gift?

Speak out loud your intentions, talk to her as you would a friend. Keep it simple – maybe you are petitioning her because you have writer's block, or need inspiration to write an essay, a poem or letter? Perhaps you need her healing as you are processing grief but feel unable to express these feelings verbally or otherwise? Perhaps you want to invite her into the space purely for the enjoyment of creative expression or learning a new craft or hobby?

When you feel ready, come out of your meditation and back into your room. Focus on your Minerva altar and pick up your pen and write out what words, phrases, inspiration, messages came to you. Write as a stream of consciousness for as long as you need.

After that, take a few minutes to sit with your breath. Place your hands on the crown of your head to give thanks to your wisdom, then place your hands over your eyes and give thanks to your insight, then place your hands on your throat and give thanks to your ability to communicate and expresses yourself, then places your hands on your heart and remind yourself to always create and express with compassion and respect. Place your hands in prayer and give thanks to their ability to make things – whether that's via painting or writing or otherwise, your hands are marvellous instruments, use them wisely, treat them kindly! Place your hands on your lower chakras and give thanks to them for their raw creative energies and finally place your hands on the earth and give thanks to the potent spark of creativity living and breathing in all things and inspiring poets and artists, just like yourself, for thousands of years!

Sprinkle water over yourself and your altar to Minerva to bless the space and invoke and activate that flow of imagination and innovation, flowing like a river, pouring out thoughts that manifest into words.

Feel free to write a devotional poem to Minerva and recite it if you wish as a way to conclude the *Invita Minerva* circle opening.

She Who Weaves Worlds with Words

May I write words more naked than flesh, stronger than bone, more resilient than sinew, sensitive than nerve. -Sappho

What is a Word Witch? Whether they are a scribe or a storyteller, a bard, a healer using sigils and spells – word witches have graced our Earth since time immemorial, since we recognised the power of our voices, words and writing. They were women who used the power of writing to invoke change. They intentionally alchemised ideas, emotions, and knowledge into methodical and lucid narratives.

- She places intention, energy, and belief into words, breathing life into each sentence and syllable.
- She alchemises one of the most foundational parts of our lives (words and language) with the ability to weave and conjure them into other things.
- She uses words as a conduit for movement, change, revelations, disruption, expression, and conjuring.
- She studies the craft of words – wordcraft or spellcraft – to beseech desires.
- She works with words as part of a prayer, having reverence for life.
- She has a deep, intergenerational, and spiritual connection to language and stories.
- She writes to call on change, big or small.
- She – writes to preserve what is hidden behind the veil, to know truth, to be a record keeper of history and to be the keyholder to the realms of the in-between.
- Someone who chants magic with their words. For she knows her words have power.

- Feel free to list other examples of what it means to you to be a Word Witch!

What does it mean to be a poetry priestess? A priestess from ancient times was a woman who served the goddess, often has temple duties and would have been the keyholder to the temple and the grain storage, she facilitated ceremonies, creates and performs hymns and lyric poetry, made daily offerings, organised important seasonal events, would have most likely been a learned woman of her time – with knowledge of the cosmos, healing remedies, divination and prayers. She would be able to write, not just record keeping but her sacred poems, she would potentially be well versed in multiple languages or dialects. She officiated at sacred rituals, managed female attendants and servants, presided over and led rituals of worship, and performed ritual sacrifices and offered counsel to the king or individuals of the community in need of her guidance. She would know how to play instruments to accompany the ceremonial poetry that she would have performed to invoke or appease the gods.

There are the poet-priestesses of ancient Sumeria, the prophetesses of Hathor in Egypt, The Damiatrix of Bona Dea, bee-priestesses (Melissae) of Demeter, woman shamans of the Lakota, druidesses of Ireland and Wales and many more. In Akkadian they are the *entu* (high priestess) or *kulu'u* (poet, singer) and in Egypt they were called the *wabet* (temple keeper) or *rekhet* (wise woman). In Greek they are called *hiereia* (she who cares for holy things) or *ergastinai* (weaver of the sacred) and *pythia* (oracle of Delphi. The Hebrew word *Tzovah* (women gatekeepers of the sacred shrine) is found in Exodus 38.8 as well as *tzovat* meaning 'women diviners using singing and offerings and *baalat ov* (witch) was a priestess who connected to the dead.

Other terms include: *chachamah* (wise woman), *konenet* (wailing woman), *kedeisha* (holy woman/priestess of a temple).

As well as the French *sage-femme* (wise woman), Norse *galdrakona* (chant-woman), German *segenoerinne* (blesser/enchantress), Polish *czaronica* (witch – from root word 'to make'), Sardinian *magliaia* (knitter, thread worker), Finnish *loitsija* (spell-weaver) and Old English *Wycce, Wicce, Witch* (twiner, spinner).

And there are so many more, you can find in the book *Witches and Pagans* by Max Dashu.

For me personally, a priestess is the antiquated ancestor of the witch and both uses words and poetry-craft for magical means. Both lead rather solitary lives, one living in a temple with sisters away from civilization, the other often living on the fringe of society. Priestesses of antiquity were revered by the community as mysterious oracles; the witch, feared, scorned and persecuted during mediaeval times when a shift began to take place in fear of intuitive and wise women. However, both do facilitate important social ceremonies and are readily available to serve the people with rites, rituals, spells, divinatory guidance and healing remedies. I use both labels interchangeably to describe my own spiritual practice. I am an initiated priestess devoted to Hellenic and Near Eastern practices and I am a hereditary hedgewitch who works with Celtic traditions as well. Why? My DNA from my mother's ancestry is Irish and French with my mitochondrial DNA having origins from the Mediterranean and Near East and my DNA from my father's ancestry is Scottish-Celtic/Pictish stemming from Norwegian and ancient Britonic tribes. Both energies flow through my blood so both energies flow out of my magical practice, as well as my writing and my mouth. I also wish to bring reverence back to the way of the priestess and the workings of the witch. It is up to you how you identify.

Today's contemporary pagan communities do have high priestesses governing covens, leading priestess initiations, officiate handfasting and other rites of passage as well as craft poetic speeches and canticles for spiritual events plus many other duties as well. So, there is a fluidity and crossover between priestess energy and that of the witch. Just as they cross between each other, they both also straddle the liminal. This is a woman of the in-between.

Both the witch and the priestess know that words are like water, words hold a density of memory that flows inside us, it is intrinsic and to write or speak with intention and reverence enables the practitioner to wield the ancient power of language, syllables and words.

> *A priestess is a service to the sacred, all that is here is sacred. All that is here is Goddess. And through mantra, prayers and offerings, we are in relationship to Goddess, meaning we are in relationship with life. The priestess is here to maintain that sacred symbiosis, she is here to maintain balance and harmony between the seen and unseen worlds. She prays not only for her own wellbeing but of the wellbeing of all beings. Because she knows that we are all One Being.* –Sharada Devi, Vedic teacher & Women's Dharmic Mentor

The Lost Voices of the Feminine Divine

Tradition speaks of the magic words that cast glamour, of 'words of power' that opened doors, of the spoken spell of the witch, of the curse of the bard. We can but wonder what compelling quality there should be about such sounds. We may divine that there were many ways of uttering 'words of power' in order to create moods of the soul or set in operation formative forces. [Our] bodies sway to the rhythm and melody of words, souls melt under the breath of the inspiring spirit, the sound of words enters the innermost being. –Florence Farr, High Priestess of the Golden Dawn, Actress, Writer and Women's Rights Activist of early 19th century

In this chapter I want to shine a light on forgotten, lesser known or lesser revered women word 'witches' throughout history. To remember these women and their magic. Men's ancient writings of literary and poetic epics have survived most in completion and are readily available on bookshelves and school curriculums yet we know so very little of their female comrades? Their works were destroyed, fragmented and lost in time. All that's left of Sappho's work is one complete poem and dishevelled fragments of papyri and the hymns created by the chantress Katebet have disappeared but we know in our bones more writings by ancient and mediaeval women existed, they are a cellular constellation within our collective unconscious deep in the mitochondrial memory, hidden like the Egyptian goddess, Amunet, ready to be awakened again.

For thousands of years, across the globe but most notably documented in the near east and mediterranean, women have been at the forefront of society as midwives, healers, priestesses and medicine women. Many were poets, drummers, dancers, weavers, oracles, and keepers of sacred spaces. Having both sacred duties to the temple and their local community, they saw the divine in the mundane, they ritualised daily life with poetic prayer and invocation, yet much of this knowledge has been lost to us with the rise of the patriarchy. Our bodies stiffened by corsets (and now jeans or work suits), our voices silenced and our worth dismantled to regimented social constructs.

Women were once poetry in motion, our chanting and hymns to the sacred feminine, the swish of our hips in time with the tides and our bellies grew like the magical phases of the moon, to be cherished and respected for our earthly magic in connection to the heavens. To be a woman meant channelling the seasons, communicating with the great goddess herself.

The *Diadema monachorum* is a mediaeval manuscript consisting of a collection of sermons archived away in the British Library. The historian Mary Wellesley discovered a note at the end of the text written by an anonymous female scribe which reads *'Salva et incolomis maneat per secula scriptrix'* which translates to 'Save the scribe, may she remain unharmed forever'. Which is rather poignant when we consider how many works by women were not saved and have become lost to obscurity.

Here are some incredible female esoteric writers and poets. There are more out there and yet they've been almost invisible to us for centuries even though for their time they were acclaimed and well respected. We know that the documentation of history tends to be controlled and rewritten by the powerful, some voices – especially women's, are usually redacted from historical or written corpus. I want to honour these women here in this chapter, honour their voices and make note of their written work. Bringing some of them to the light will empower and illuminate the way for our voices. Their poetry and writings are like the scatterings of small dandelion seeds floating through time to reach us.

Near East and Middle East

Enheduanna was a high priestess, princess and poet of ancient Sumeria (2300 BCE), she governed the temples and community responsibilities such as overseeing grain, food storage, agriculture and harvest for the city. She also interpreted dreams and presided over new moon festivals, equinox rituals and wrote temple hymns. As a writer she unified the older Sumerian culture with that of the new Akkadian civilization, acting as a diplomatic bridge soothing any conflict arising between people by combining both mythologies together in 42 poetic hymns respectfully uniting all their deities into one pantheon. This was during a time when writing was mainly for record keeping and accounting, therefore Enheduanna is the first known person to write as a form of expression. She is recorded as the world's first known author who also used the 'I' pronoun which marks the first-time writing has been used to explore deep, private emotions. Enheduanna's most celebrated and cherished literature were three beautiful epic poems dedicated to Inanna, goddess of war, love and desire-the divine chaotic energy that gives spark to the universe (from whom Ishtar, Isis, Aphrodite and Venus descended from). She gave a voice to Inanna and made her the most powerful goddess of that time. These poems were also used as invocations to Inanna for ceremony.

Bulluṭsa-rabi was a Babylonian author and poet from the first millennium BCE. Not much is known about her life but her name translates from the Akkadian to 'Her Curing is Great', and refers to her being given this name as a title which associated her with the Mesopotamia goddess Gula who was the goddess of healing. Knowing this, it is implied Bulluṭsa-rabi was a renowned healer and priestess of Gula. The only surviving manuscript of her work is a poetic hymn to Gula. The hymn is written in first person addressing Gula and asking for her love. Among the goddesses identified with Gula are Nintinugga,

Ninmadiriga, Nanshe, Ninkarrak, Ninigizibara, Bau, Ungal-Nibru, Ninsun and Ninlil each assigned with their own roles in the hymn.

Katebet (1320 – 1280 BCE), Henettawy (980 BCE) and Lady Henutmehyt (1279 BCE) were all ancient Egyptian priestesses whose primary temple duty was that of 'Chantress'. They wrote and performed their hymns to the gods, particularly Amun-ra in the temple of Karnak and Thebes. Their songs and poetry would have been accompanied by musical instruments such as the lyre, flute, sistrum and drums plus other ritual ornaments and adornments for specific ceremonies. All three were very wealthy women, suggesting this was a high-status position and they were very well respected. Sadly, none of their hymns survived but you can visit these ladies at the British Museum. Interesting to note: The name *Kateb(et)* means *'writer'* or *'scribe'* in Arabic. In ancient Egypt wise women known as *rekhet,* meaning "female knower" were thought to have the ability to communicate with the gods and the dead. They were consulted as seers, and their clairvoyant abilities were apparently passed down through families. The goddess Isis was often associated with these women as their patroness.

Jahan Malek Khatun- Was a Persian poet and princess from 1324 Iran. It was common practice in this time for noble women and girls to receive a good education and so Jahan excelled, especially since she was also an only child. Her poetry was written in the form of Ghazals which were amatory odes on the topics of spirituality and love. This style of poetic expression explores both the pain of loss or separation from the beloved and the beauty of love in spite of that pain. It is suggested she chose to write poetry as a means to leave something behind after her death, and to deal with her tumultuous life at court. Her divan is the largest known divan from any woman poet of pre-modern times, containing four *qasidas* (odes with single elaborate metres), one *strophe-poem* (Verse), one lengthy elegy, 12 fragments, 357 *rubai* (poem consisting of four lines like a Haiku) and 1413 *ghazals*.

Mahsati was a mediaeval Persian poet who was reportedly one of the first poets to compose *ruba'iyat* (quatrains) in her native language. She gained the attention and favour of the ruler Sanjar by performing a speech which she had improvised. The term *dabīr/dabīra* (professional scribe) is often associated with her name, but it is uncertain if she ever held this function. Most sources present her as a singer and a musician, as well as a poet of a court. Not much else is known about her, except she must have been exceedingly revered because she later becomes a semi-legendary figure as the heroine of romantic tales. The vast majority of her poems are erotic in nature plus other themes such as complaints about lovers, the cruelty of love and the lack of attention. Iranianologists considered her to some extent to have lesbian inclinations and there are accounts that she was a courtesan who entertained the sultan with her poetry.

Al-Khansa Was a 7th-century tribeswoman, living in the Arabian Peninsula. She was one of the most influential poets of the pre-Islamic and early Islamic periods. In her time, the role of a female poet was to write elegies for the dead and perform them for the tribe in public oral competitions (similar to poetry slams today). Al-Khansāʾwon respect and fame in these competitions with her elegies, and is widely considered as the finest author of Arabic elegies and one of the greatest and best-known female Arab poets of all time. Her funerary poetry rituals had a traditional sense of despair at the irrevocable loss of life.

Rabia Balkhi was a 10th-century Persian writer who composed poetry in Persian and Arabic. She is the first known female

Persian poet. Her shrine is located in the mausoleum of the 15th-century Sufi Khwaja Abu Nasr Parsa in present-day Afghanistan. She is celebrated in the Balochistan province of Pakistan, Afghanistan and Iran through various schools, hospitals, and roads being named after her. Rabia later became a semi-legendary figure who putatively wrote her last poems with her blood on the prison walls of the jail in which she had been incarcerated because of her love for a slave named Bektash. She later became known as a mystical poet because of her devotion to Sufism.

Rabia Basri was an 8th century Sufi poet and mystic. Growing up she came from a poor family, and when her father died, famine overtook the area of Basra and so Rabia parted from her family, went into the desert to pray and became an ascetic (asceticism is a lifestyle of abstaining from pleasures and adopting a frugal, secluded lifestyle). She is cited as the queen of saintly women and she became completely devoted to the divine. She is also said to be the founder of Islamic love mysticism which is similar to the practice of Bhaktism. It is stated that her poems were so divine that Allah enabled her to perform miracles. Often writing and chanting poetic prayers, one story claims she was seen surrounded by pure golden light as she spoke celestial poetry.

Khurshidbanu Natavan was an 18th century Azerbaijani poet and philanthropist. She wrote her poems in both Azerbaijani or Persian and was considered the best lyric poet of her time. The style she wrote in was called Ghazals or *Rubāʿiyāt* which is a form of spiritual romantic poetry with sentimental lilt to express the sufferings of women. Her name Khurshid Banu is Persian and means "Lady Sun" and Natavan is a pen name, is also Persian and means "Powerless", perhaps a play on words to show she was a lady of contradictions? She founded and sponsored the first literary societies in Shusha and in the whole of Azerbaijan and she funded a water main and aqueduct in her local town so the people had cleaner drinking water which is now named in honour of her as 'Natavan Springs'. A monument was built after her death which has become a local shrine and many of her poems have become traditional folk songs.

Miriam of Magdala (Mary Magdalene) Born in the 1st century during Roman Judea and has infamous tales attributed to her such as that of 'prostitute' and 'mad with demons'. Possibly the patriarchy demonising her? But she was a writer, teacher and mystic. Much of what is written about her is up for debate. Yet she was one of Yeshua's followers. Some Historians believe she was actually a wealthy woman who financed Yeshua's spiritual campaign and was given the same respect as his male followers. There is one gnostic gospel (non-canonical text) written in Sahidic Coptic on papyrus potentially considered to be written by her and in it she discusses women's roles within this spiritual mission, documents her visions as well as scripture entitled 'The Sophia of Christ' which is the feminine aspect of God. *Sophia* means 'wisdom' and she was considered a great goddess and wife of God. She was also depicted with her seraphim, described as heavenly dragons called 'The Burning Ones' and was known as the creatrix (great mother) of earth. I felt it important to mention Mary Magdalene and her potential writings honouring and teaching about the goddess Sophia, whilst a very obscure lady, I feel her true importance and her voice has been tarnished and lost. Today, Mary Magdalene is finally identified by the Catholic Church as a saint. The Magdalene (and Saint Sara) are much beloved by the Romany in France in the French coastal town of Saintes-Maries-de-la-Mer and by the current priestess movement of the early 21st century for her energy represents that of 'the priestess who was forbidden to be a priestess' yet she persevered anyway. I think many women can identify with her struggles and hardships, she is a physical symbol of hope and a pioneer teaching of feminine divinity being equal to that of man and God.

Greek & Roman

Sappho was a 6th century Greek poet, known as the 'mortal muse', the '10th muse' and simply 'The Poetess'. She wrote nine books of lyric poems, she invented the plectrum and she also wrote epigrams, elegiacs, iambics, solo songs, wedding songs and folk songs for intimate festivities. Much of her work is lost, only fragments remain. Her 'Ode to Aphrodite' epic poem is her most famous. Sappho's work was in the style of Lyric Poetry accompanied by the Lyre. Her poems are both erotic and mystical. It is debated as to who she really was; priestess to Aphrodite? Courtesan? Chorus organiser? Music teacher? Or simply a performer at banquets? Or an amalgamation of all of these titles? She wrote hymns to goddesses, and taught other women how to perform so perhaps ran a school. Or she could have been a high-class courtesan because sacred prostitution was practised and often these women were also entertainers, or perhaps a musician commissioned to create and perform poetry and songs for all kinds of gatherings from weddings to parties to ceremonies. She is the only historical woman ever to have been depicted on an ancient Greek vase. On this vase she is painted with her lyre, scroll of poetry and being attended by a group of women. One woman places a crown on her head – this suggests she has won an award of some kind. This Athenian vase was made in 440 BCE a century and a half after Sappho had died. This suggests that a poet from a small island far away near Turkey had such a great reputation that it spread across the classical world.

Erinna, an ancient Greek poetess from the 4th century, is best known for her long poem *The Distaff,* a 300-line lament for her childhood friend which she composed when she was just

19. Along with the fragments of the *Distaff,* three epigrams attributed to Erinna survive. In antiquity, Erinna was highly regarded; the only Greek woman poet to be better thought of was Sappho, sadly today she is little-known. Antipater of Thessalonica included her in his list of "nine earthly muses". She is said to have died at the age of 19.

Nossis, was an ancient poetess from the 3rd century from a noble family. She, herself, claimed to rival Sappho. Twelve of her epigrams have survived. Most of her poems were about women and love as well as for religious dedications and epitaph, mainly to Aphrodite as well as Hera. Sometimes Sappho would be mentioned in parts of her poetry and four of her poems are dedications of women's portraits. Nossis idolised Sappho and said *"She was the flower of Lesbos, and may the Muses love me as they did her."*

Anyte of Tegea from the 3rd century was a Hellenistic poet from Tegea in Arcadia. Little is known of her life, but twenty-four epigrams attributed to her are preserved in the *Greek Anthology*. She introduced rural themes to the genre, which became a standard theme in Hellenistic epigrams and her works were adapted by several later poets, including Ovid. She wrote in the Doric dialect and many of her poems were invocation hymns to the God Pan. Not much else is known about Anyte, except for one story that was preserved: Anyte claimed that she was once visited by the God Asclepius while she was asleep, and told to go to Naupactus to visit a certain blind man there. On doing so, the man was cured, and he built a temple to Asclepius. She was famous as a lyricist and epic poetess yet none of those poems survived. She also wrote poems about death as well as epitaphs for animals and pastoral epigrams describing idyllic landscapes. She has a crater on Mercury named after her.

Korinna a 5th century BCE Greek Choral lyric poetess. Her work has only survived in 40 fragments. She wrote an invocation of Terpsichore, the Muse of dance and chorus, in one of her fragments. One of her poems tells the story of a singing contest between the mountains Cithaeron and Helicon and a second poem narrates the tale of the daughters of the river-God Asopus. Similarly to Sappho, Corinna's songs were composed for performance by a chorus of young girls in religious festivals, and were related to the ancient genre of *partheneia* (Maiden Songs). The poems may have been performed at cult celebrations in the places which appear in her poetry.

Telesilla of Argos was considered one of the nine great poetesses by Antipater of Thessalonica yet only two fragments of her work exist. Active as a renowned poet in the 5th century she wrote poetry to the gods, mainly Apollo and Artemis. According to Pausanias, there was a stele to Telesilla in front of the temple of Aphrodite in Argos which depicted her holding a helmet and with her poems on the ground around her. She was quite sickly in her youth so she consulted the Pythia oracle at Delphi, the oracle told her to dedicate herself to the nine muses, so she devoted her time to the study of poetry and music. Others have documented her as being greatly loved and famous for her poetry. As well as her poetry, Telesilla is also remembered as being the defender of her hometown against the Spartans in 494 and 493 BCE, she encouraged the women, youth and elders to rise up in defence after learning how their men were captured and killed in a nearby grove.

Praxilla of Sicyon was a Greek poetess and courtesan of the 5th century BCE. Five quotations and three paraphrases from her poems survive. Three of the poems attributed to her are drinking songs, two are religious, and the three paraphrases are all versions of myths. She was known for erotic and hymn poetry to Adonis. Antipater of Thessalonica considered her one of the "immortal tongued women".

Kassia was a 9th century Byzantine-Greek composer, hymnographer and poet who wrote sacred hymns. She was an abbess of a convent in the west of Constantinople. Many of her hymns are performed in Byzantine liturgy to this day. Not only did she write spiritual poetry but she produced music to accompany it, her style is a scope between lyric and epic poetry. Her most famous is 'The Hymn of Kassia'. Kassia is also known for the 'hymn for Holy Wednesday', in which she gives voice to a nameless woman from the gospels. The woman appears in an episode in the gospels, whereby Christ, dining in the house of a wealthy man, is anointed by a woman who is considered to have led a sinful life. A fine copy of Kassia's poem survives in a 16th-century manuscript held by the British Library, where Kassia imagines the woman's lament. It's wonderful to imagine that this woman was possibly Mary Magdalene and that a woman poet gave her a voice!

Sulpicia is the only surviving woman poet of 1st century BCE Rome. Six of her poems, written in Latin, were published in a poetry collection called *Corpus Tibullianum*. All remaining six poems revolve around love and its many forms, from falling in love to yearning after separation to unfaithfulness. The first poem invokes Venus to say a thank you prayer for being allowed to make her love public rather than hiding it and being modest.

Sulpicia (The Satirist) from ancient Rome CE 81–96 during emperor Augustus's reign. A seventy-line hexameter poem and two lines of iambic trimeter attributed to her survive. Sulpicia wrote love poetry discussing her desire for her husband, and was known for her frank sexuality. Sulpicia may not have been her real name, possibly a pseudonym or pen name borrowed from 1st century poetess Sulpicia in order to hide her real identity because her poetry was rather erotic and scandalous for the time. Much of her poetry was also satirical. She is the only woman known from antiquity who was associated with a comic genre. Surviving testimonia on Sulpicia documents that she openly wrote poetry about her sexual desire for her husband; this outspoken and bawdy centering of female sexual desire is extremely unusual amongst ancient women poets.

India and South Asia

Gargi Vachaknavi, born in the 9th to 7th century BCE, was an ancient Indian sage, philosopher and Vedic poet. She was a leading scholar who also made rich contributions to propagate education and she has written many hymns in the Rigveda that explore the origin of existence. She was greatly honoured and respected for her mastery of the science and the philosophies of the Vedas. She participated and gave lectures in Brahma Yagnas and was bestowed with the title of Brahma Vadini. It was a testimony to her greatness that she was recognized as one of the *Navaratnas* (Nine Jewels) in the court of King Janak of Mithila.

Lalleshwari 'Lalla' Ded of Kashmir, was a 14th century Hindu mystic, poet and yogi. She was the creator of the style of mystical poetry called Vatsun. Her poems represent some of the earliest known works of Kashmiri literature. Lalla is renowned for being a wandering naked pilgrim, chanting divine poetry as she roamed in the forests. She became a Bhakti saint – Bhakti means 'devotion' or 'love' in Sanskrit. Bhakti yoga is the yoga of chanting devotional songs. A total of about 285 poems are attributed to her.

Andal was a 7th century Tamil Bhakti Poet-saint. She was also known as Kothai, Nachiyar, and Godadevi and was the only female Alvar (Bhakti devotional poet) among the twelve Hindu poet-saints of South India. She was posthumously considered an avatar of the goddess Bhudevi (an aspect of Lakshmi as Mother Earth). Andal is credited with two great Tamil works, *Tiruppavai* and *Nachiyar Tirumoḻi,* which are still recited by devotees during the winter festival season of Margaḻi. In the Tiruppavai she imagines herself as one of the gopis (maidens) devoted to Krishna. The *Nachiyar Tirumoḻi* is a poem of 143 verses. *"Tirumoḻi"* translates to "Sacred Sayings" in a Tamil poetic style and *"Nachiyar"* means 'Goddess'. The full translation means "Sacred Sayings of the Goddess." Through their devotional poetry women were thought to be able to connect with God directly and those words are thought to encapsulate their personal emotions.

Gangasati was a 13th century mediaeval saint poet of bhakti tradition of western India who composed several devotional songs in Gujarati language. Not much is known about her life because everything about her was passed down through oral tradition. She, alongside her husband was a follower of the Bhakti movement and their home became the centre of devotional activities which was a small abode that sometimes housed a number of sadhus (holy men). Gangasati composed a number of Bhajans, each with a spiritual teaching about grace, nature and the life of a devotee of Bhakti. Her bhajans are still popular in Saurashtra and are traditionally sung by devotional singers.

Kanhopatra was a 15th-century Marathi saint-poet. Not much is known about her. According to most traditional accounts, Kanhopatra was a courtesan and dancing-girl. She wrote in a style called *Marathi ovi* and *abhanga* poetry telling of her struggle to balance her piety with her profession. In her poetry, she implores Vishnu to be her saviour and release her from the clutches of her profession and she expresses disgust for the society which adored her as an object of beauty rather than as a human being. She describes how she has been the object of lustful thoughts but wishes to devote herself to Vishnu. She worries that she is beyond the "scope of God's love".

About thirty of her *abhangas* have survived, and continue to be sung today. She is the only female Varkari saint to have attained sainthood based solely on her devotion, without the support of any guru, male Varkari saint, or tradition or lineage.

Madhavi Pattanayak (or Madhavi Dasi) born in the 16th-century CE was one of the earliest female poets to write in the Odia language which is Indo-Aryan classical language in the Indian state of Odisha. Pattanayak was devoted to the God Jagannath who is considered to be 'Lord of the Universe'. She wrote mystical, hymn-like poetry. She was a disciple of the Hindu saint Chaitanya Mahaprabhu and a contemporary of the Pancha Sakha poet-gurus of Odisha.

Habba Khatoon was a 16th century Kashmiri Muslim poet and mystic. Habba also lived her life as a Sufi ascetic and was given the honorary title 'The Nightingale of Kashmir'. she was nicknamed Zoon because of her great beauty. According to legend, one day Yousuf Shah Chak, the last independent emperor of Kashmir, was out hunting on horseback. He heard Zoon singing under the shade of a chinar tree, and the couple met and fell in love, however, one day he was captured and imprisoned by the Mughals, never to return. She became a solitary mystic, abstaining from worldly pleasures when her lover did not return. As an ascetic she spent her life wandering across the valley singing her songs. It is claimed that she introduced *"loal"* to Kashmiri poetry, "Loal" is more or less equivalent to the English 'lyric' and her poems are brimming with yearning, melancholia and romantic expressions.

Akka Mahadevi was one of the early poets of Kannada literature and a prominent person in the Lingayat Shaiva sect in the 12th century. Her 430 extant Vachana poems, and the two short writings called Mantrogopya and the Yogangatrividh are considered her most notable contribution to Kannada literature. She is considered by modern scholars to be a prominent figure in the field of female emancipation. She wrote that she was a woman only in name and that her mind, body, and soul belonged to Shiva. As a wandering mystic and ascetic, she renounced worldly possessions, even clothing and befriended animals, flowers and birds as her companions, she rejected family life and societal values. Akka's poetry is considered 'enlightenment poetry' of which she explores the rejection of mortal love for everlasting love for the divine.

Mirabai was a 16th century Hindu Bhakti poet and mystic from Rajasthan. She was a devotee of Krishna and many devotional hymns called Bhajans and poetry dedicated to Krishna are attributed to her. According to a popular legend, her in-laws tried many times to assassinate her, such as sending Meera a glass of poison and telling her it was nectar or sending her a basket with a snake instead of flowers. According to the hagiographic legends, she was not harmed in either case, with the snake miraculously becoming a Krishna idol. She was often recorded as going on numerous spiritual pilgrimages and legend has it that she never died, she miraculously disappeared by merging into an idol of Krishna in 1547.

Muddupalani was a 17th century Telugu speaking poet, scholar and devadasi. She wrote the erotic epic *Rādhikā-sāntvanam* "Appeasing Radha" as well as erotic devotional poetry. Renowned at court as a talented musician and poet she was adept at 'Nava rasa' which is a concept in Indian arts denoting the aesthetic flavour of any visual, literary or musical work that evokes an emotion or feeling in the reader or audience, but cannot be described. Someone who performs Nava Rasa is considered one who 'has heart.' She also studied and translated other songs and poems by others. Although a courtesan, she desperately wanted children and adopted a boy and a girl. Not much else is known about her.

Avvaiyar was a 9th century Tamil poet who lived during the Sangam age of India. In these literary tomes she is attributed as the author of seven verses in Naṟṟiṇai, 15 in Kuṟuntokai, four in Akanaṉūṟu and 33 in Puṟanāṉūṟu. Legend states that whilst she was a poet at court, she travelled all over the country, from village to village sharing the gruel of the poor farmers and composing songs for their enjoyment. She became revered as a wandering saint and she was a devotee to Ganesha. The name 'Avvaiyar' isn't her real name, it means 'grandmother'.

China and Far East

Senshi The Japanese Kamo High Priestess, princess and poet who wrote devotional Buddhist poems and scriptures whilst attending to shrines. Senshi was a renowned master of the *waka* form of Japanese poetry and held her place as Kamo high priestess from the age of 12 until she was 68, it is unusual for a priestess to hold that title for so long and it is unclear as to why. Senshi went on to preside over court, educate women in the arts of poetry and scripture, and continue to create beautiful poetry for the emperor; however, her true desire was to become a Buddhist nun and dedicate her poetry to Buddha. In the early years of the 11th century, Senshi produced a poetic collection called *Hosshin wakashu,* "A Collection of Poems for the Awakening of Faith", Each *waka* poem was written in response to an excerpt from a sutra and throughout the collection, she explores themes such as the role of women in Buddhism. Six days after turning 68 she finally took her vows as a Buddhist nun. There is evidence she was queer because in her life she did exchange love poems with another woman, as a Kamo high priestess it would have been forbidden to have relations with men, however, love between two women may have been overlooked.

Consort Ban was a Chinese scholar and poet from the western Han dynasty 206 BCE.

She began her life as a maid, then became a concubine to the emperor and quickly rose to prominence at court. She is credited with two 'fu' poems (rhyming prose) and was most famous for her "Yuan Ge Xing" or "Song of Resentment", in which she compares herself to a discarded autumn fan. It describes the sorrow she felt at being abandoned by the emperor.

Zhuo Wenjun was a poet from 2nd century BCE China. From a noble family, she had the best education, predominantly in music and poetry. She was married and widowed by sixteen and after returning to her father for a spell, she fell in love and ran away to be with a famous poet called Sima Xiangru. Through his anger her father denied her any support, she lived in poverty so she opened a wine shop and became an innkeeper. When her husband died, she wrote an epic funerary ode to him, the poem *Baitou Yin* (White-Haired Lament) which complains at the inconstancy of male love, is also attributed to her.

Murasaki Shikibu was a Japanese novelist, poet and lady in waiting at the Imperial court in the Heian period. She is best known as the author of the world's first novel 'the *tale of Genji*'. She also wrote '*The Diary of Lady Murasaki*' and a volume of poetry. As a member of the imperial court, she entertained the empress with her stories and poetry. Murasaki became a popular subject of paintings and illustrations highlighting her as a virtuous woman and poet. She is often shown at her desk in

Ishimyama Temple, staring at the moon for inspiration. A plant with purple berries has been named after her.

Ono no Komachi was a Japanese Waka Poet and suggested lady of the bedchambers. Not much of her life is known. But she was renowned for her unusual beauty, her name Komachi is used as a synonym for feminine beauty in Japan to this day. Almost all of her poetry is melancholic, her poetry and her life have been used as inspiration for writers of Noh plays that communicate Buddhist themes.

Zhou Xuanjing was a 12th century Chinese Taoist mystic and poet. She dreamt that she was immersed in a scarlet mist (considered an auspicious sign) just before the birth of her son. Her Taoist teacher gave her the title "Free Human of Mystic Peace." The emphasis in her poetry was the power inherent in stillness. She often referenced the moon in her poetry as she believed this was a symbol of the eternal sky. She taught that meditation and poetry as an act of meditation would bring clarity and dissolve the dramas of the ego.

Kishi Joo was a Japanese princess and poet of an imperial family during the middle of the Heian period, became a consort to emperor Murakami. Prior to becoming a consort she served as the Ise Priestess, chief priestess of the Ise Shrine. Not much else is known about her.

Akazome Emon was a Japanese Waka poet and early historian of the Heian period. She presented devotional poems as offerings to Sumiyoshi Shrine; her poetry was incorporated into court anthologies and she wrote a personal poetry collection called the *Akazome Emon Shu.* Throughout her life she presented her work to numerous poetry competitions and when her husband died, she became a Buddhist nun. Her poems are applauded for her captivating words about loss and unsaid goodbyes, often expressing her sadness through seasons and relating to nature. These poems are known collectively as *wakare no uta*. It is believed that she was the author of an epic known as the 'Tale of Flowering Fortunes' which chronicled the lives and works of the Fujiwara clan and royals at court, thus documenting historical information.

Yeo Ok is often regarded as Korea's first woman poet. Her poem, the *Gonghuin* "A Medley for the Harp", is one of only three poems from the ancient Korean kingdom, Gojoseon (approximately 1500–108 B.C.) and the first by a woman. One version of the poem tells how one day at dawn as Yeo Ok's husband, Gwakri Jago, was rowing across a river, he saw an old man jump into the river and try to swim across it. His wife had tried and failed to prevent him from entering the water. He was swept away and drowned. The old lady, stricken with grief, followed her husband into the water singing and playing her lyre and met the same sad fate as her husband. Gwak Rijago told his wife Yeo Ok about the sad event and this moved her to set the old lady's words to music and to be accompanied with a lyre. *The Gonghuin* was later introduced to the Chinese courts in the Jin dynasty, making Yeo Ok quite renowned across both Korea and China.

Heo Nanseolheon (1563 – 19 March 1589), was a Korean painter and poet of the mid-Joseon dynasty. Her own writings consisted of some two hundred poems written in Chinese verse (*hanshi*), and two poems written in hangul (Korean alphabet). From an early age, she became recognised as a prodigal poet, though due to her position as a woman she was incapable of entering into a position of distinction. Her early piece, "Inscriptions on the Ridge Pole of the White Jade Pavilion in the Kwanghan Palace" (*Kwanghanjeon Paegongnu sangnangmun*), produced at the age of eight, was lauded as a work of poetic genius and earned her the epithet "immortal maiden." After both her little children and also her brother died, she died of illness at the age of twenty-seven in 1589. A significant amount of Nanseolheon's writing was burned upon her death per her request, and the surviving poems are collected in a 1913 poetry collection *Nansŏrhŏn chip*. The collection consists of 211 poems, in various Chinese styles. These include *koshi* (traditional verse), *yulshi* (metered verse), *cheolgu* (quatrains), and a single example of *kobu* (rhyming prose). Much of her poetry explores Confucian teachings which is the practice of ancestor worship and living a peaceful life.

Yeshe Tsogyal was a princess born in Tibet, 777–817 CE. Known by epithets as 'Victorious Ocean of Knowledge' and 'Lake Empress', she attained enlightenment in her lifetime and is considered the mother of Tibetan Buddhism. Some schools of Buddhism recognise her as a female Buddha. In her lifetime as a spiritual master teacher, she wrote many devotional poems such as: *"Now until the dualistic identity mind melts and dissolves"*, *"The Supreme Being is the Dakini Queen of the Lake of Awareness!"* and *"This self-sufficient black lady has shaken things up"*.

European

Marie De France was a 12th Century French poet and earliest named female writer of literature in European tradition living in England. Little is known of her life, other than she was probably the Abbess of the abbey at Shaftesbury, she performed at an unknown court, her work was much beloved by Henry II and She is considered by scholars to be the first woman known to write francophone verse. Her style of poetry centred on romantic and magical themes; she was one of the first people to write folklore down as bardic poetry. She was fluent in Francien, Latin, Middle English, Anglo-Norman and Breton. 102 French fables have been attributed to her. Some historians believe her to be the illegitimate daughter of Geoffrey Plantagenet and therefore the half-sister of Henry II of England.

Marguerite Porete was a 13th century French-speaking mystic and the author of *The Mirror of Simple Souls,* a work of Christian mysticism dealing with the workings of agape, teaching of freeing the spirit from logic to know divine love. Much of her writing reflected the style of courtly love which was popular at the time. She is known for expressing the Love Mysticism of Beguine spirituality. She was burnt at the stake for heresy in Paris in 1310.

Hildegard was a German Benedictine Abbess, poet, mystic and polymath. She is best known for her spiritual concept of Viriditas – "greenness" – the cosmic life force infusing the natural world. For Hildegard, the Divine manifested itself and was apparent in nature. Hildegard wrote theological, botanical, and medicinal works, as well as letters, hymns, and antiphons for the liturgy. She wrote poems, and supervised miniature illuminations in the Rupertsberg manuscript of her first work, *Scivias* There are more surviving chants by Hildegard than by any other composer from the entire Middle Ages, and she is one of the few known composers to have written both the music and the words. The Ordo of Virtutum is a liturgical drama written by Hildegard, it is considered the oldest surviving morality play. She is also credited for the creation of a constructed language called Lingua Ignota. Throughout her life she had many visions, one of which she called 'The shade of the living light' and another vision told her to write her poetry in devotion to spirit.

Bieiris de Romans was a 13th century French *trobairitz* (feminine title of a troubadour), she wrote poetry about courtly love. One of her love poems is sapphic in nature and is dedicated to a woman named Mary. Not much else is known about her.

Christine de Pizan was a 14th century Italian-born French poet, lady of letters and court writer for King Charles VI of France and several French dukes in mediaeval France. She served as a court writer in mediaeval court after her husband died. Her work is considered to be some of the earliest feminist writings, which includes novels, poetry, and biography, and she also penned literary, historical, philosophical, political, and religious reviews and analyses. Her best-known works are *The Book of the City of Ladies* and *The Treasure of the City of Ladies* of which Christine created a symbolic city where women are appreciated and defended. Her books of advice to princesses, princes, and knights remained in print until the 16th century. Her writing career flourished when her father (the court physician and astrologist) and her husband died of the plague, so she needed to find a way to earn money to support her children and her mother. Her love ballads gained attention from wealthy courtiers and she soon became a prolific writer which earned her the title of the first professional woman of letters in Europe. Christine only ever collaborated with other women artists, her illustrator for her manuscripts was a woman named Anastasia. Christine's notable works include: One Hundred Ballads (1393), Letter of the God of Love (1399) and The Tale of the Rose (Poem, 1402).

The Comtessa de Dia was a 12th century Female Troubadour entitled *"chantar"* meaning the poems are written in a style and from the point of view of a woman who sings of the pride and disdain of her male lover. Five of the Comtessa's works survive, including four cansos (song-poem) and one tenson (lyric poem). She is sometimes called Beatritz or Isoarda. She wrote in the Occitan language about unrequited love or feeling betrayed by a lover but despite these emotional wounds, she sings praise for herself and of self-worth.

Gabrielle de Coignard was a 16th century Toulousaine devotional poet. She is renowned for her religious poetry. She wrote the *Les oeuvres chrétiennes* which is a compilation of 129 individual sonnets (*Les sonnets spirituels*, or "Spiritual Sonnets") and 21 other poems. Many of her writings transpired after the death of her husband, whom it is documented she had a happy marriage with, which was rare in those times. Whilst the majority of her work is mystical in nature Gabrielle received praise for her inclusion of the more worldly themes of widowhood, the body, and illness and for offering a unique perspective on womanhood in early modern France. Although her work was popular in the 16th century, she fell into obscurity by the mid-17h century.

Hadewijch, was a 13th century Dutch poet and mystic. Most of her extant writings are in a Brabantian form of Middle Dutch. Her writings include visions, prose letters and poetry. Not much is known about her life other than what can be read from her letters, she writes she was the head of a beguine house (religious abode) but experienced opposition which drove her to become a wandering mystic. Her forty-five *Poems in Stanzas* (*Strophische Gedichten,* also *Liederen,* "Songs") are lyric poems following the forms and conventions used by the trouvères and minnesingers of her time. She also wrote hymns as well as troubadour styled courtly love poems too.

Cecilia Ferrazzi was a 16th century Italian Counter-Reformation Catholic mystic whose life was extensively involved with the establishment and maintenance of women's houses of refuge in 16th century Italy. Her entire life she struggled to become a nun, for a variety of reasons she was rejected, considered too independent and rebellious. She wrote autobiographies chronicling her life, documenting visions she claimed to have had, including her battles with the devil, her visions of saints and the Virgin Mary, and examples of divine grace that enabled her to foresee future events or cure the sick. Cecilia Ferrazzi was convicted of heresy and sentenced to seven years in prison by the Italian inquisition. Her book *Autobiografia di una santa mancata* (autobiography of an aspiring saint) is still available in print.

Antonia Tanini Pulci was a 15th century playwright and poet from Florence, Italy. Her father was Francesco d'Antonio di Giannotto Tanini, an Italian merchant. Her mother was Jacopa di Torello di Lorenzo Torelli, a Roman from Trastevere. Pulci had five sisters and a brother along with a half-brother and a half sister, who were her father's natural and firstborn children. Antonia married Bernardo di Jacopo Pulci in 1470. Bernardo Pulci was notable in the literary sphere. He also held a notable position at the University of Florence. Antonia Pulci established herself as a prominent playwright by creating several 'miracle' plays, or *sacra rappresentazione*. A play of this genre is heavily based on religious stories. Typically, these plays are narrated by an angel, who covers all of the actions of the characters in the tale. The angel ends by explaining the lesson to be learned from the tale in an epilogue, called *l'angelo che licenzia*. In the later years of her life, she studied Latin and Scripture and wrote spiritual poetry and epic verse. She also used part of her returned dowry to purchase land and established a convent there. She also coordinated the building of the chapel of Santa Monica in the church of San Gallo. All of Pulci's plays were published in various editions throughout the fifteenth and sixteenth centuries. The works probably sustained their popularity because nuns could use them for convent theatre and devotional reading.

Teresa of Ávila was a 16th century Spanish Mystic, poet and memoirist. She wrote prominent works of Christian mysticism and meditations. She was a devotee to Mother Mary. Throughout her life she experienced dreams, visions and bouts of religious ecstasy which actually made her quite unwell. In one vision, the famous *transverberation*, a seraph drove the fiery point of a golden lance repeatedly through her heart, causing her an ineffable spiritual and bodily pain. Some suggest her visions are highly eroticised and she became known for her raptures, she is even reported to have levitated.

Anne de Marquets was a 16th century French Catholic nun, who wrote devotional sonnets. She entered a convent at a very young age and she proved to be gifted at ancient languages as well as creative writing. She was a talented Latinist and published a collection of Latin devotional poems. A book of her sonnets, *Les Sonets spirituels,* was published in 1605. Anne de Marquets' sonnets are also noteworthy because they exhibit the influence of post-Tridentine (North Italian) spirituality, in particular an interaction with contemporary meditation techniques.

Madre Cecilia del Nacimiento was a 16th century Spanish nun, mystic, writer and poet. She wrote in both verse and prose, primarily of her mystical experiences, but she also wrote romance poesia (romantic poetry), Christmas carols, limericks, redondilla (Spanish Stanza) and theatrical works. Copies of two of her works, *Cántico espiritual* and *La Noche Oscura,* are held in the convent of Valladolid, letters of hers have also been preserved, they describe her life in the convent and of her mystical experiences.

Tibors was an 11th century trobairitz (woman troubadour) of mediaeval Occitan literature. She was a lady of noble birth and her prose; ballads and poems were very popular in the Occitanic south of France courts. Like many of her troubadour comrades she wrote and performed poetry about mystical courtly love influenced by Arthurian legends and the concept of a beautiful, ethereal woman whose beauty is so astounding she is able to cast a spell over the knight who must serve and protect her.

Azalais de Porcairagues was a *Trobairitz* and *Joglar* (woman troubadour & minstrel), who composed in Occitan in the late 12th century. Coming from the area of Montpellier, Azalais was educated and a gentlewoman. One poem of hers that survived was an elegy (with an envoi) in dedication to Raimbaut of Orange who was a very famous and influential troubadour.

Vittoria Colonna was a 15th century poet and Italian noblewoman. She was very much in love with her husband and upon his early death, she took refuge at a convent in Rome because she couldn't bear to remarry and be without him. As a laywoman she experienced strong spiritual resumption and remained devout for the rest of her life.

In her love poetry dedicated to her deceased husband she employed figures from Ovidian myth, including characters such as the goddesses Diana, Europa, Danaë and Leda. In one sonnet she challenges love to transcend to heaven so she may see her husband again. She was an active participant in Italy's religious Reform movement in the 1530s and 40s and began to focus instead on spiritual matters. Her devotional poems caught the attention of the master painter Michelangelo and a very intimate (platonic) friendship ensued and they inspired each other's artistic expressions. She became his muse and he drew her a collection of drawings and she wrote a collection of religious verses. Mary Magdalene, is a figure who appears frequently in her spiritual poetry. She published a plethora of spiritual poetry in her lifetime.

Britain

Bandrui was the title given to a woman druid, as part of the initiatory process of becoming a druid. Within the initiations and training there was the Bardic stage – becoming mystical poets of the druid order. The name given to poetesses once they attained the bardic title, were called *Banflaith*.

Brigid or Brigantia was the goddess of poetry and divination to the ancient Celtic Britons, equivalent to Roman goddess *Minerva* and India's *Saraswati*, Brigid was a popular deity for the Druids and Bards to petition for inspiration. Many poets were bards and bards would have been initiated as Druids. Bards were keepers of sacred knowledge passed on through song, poetry, storytelling. Much knowledge of these women and their poetry are lost but I can name them here: Ness, Accuis, Col, Erase, Eirage, Eang, Banbhuanna, Gaine are all documented druidesses and most likely performed sacred poetry. Beaferlic was a renowned priestess of Northumberland, Fedelm was a poetess and prophet in Irish mythology and Brigid of Kildare was a priestess of pre-Christian Ireland later turned patron saint of poetry, midwifery, newborns and more.

Thrutgeba Leoba was an 8th century abbess of Tauberbischofsheim, lady of letters, scribe of scriptures and composed poetry. She was part of the Benedictine double-monastery in Dorset. She is considered the first named female poet of England. One of her only surviving manuscripts was a letter she sent to St Boniface, a Christian missionary in Germany who was her cousin, and within this letter she included a poem. She was also a disciple of Abbess Eadburga of Thanet who taught her to study and write poetry.

Hugeburc was an 8th century English nun, hagiographer and poet. She lived in the Bavarian monastery of Heidenheim and travelled extensively from England to Germany as a missionary for Bishop Boniface. Hugeburc composed poems and ballads of the lives of saints Wynnebald and Willibald. She is the first known Englishwoman to have written a full-length literary work and the only woman author of a saint's life from the Carolingian period. She had also written a secret code in the space of two texts which was not deciphered for 1,200 years. In

1931 the scholar Bernard Bischoff unravelled it from *'Ego una indigna saxonica nomine Hugeburc ordinando hec scribebam'* which translates to 'I, an unworthy Saxon nun named Hugeburc, composed this.' Hugeburc probably understood that women weren't encouraged to take credit for their work, often their names erased and their work later attributed to a male comrade, she was ensuring we knew she was the author of these poems.

Princess Gwenllian was a 12th century Welsh princess. Historians speculate she is the authoress of the epic and mystical poem-story the *Mabinogion.* Because the Mabinogion details female characters in such an honest and sensitive way, Celticist and Lecturer Dr Breeze believes there is no way a monk would have wanted to write about, let alone understood the complexities and even the humanity of womanhood such as child-bearing, childlessness, wet-nursing, fostering and the upbringing of children as well as women's grief, among other themes such as women having strong personalities and backstories in their own right. The female characters also all seem to be the ones getting the men out of the messes they made, making the women subtle heroes of the entire epic, this is therefore a feminist epic poem. Princess Gwenllian was a mother of four and a warrioress, she died leading an attack on the invading Normans in 1136.

Julian of Norwich was a 14th century English writer, mystic and anchoress hermit. Her writings, now known as *Revelations of Divine Love,* are the earliest surviving English language works by a woman. Julian lived in permanent seclusion as an anchoress in her cell, she felt this was a calling to live a life in isolation in a tiny room which was attached to St Julian's Church, Norwich. There was a little window that opened up into the church so she could participate in religious service. At the age of 30 she became seriously ill and it was thought she was on her deathbed, she believed she could feel her soul transcending the suffering of the body; however, Julian received a series of visions and revelations of the *Passion of Christ,* which she wrote down in a manuscript known as the *Long Text* as a way to teach us of our sacred vulnerability and how we can still know love and healing regardless of suffering. Julian is today considered to be an important Christian mystic and theologian.

Gwerful Mechain is the only female mediaeval Welsh poet from whom a substantial body of work from the 15th century that is known to have survived. She is known for her erotic poetry, in which she praised the vulva among other things. She unabashedly wrote and performed bawdy playful poetry celebrating a woman's body, eroticism and sexual desires. Some of her work is religious and devotional in nature, oftentimes linking religiosity with sex – the sacred with the profane. It is said much of her poetry was born on a whim of the moment, it is stated she wrote a beautiful poem-hymn about the passion of Christ, she was also deeply moved by jealous wives and scandalous poets!

Anne Cary (Dame Clementina) was a 17th century poet and nun born in England and died in France. She was the daughter of Sir Henry Cary, Viscount Falkland, her mother Elizabeth was a dramatist and her sister Lucy was a writer. After spending her childhood in England, she was sent to Europe with siblings to be in the care of Benedictine monks within the joined order of Benedictines in Cambrai. Later in her life she founded the abbey 'Our Lady of Good Hope' in Paris (1652) and remained there until her death (1671).

She wrote devotional poetry and songs, some of her works include: Eight Collection Books, Psalms and spiritual songs (in three parts). Her writings can be found in *"Glow-Worm Light," Writings of 17th Century English Recusant Women from Original Manuscripts* (1989).

Margery Kempe was another 14th century writer, mystic and traveller from Norfolk, England known for writing through dictation *The Book of Margery Kempe*, a work considered by some to be the first autobiography in the English language. Her book chronicles her domestic tribulations, her extensive pilgrimages to holy sites in Europe and the Holy Land, as well as her mystical conversations with God. After the birth of her first child, Kempe went through a period of crisis for eight months, which was potentially an episode of postpartum psychosis. During this time, she claimed to have had visions of numerous devils and demons attacking her. She also had visions and visitations of Jesus Christ, Mary and other religious figures. These visions and hallucinations physically affected her bodily senses, causing her to hear sounds and smell unknown, strange odours. She also wrote in her book of hearing a heavenly melody that made her weep, it is later documented she visited Julian of Norwich who confirmed her visions and incessant tears of devotion were genuine experiences connecting her to God. She was tried for heresy three times but never convicted.

Anne Askew was an English writer, poet, and Protestant preacher of the 16th century. At 26 years old she was condemned as a heretic during the reign of Henry VIII. She is also one of the earliest known female poets to compose in the English language. Anne Askew wrote and published a memoir called *Examinations* which chronicles her persecution and offers a unique look into sixteenth century femininity, religion, and faith. Her writing is unusual because it deviates completely from what is expected from 'Tudor women' or, more specifically, 'Tudor women martyrs'. Anne was the first and only woman ever to be tortured in the Tower of London. Her poetry was devotional in nature and also explored themes of womanhood in a man's world plus ballads documenting her persecution and imprisonment.

Christina Rossetti was an English writer and poet of 18th century England. Considered the High Priestess of Pre-Raphaelitism, Christina had a genuine lyric gift that could articulate both the joy of being alive and the bitterness of loss. Her poetry was devotional with magical undertones and inspired by the romantic stylings of the pre-Raphaelite movement. Her most famous poem is 'The Goblin Market'. Rossetti worked voluntarily in 1859–1870 at the St Mary Magdalene house of charity in Highgate, a refuge for ex-prostitutes. It is suggested that 'The Goblin Market' may have been inspired by "fallen women" she came to know.

Catherine Crowe was an 18th century novelist, playwright and spiritualist. Two of her plays, the verse tragedy *Aristodemus* (1838) and the melodrama *The Cruel Kindness* (1853) were both published in London in 1853. Crowe turned increasingly to supernatural subjects, inspired by German writers. Her collection *The Night-side of Nature* (1848) became her most popular work and was reprinted as recently as 2000. According to historians she is accredited as the first 'paranormal investigator' because she investigated and wrote about supernatural experiences and hauntings. She also brought to light a variety of phenomena such as: Out of body experience, near deaths, prophetic dreams and extrasensory perception. Catherine introduced the concepts 'doppelganger' and 'poltergeist' into English usage. It is stated that Charles Dickens slandered her work and ruined her reputation which is why she isn't as widely known today.

Pamela Colman Smith was a late 19th century British-Jamaican Artist, poet and mystic. Best known for her illustrations of the globally known Rider-Waite-Smith Tarot deck. She also illustrated over 20 books, wrote two collections of Jamaican folklore, edited two magazines, and ran the Green Sheaf Press, a small press focused on women writers. Working as an illustrator and theatre set designer in London, she was given the nickname 'Pixie' by the group leader of a theatre group. She joined the Hermetic Order of the Golden Dawn in 1901 and in the process met A. E. Waite, who commissioned her illustrations for his tarot deck being published with Rider & Sons publishing house (A Penguin Random House division). Pamela also wrote poetry but only two poems have survived, one called 'A dream' of which she describes a dream she had of meeting lovely spirits holding hearts as they floated out of a tomb and into a church with a blue door. Another poem entitled 'Alone' she describes her sadness of feeling isolated in the world. Both poems are accompanied by illustrations. She died in Bude, Cornwall penniless. She wasn't paid much for the work she created for the Rider-Waite deck (over 80 illustrations) and she never received royalties or mass commercial success once the deck was published either.

I could write an entire book about women writers and poets, as there are many more, I chose to focus mainly on the devotional poets and mystical writers or those of a rebellious nature that didn't fall into the confines of society and have become obscure or lesser known than their male comrades. The lives of these women are varied, many were philosophers, feminists, queens, courtesans, scholars, scientists, playwrights, scribes, warriors and more. All of them follow the path of the liminal world in their own way and document that in their magical writing – whether priestess, witch, mystic or occultist – different threads of the same tapestry seeking to explore and surrender to a mighty and feral energy beyond their personal egos and humanness, all of them from varying cultures and faiths. These women understood that space between the notes, that wordcraft or poetry straddles those boundless mysteries, harnessing language as a tool to manifest something so ethereal, where shadows and light weave together in the signature of all things. Their work, although whispers and fragments, still scream loudly, carried through time like a spell hurtling through quantum trajectories and aether to be heard, to be remembered.

Make a Connection

If you feel drawn to a particular poetess that I've mentioned, her spirit may be calling to you. Try to do more research on her or the form of poetry from that time, bring her into your rituals as a guide for your magical writing and word witchery.

Women are now reclaiming the archetype of the witch and the priestess, we are reclaiming our voices, whether that is speaking up against oppression in a protest, casting spells against corrupt world leaders, topping the charts with hypnotising melodies or becoming famous Instagram poets influencing the masses. The voices of these creatrixes today are the same frequency as the women who came before us.

These ancient and mediaeval poetesses connected with the divine through written and spoken word. All of them lived, loved and created with freedom. And yet somewhere in our recent history women's voices, creativity and sacred femininity has been crushed. Enheduanna and her descendants are living proof of a time when women's voices, wisdom and magic were once revered.

The Weaver Priestesses

> The word *Text,* is in fact, etymologically linked to *Textiles,* the word comes from the Latin *Textus* which means *That which is woven, 'web'* or *texture. Textus* itself is derived from *Texere* which means *to weave.* –Mary Wellesley, Historian and Author of 'Hidden Hands: The Lives of Manuscripts & their makers'.

According to the book *The Hebrew Priestess* by Jill Hammer, poetry priestesses and word witches work with the energies of 'weaving' and are known as 'weaver priestesses'. Rachel Koppelmann says:

> *...the experience of the Weaver is an experience of fluidity, being able to channel whatever is appropriate or necessary to best serve the higher good. It's about letting something come through, she can take individual divine strands, disparate things and make this synergistic new thing. Weaving is a process that happens infinitely across time and space.*

Basque wise women were called *Azti* and they worked with spirit helpers called *Mamarro* or *Galtzgorri*. These women were said to keep these helpful spirits in their needlecases called *Kuthun,* which also translates to "amulet, book or letter". Magically charged vessels also utilised for craft and writing.

In mediaeval Spain some wise women were called *Carminatrix* from the name 'Carmen' which is Latin for 'Charm'. These women were local healers of their community who chanted healing poems as they performed ritual cures, thus weaving magical words into the cure.

In Old English these women were called *'Wyrtgælstre'* which means *'women who chant over herbs'*.

The *Völva* were Germanic wise women (also described as priestesses and seeresses). These were important women in their communities who were well versed in ritual, herbalism, charms and poetic incantation for healing and speaking with spirit. Spirits had to be called at night using chants for protection or ceremonial song.

These are women who channel the goddess and magic from liminal realms by weaving words as poetic incantations, prayers and spells – *she who weaves worlds with words*.

The Poetic Priestess of antiquity to the Wise Word Witch of the mediaeval world to the present day – they are one and the same, they just lived in different abodes! The priestess in her temple, the witch in her cottage on the fringe of society.

Women for centuries have been working with the inherent power of the word through art, poetry, sigil creation, charms, weaving words into fabric, dream journaling, diaries, letters, writing spells and rituals as well as singing and chanting. Wordcraft enables us to manifest our intentions into reality. When we write for magical or sacred purposes consciously, our bodies become an expression of that magic. It awakens our sacral chakra- the womb space that births all forms of creativity. It opens our hearts to create with love, our throat chakra blooms with self-expression and communication, and the third eye is unfurled because writing acts as a gateway for daydreaming, connecting us to the heavens and the stars.

Weaving words like thread on a magical spinning wheel reminds us just how powerful and divine poetry can be and how it can be a great catalyst for personal, social and planetary change.

Conjuring Poetica

The writing of poems is an alchemical process. Concrete words can frame more ephemeral thoughts and emotions. To be an alchemist is to work with the transmutation of one substance to another, while poets need to utilise both realism and symbols, and be able to shift seamlessly between conscious and unconscious levels as well as divine beyond our human experience.

Letters and words are symbols that become vessels – containers of potent word magic. The poet or writer becomes the conduit of that magic. The craft of words can be incredibly prophetic, a formidable force erupting from the subconscious and the great beyond, divining messages from dreams or deep primal feelings channelling symbolic wisdom.

Do you feel poetry magic or writing for healing is for you? Creating poetry and working with the innate wisdom of language has been a practice for thousands of years. What's so great about utilising poetry, journaling and writing into your magical application is that it's affordable and accessible. You just need a pen or pencil and scraps of paper or notebook. You may wish to incorporate your poetry-craft into your grimoire at a later date too.

The process of writing poetry takes place in a liminal space. Throughout this book create your altar, your place of sanctity. Light candles, work with stones such as clear quartz, tiger's eye, labradorite, sunstone and blue lace agate or simple stones found in your local woodland and shells found in the sand dunes.

Play music to inspire you, depending on the poem-spell focus. Perhaps it's love? Manifestation? Exalting a goddess? Cord cutting? Inner child healing?

Take deep breaths and meditate. Take yourself on a visual journey, summon a deity that would enjoy your poem or perhaps poetesses from the past as guides? Light incense, and ignite all your senses. You may wish to consider which moon phases you wish to perform your poetry and include local herbs and flowers as part of your offering. Create a space that sets the tone for conjuring a poetic spell or ritual. The activities throughout the book are not set in stone, as you weave your world with words you will create what is best for you and can substitute items you feel better suited depending on what you have to hand or what's local to you.

Part II

"Long before the Soul incarnates, it is sound. It is for this reason that we love sound."

— Hazrat Inayat Khan

Welcome to the Temple

Poetry, Magic and Writing Rituals

Magic…is the ancient and absolute science of nature and Her laws. –A.L Constant, *The history of magic*, London 1922

In the second half of the book, I've created ritual activities for readers to incorporate into their own practice if they wish. These are sample rituals and spells that you can adapt or utilise as inspiration to create your own. All of the rituals include the encouragement of blending poetry, journaling, sigils, letters and more into your magical practice to connect to the numinous.

My intention is to bridge our modern praxis with those of the past. Ancient scriptures, mediaeval incantations and manuscripts and folk customs often contain a form of poetic prayer or song because words and language are the heart and soul of magic, it is your essence communicating with everything around you, giving it a pulse, giving it life. Poetry and the written word as a vessel of devotion is a universal act of worship around the world that helps us not only make sense of the signature of all things and commune with the elements within it, but to make the intangible tangible and to recognise how sacred it all is. Utilising the generative power of wordcraft enables the practitioner to wield their wands of inspiration, craft and manifest their pentacles, swish their swords to sever energy that does not serve and overflow with intention and love of their chalice.

Included are rituals written by some dear friends I wanted to be a part of the book. The chapter about lost women poetry priestesses and word witches inspired me to reach out to witchy women in my life to contribute. Whilst most of these rituals are created by me, I wanted other women to have a voice as a way to invoke the collective and timeless sisterhood.

Poetic Hymns to Invoke Goddess

I've held the opinion for a long time that the gods and goddesses choose the humans they want to work with, not the other way round; that they choose people who are similar in nature to themselves...Exploring deities through poetry can help us discover who they are – and who we are in their reflected light.
–Fiona Tinker, *Pathworking through Poetry*

As you've seen in the first half of the book and in your own research, there are so many poetic hymns and prayers that have been unearthed or found as inscriptions on temple walls or scribed onto offerings since the dawn of civilisation (happening around early 9th millennium BCE in what is known today as the 'fertile crescent' – Turkey, the Levant, Iran, Iraq, Syria etc, where the two sacred the Tigris and the Euphrates, regularly flooded the region). The Nile River also runs through part of it. These hymns were dedicated to numerous deities with the earliest intact recorded hymn by the high priestess Enheduanna of Sumeria to a goddess named Inanna who is the ancestor of Ishtar, Aphrodite and others. And we find devotional poetry to the divine throughout antiquity with the works of Sappho to Aphrodite, Muddupalani's erotic hymns to Radha and mediaeval bardic bawdy prose by Gwerfal Machain. And we know it's been common practice for witches of old to modern practitioners, to create rhyming chants when they call forth a supernatural being.

And it is poetry that is the most marked form of speech. It is always the most common form of prayers in ancient times; even many prayers that seem at first to be prose have been shown to be structured as poetry [in their own language] –Ceisiwr Serith, *The big book of pagan prayer and ritual*

Magical writing and devotional poetry act as gifts to the gods. The gift of words especially created for them as well as the gift of quality time to craft such reverence plus any offerings as part of the ritual show thoughtfulness and respect, like when you visit an old friend and you remember their favourite wine or cake and out of respect you wish to bring them these gifts on arrival. As with any communion – whether meals with a close friend or in the presence of the numina it is wise not to be empty-handed to ensure sincerity and altruism, offerings also remind us that the material is sacred, keeps us grounded as we connect to other realms. Just like us, deities don't want one-sided relationships. If you want to form a good relationship with sacred beings and petition them for help, you have to do the work and give offerings as an exchange or as a thank you for their time and generosity.

Which Goddesses or Gods are you Drawn to?

My Vedic teacher always says to me *'What you see in me, is also in you, the qualities of the goddess that we pray to, shine through us like gold. We already are whole and complete as we are'* meaning, we see attributes of what we worship in ourselves, or 'what we worship, we become'.

> *All mortals who live on the limitless Earth, Thracians, Greeks and foreigners, utter Your Glorious Name, which all honour, each in his own language, each in his own land.*
>
> *Syrians call you Astarte, Artemis, Nanaea. The tribes of Lycia call you Mother of all Gods, Greeks call you Hera of the lofty throne, and Aphrodite, kindly Hestia, Rheia and Demeter...*
>
> *My Lady, I shall not stop hymning your mighty power, Immortal Saviour, Goddess of the Many Names, Almighty Isis!* – Ancient Egyptian hymn to Isis

Most people don't know that before Shakespeare's Macbeth, Hecate was not the Goddess of Witches, this is a modern interpretation. All goddesses are goddesses of witches! It just so happens that when Shakespeare wrote *Macbeth*, he picked Hecate to be summoned. Hecate is not just the goddess of ghosts and necromancy, to the ancients she was the anima mundi (world soul), goddess of the seas, earth and heavens among many more things.

Aphrodite is not just a goddess of love and beauty she has epithets as a funerary goddess and as great queen mother goddess of Cyprus. Her Roman equivalent Venus was once a cabbage goddess of agriculture before Aphrodite's qualities were added to her.

Kali is not just a ferocious goddess of destruction; she is also the goddess of time – *Kala* means time in Sanskrit and so her name means *'she who has time'* and often we mistakenly petition her to vanquish our so called 'enemies' but her skull necklace is symbolic of the demons of our egos we need to conquer and slay within us. She is the great judge of our karmic actions, the epitome of what you send out, will be sent back to you threefold. If you invoke her to try and seek revenge on others, it's more likely her ruthless energy will come back to you. She is, however, a goddess of cutting cords, new beginnings and destruction as a way to make space in your life for self-transformation and rebirth. Kali is the freedom you gain from death.

It is a good thing to do thorough research, read archeology papers and history books to garner a deeper connection and understanding to your deity. A lot of information out there creates very diluted and superficial depictions of deities and so if you feel drawn to a particular goddess, it is important to dig deep into her ancient origins and evolution, you'll be surprised what you discover!

It is also important to learn the variety of epithets attributed to your deity, you'll be surprised they are so much more than just 'god of war' or 'goddess of wisdom'

For example, here are just a few of Hekate's:

Abronoê 'Gracious-minded', 'Providing Grace', 'Gracious'
Aktinochiatis 'Radiant haired', 'With Rays for Hair'
Alexeatis 'Averter of Evil'
Dadouchos 'Torch-bearer'
Daeira 'The Knowing One'
Enodia 'Of the crossroads', 'Of the Roads', 'Of the Path'
Genetyllis 'Birth-Helper', 'Goddess of Childbirth', 'Midwife'
Kardiodaitos 'Heart-Eater', 'Feasting on Men's Hearts'
Kleidouchos / Kleidoukhos 'Key-holder', 'Key-keeper'
Potnia Theron 'Mistress of Animals', 'Lady of Wild Beasts'
Zootrophos 'Nourisher of Life'

And Aphrodite:

Anaduomenê the goddess rising out of the sea
Antheia the blooming, or the friend of flowers
Apotrophia the expeller of the hearts of men
Despoina the ruling goddess or the mistress
Cypris Queen of Cyprus/Born on the shores of Cyprus
Genetullis the protectress of births
Limenia protectress of the harbour
Peithô The personification of Persuasion
Ourania Queen of heaven
Epitumbidia she upon the graves
Androphonos Killer of Men

As you can see, they are both multifaceted goddesses and it seems sometimes they switch places! Who'd have thought

Hecate would be described as 'Nourisher of life' or Aphrodite as 'She upon the graves'? Aphrodite is *not* just a love goddess and Hecate is *not* just a goddess of the dead.

It is important to really get to know your chosen deity – their origin stories, historical evidence, potential excavated charms and spells invoking them, their folklore, corresponding symbols, animals, moon phases, gifts they like to be given and more so that you have a good relationship with them, wouldn't you want to be treated the same way?

As well as this, knowing their multitudes enables you to be precise with exactly what you wish to praise or petition them for.

When you create and chant your devotional poem make sure you also create a sacred sanctuary with an altar, candles, incense and ritual oil as well as images or statues of them, perhaps including objects associated with the elements and even their favourite symbols or food offerings.

Harness the priestess energy within you and chant with respect and love, deities love to be appreciated. Your votive words don't even need to petition them for anything, you could just create a votive poem purely to praise them as part of your offering in a devout ceremony. Taking time to create a space and work your word craft with intention enhances the frequency. Before you create your hymn you may want to sit a while in reflection with your journal and consider why you feel connected to this goddess, being or spirit? Can you describe them? Can you relate to their qualities and stories? What feelings arise when you contemplate the reason why this deity is calling to you? Is it an internal reflection of yourself in the present moment?

Once you've set up your ritual space, created and recited your hymn, don't forget to praise and thank them for their presence or for assisting you before you close the circle.

Devotional Poems to the Sacred Feminine

This poem imagines myself as an ancient priestess telling Inanna I love her darkness, her contradictions and therefore helps me to accept myself and my shadows. This came from when someone with malicious intent, spitefully called me "always the paradox", which now looking back is quite an ignorant and redundant thing to say, because don't we all straddle between a variety of contradictions and paradoxical natures? It's what makes us human.

I ask her to guide me through my underworld – my descent so I may rise from my shadows and the shadows projected onto me. It's an invocation to her as goddess of both life and death, of shadow and light.

I wanted the poem to feel ancient and as if archaeologists have just discovered it on a clay tablet somewhere, which is why some of the words have been left to look untranslated.

Inanna is the heavenly queen of both love and war; two seemingly paradoxical forces of divine womanhood, she celebrates what stirs the blood, our passions, our humanity. Inanna was also severely punished and demonised by her sister Ereshkigal and sent deep into the underworld but as the evening star she transcends the pain and rises to heaven, something I can also relate to!

Inanna: *High Queen of queens*

High-Queen of the dark-light,
With all this lethal light,
Resolute in your fanged bright night,
A frightful swift Empress of swords and dust.
Forceful are your fruitful twin rivers,
Fruitful are your unfaltering Zagros mountains.
Unfaltering is my devotion to you.

Star-knowledge from the beginning of time,
The red egg of the Kur serpentine universe.
Wind haunted junipers and the rain-veiled dark roses,
cry out from their bloody buds;
a choir keening to your golden rage,
Death-vesseled lady of the hunt and the resurrection.
Swaying in the sands sauntering to hidden places of the Shanidar cave.

You sing the alchemy of the dead,
You sing the shadowed origins of the blackest oceans,
You strike the ground and out sprang a lion,
A war-like gift, a lion on fire, a heart stirring lioness.
You sing out the ash of new gods and choke their ruinous Adamic scriptures,
You shriek with desirous dragon-delight with your vagina dentata,
Feasting with the beasts of Ki.

Enrobed in violet flamed sovereignty,
From the birth of the garden to your comet garlands,
A governess of the grain and the harvest.
Your eyes are a wilderness of snares,
Your diamond feet crushing the red clot of poppies,
freckled across the valley in a cosmic sanguinary gush.
Birthing and culling, thriving and waning.

Mistress of the muses, of desert sands and secrets.
Dancing with Kuliana along the Tigris and Euphrates waters.
Gorgeous lady! You are the beginning,
Lady of the first cuneiform gleaming.
Mountain born! You rose from the primordial sea.

At the dawn I seek thee, in the glory of the kipur,
I pray to you from the Opal-mooned ziggurat.
And give offerings to you at the Huluppu tree by the marsh reeds.
Serpent Queen – mistress eagle, great Nin-dingir!
Breathe into me your truth and beauty.
I am your priestess of the Gipar,

High Priestess of the grain and the grave,
Of song-weavers and scroll keepers of your apocrypha.
I offer you Arazoles and dreamy Hul-Gil from Alashiya's bilbil juglets,
Sweet Kyphi and Nymphaea Caerulea from the kingdom of Kemet,
Lapis, honey and kangina of grapes from the river valley of Ariana,
Pomegranates and lemons from Sikelia's Mount Eryx,
Gold, Nerium Oleander and apricots from the Lydian coast,
And Jasper, Jet and strawberries from the isle of Albion.

From the Kopet Mountains to the Caspian Sea,
From my heart to the vault of the skies,
I am devoted to you in all languages and in all hearts,
in all the rain-soaked earth and in all the stars.
Inanna, I cherish you,
My unbridled Queen of queens,
I bow to you,
I am bound to you,
Oh, Sacred heart,
Great goddess of love and hate,
Of life and death, of passion and peace,
Of all the holy contradictions,

maiden of the ascension and descension,
of the looping serpent's Ouroboros,
Guide me through my darkness,
So, I may see the light.
So that I may rise from the fall,
With the wings of the dawn,
of your everlasting Arammu.

Nemetona, Celtic Goddess of Groves and Sanctuaries

Scholars believe her to be the Celtic variant of the Greek goddess Nemesis. The etymology of this name means *'dispense justice'*, making Nemesis the goddess of divine retribution.

In proto-Celtic *'Nemos'* means 'heaven, sky', in Latin *'Nemus'* means 'grove' and in Old Breton *'Nimet'* means 'sanctuary'. Nemetona was often conflated with the Roman goddess Victory and petitioned with Mars before battle. Making this goddess both a deity of sacred groves and divine justice.

Having done some research of who Nemetona is, what her symbols are and learned a bit about her history gave me a solid foundation to create a hymn to her.

Here is an excerpt of a devotional poem I wrote for Nemetona as her aspect of karmic goddess of divine retribution and protectress of sacred borders.

Divine lady on the hillside,
Watching over the land and skies,
Queen of the borders,
The keeper of this land,
Protect this sacred place from all that is dark,
Spirits of evil shall not pass,
Show me the wise way through the groves,
To my heart,
To imbue me with courage,
You fight for justice to keep me safe,

Nemetona, she of the sword,
Banish what does bring peace
to my sanctuary of being.
Reflect it back with the light of your stars,
And the sheen of your shield,
May they know their own darkness,
May my garden and home always know serenity.
I praise you Nemetona,
Goddess of boundaries and karmic reckoning.

Saints

You can also petition saints; this is a common practice with both pagans and Christians today. There are many locations around the world dotted with shrines of saints that are covered in blessing rags and prayers for healing, protection, safe voyages and love.

Here is my prayer-poem to Saint Sarah, patroness of infertility, the Romany, laughter, protectress of outsiders, voyages, travel and safe seafaring.

Her name and story is obscure, some legends say she was an Egyptian or Hindu maid who journeyed with the three Mary's to the south of France, others say she was Mary Magdalene's daughter, there are accounts that she was a local wise woman welcoming the three Mary's upon arrival and some say her name is an amalgamation of the three Hindu goddesses Saraswati-Lakshmi-Kali (which to me seems the most plausible given her name and she is depicted with beautiful dark south Indian features, plus the Roma originated from Punjab and Rajasthan areas, they were misidentified as 'Egyptians', later shortened to 'Gypsies' just like Sara-La-Kali). She is beloved by the Roma during the Saintes-Maries-de-la-Mer ceremony in Camargue.

Given my partial Romani roots from my mother's side and surviving an ectopic pregnancy I felt called to devote a poem to her as a way to connect with my female ancestors and for womb healing. Here is a sample of it:

Sarah-La-Kali

Shadow of the Madonna,
Beautiful dark-mooned face lady of the Rom,
Hands holding the blue cloth of the womb,
Lady saint of the wanderers,
You who sailed the seas and stars,
You are the anchor for all that is holy hurt,
My birth cut to death,
Cut the cloth of my bloodline,
My blood poured out in rivers,
The way your tears flow for the discarded,
Cut away my pain,
Cut away the grief,
Cut out the shine of stars
And stitch up my wounds with light,
Anchor my heart to the breath of the sea.
May your gentle palms, hold all neglected
Women, who walk alone in the ache of the womb.

Working with the Muses and Nymphs

Muses were associated with sacred springs, the water symbolic of divine flow of inspiration that swirls through a poet or artist. *Erato* was the muse of lyric and erotic poetry, *Polyhymnia* was the muse of sacred poetry and hymns and Calliope was the muse of epic poetry, song and dance. Nymphs were associated with nature and so pastoral poetry was commonly crafted to connect with these beings. This type of poetry originated in ancient Greece and it is usually centred around rural life.

Here is a snippet of my hymn to commune with the three muses of Poetry.

Three ladies of the water's way
And of the sacred word,
I invoke thee to dance with thee,
By the rivers so sweetly you play,
I hear the laughters and song and harp,
The majesty of your honeyed spirits,
May I join you?
Erato calls fourth Catarina del la mer
And her silk bodied universe.
Unbridled passions gallop in the undertow!
Polyhymnia make my words shine like
Gold for the goddess!
Calliope, imbue me with your pure voice.
Like a rainstorm melting into seas,
My clear watered dreams and poems
Flow down the mountain and into my heart,
From your generous and perpetual chalice.

Poetry Rituals for the Pagan Sabbats

The Sabbats celebrate the earth's journey around the sun. The year is broken up into eight festivities which are observed by modern pagans. These seasonal events differed throughout Europe, the Anglo-Saxons marked the solar stations while insular Celtic tribes marked the mid points between them. As this is a popular topic for many pagan and witchcraft books, I have only selected three sabbats as examples to create writing rituals. You can utilise other sources as frameworks to create rituals for the sabbats that are not included in this chapter.

Imbolc Three Wish Spell

According to historians, prior to early Christianity, priestesses used to gather on the hill of Kildare to tend to their ritual fires to invoke the goddess Brigid for protecting their community, their livestock and providing a fruitful harvest.

This is a very simple and sweet spell to invoke the loving and healing energies of Brigid and send them out to others during Imbolc. As a triple goddess associated with healing and poetry, she will grant you three wishes.

You will need:

Small wooden hoop
Three ribbons
Small blue pouch
Pen and paper
Snow drops
Feathers
Twine
3 White candle
Image or icon of Brigid

Light your candle and connect with the spirit of Brigid. Say a sweet prayer to call her presence to you. Write out three poem-wishes. One for each of her aspects:

- The first: a wish for the good of others such as animals, the planet, humanity.
- The second: a wish for a loved friend, partner or family member.
- The third: a wish for yourself.

As you write out each wish, light the three candles to ignite and breathe life into all three wishes.

- Next hold a ribbon in your hand and recite the wishes out loud to enchant the spell into the ribbon. You may wish to sprinkle a bit of water onto the ribbons to represent Brigid's healing waters.
- Once you have done all three, tie them onto the small wooden hoop.
- Fold or roll up your wishes with the feathers and place them in the pouch then tie the pouch onto the hoop so it dangles in the centre.
- Add your bunch of snowdrops gently to the hoop with string or twine.
- Leave the candles to burn down completely and hang your cute little wreath – wish bag on the handle of your front door for Brigid to collect, she will make sure your wishes are granted.

Rhiannon Beltane Fire Release spell

Rhiannon is a beloved Celtic deity of mine. She is the first goddess of the Celtic pantheon I connected with. Just after surviving an ectopic pregnancy, I began having dreams of a lady on a white horse and I confided in my dear friend Dan the Druid about this. I said "I don't know who she is and I don't really connect with the symbolism of horses." Dan replied "My dear, it seems to me that Rhiannon is visiting you, don't you know she is the goddess of many things, including the otherworlds, particularly grief of losing a child? I will say, from my years of studying all things Celtic, out of all the Celtic deities, you are most like her, you have her Awen." Which cheered me up immensely to be told such a lovely thing.

In Ireland there is an old folk custom that believes if you light fires just before dawn at each corner of a crossroad and you sit quietly there, you can see Rhiannon ride by, galloping from the darkness of the West to the saluting sunrise.

Beltane, although a time of summery festivities, is also when the veil between worlds is at its thinnest. Rhiannon being a psychopomp can walk between the realms of mortals and the faery kingdom. Her Gaulish name "Rigani" means 'Great Queen' and her energy reigns over a multitude of attributes such as motherhood, forgiveness, sovereignty, independence, mercy, patience, the moon, groves, the spirit world, animals, grief, love, abundance, leadership and more.

This simple spell invokes her for her guidance on all things related to self-love and lightness of being as we walk into the first days of summer, we can turn our winters to dust and ash. Rhiannon, in the epic Mabinogion was betrayed by humans and accused and punished for a crime she never committed and this was during the time she was also grieving her son! Harsh moments like this in life can lead to self-doubt and low self-worth. Often women especially can doubt themselves – from their beauty to their intelligence and even our gut intuition! Like the events that happened to Rhiannon, we can end up believing lies told about us and we can also re-tell those lies to ourselves. Carrying the burden of other people's projections can be debilitating and limiting of our own light and personal power. The worst is our own self-criticism held in our hearts.

Rhiannon, with the fiery flicker of flames of the borderlands will transmute your pain into *your truth* and encourage feelings of summery grace, abundance and joy.

This ritual is to lighten your heart and alchemise your hurt with gentleness.

You will need:

Small fireproof pot or cauldron
Pen and paper
A jar or box
Matches
Rose petals
Water for safety
A key

On the first day of May begin to contemplate moments in your life that were hard, when you were bullied, ridiculed, criticised, judged, slandered, mocked, ostracised, controlled, made to feel unworthy or unlovable. Think about how this reinforced negative beliefs about yourself, made you doubt yourself or even fragment your own sense of self because these projections stole your confidence and self-actualising. How did this affect your life, your heart, perception of how you relate to yourself and the world?

On small strips of paper, write a small sentence every day of negative things said about you or that you've experienced and they've been ruminating in your heart and mind for a long time. Write down one a day and then roll it up away from you and place in your jar.

Over the whole month as well, begin to craft a devotional hymn to Rhiannon to petition her as queen of grief who can comfort you and expel your hurt.

Here is an excerpt of my hymn to Rhiannon to give you inspiration.

Rhiannon, great queen! The great mothering mare,
Carry my grief with you into the sunrise,
So with each new dawn it dissipates into golden dust!

On the 31st May, the first eve of the beginning of Summer, pour your slips of paper into your fire safe cauldron and carefully light them aflame! As you watch the negativity burn you may chant your hymn out aloud to Rhiannon! You have created your own personal Beltane fire!

As you chant your hymn, carefully hold your key over the flames and smoke, this key is a talisman for your connection to Rhiannon – unlocking portals to her realms to commune with her and it is also a symbol of opening doors to your heart to release the past hurt, sweep it out you and into the fire *dust to dust – ashes to ashes!*

Once the slips of paper are burned to ash you may want to rub some ash onto your key and throw the rest out into the aether. Send your rose petals out into the wind as an offering to Rhiannon.

Sit for a while with your journal to write down positive things about yourself and lovely things people have said about you. In the folklore of Rhiannon, she has blackbirds flying around her singing beautiful songs so imagine all positive words about you flying towards you and being sung to you on the wings of birds – these are songs of your truth, beauty, worth.

The Hearth of Hestia, Ritual for Samhain

Hestia is the Greek Goddess of the Hearth, Fire and Home. More than that, she is the personification of the hearth and represents community and domesticity; her name means altar, hearth and fireplace. The worship of Hestia was centred around the hearth, both domestic and civic, which was essential for warmth, food preparation, and the completion of sacrificial offerings to deities. As the guardian of the sacred flame on Mount Olympus, home of the Gods, Hestia was often given the first and last libations of wine or food, before any other sacrifices were made.

Invoking Hestia's name at the beginning of a ritual helps us establish a connection with our inner fire, with the energies that link us back to our families, our ancestors, our roots as part of our culture. Hestia reminds us that, even when alone, we are part of something greater and that as long as we keep the fires burning, we will always find purpose, community and warmth.

This invocation can be used when casting a circle as a coven or as a solitary practitioner, and as part of a festival celebration.

Burn your favourite incense. Frankincense and Myrrh were the most commonly used in religious ceremonies in ancient Greece and are excellent choices. Iris, lavender and peony are also specifically associated with Hestia.

Light a candle of your chosen colour, this can be relevant to the spell or ritual you are performing, or to the festival you are marking. Green candles are great for fertility, good fortune and abundance spells. Brown candles can be wonderfully grounding. White candles can be used when looking to connect with esoteric energies, perhaps for ancestral work, or past life healing, and they also represent the Maiden aspect of the Goddess, and so they are particularly appropriate for working with Hestia, who is a Virgin Goddess.

Offer wine or food to the fire and chant this invocation to attune to Hestia's energies.

"Brightest Hestia, Sacred Flame,
I call upon your blessed name.

I offer you this first libation,
and welcome you to this celebration.

First and Last, daughter of Time,
I worship at your Altar divine.

Hearth and heart, together or apart,
You connect us to the very start.

Your silver thread binds us together,
Your eternal fire a shining tether.
To our ancestral wisdom, to our roots,
To the fruits and truths of our earthly pursuits,
As it is now, as it was before,

Merry meet, merry part and merry meet once more."

Write a short poem-prayer to Hestia to ask for her warmth and protection over the hard winter months and throw it into the fire. May her soft glow carry you through the darkness.

Warm your hands by the fire and then place your hands on your heart with eyes closed to call her energy into the room.

This ritual was created by Ninfa Sferlazzo-Hayes, author, writer, mother and witch. She lives in Manchester with her family and cats. She loves researching new divination methods and mythology.

Moon Phase Poetry Magic

In astrology the moon is a divine feminine entity and governs the tides of our emotions. Artemis is a Greek goddess often venerated and associated with the moon and young girls between ages five and ten in ancient Athens were sent to a sanctuary of Artemis for one year. Artemis later became associated with Selene, another goddess of the moon and Hekate is often depicted as a dark moon goddess, she is wonderful to petition for shadow work or celebrate her during the *Deipnon* (A feast on the last sliver of moonlight before the new moon). In many cultures around the world the moon is also linked with the realms of the dead due to its cyclical nature and its ability to disappear and reappear in our night skies – symbolic of a soul's descent and ascension between death and rebirth. In ancient Egypt it was common practice to have bathing rituals as it was believed with the help of the water, you could soak up and harness the moon's life-giving powers. The ancient Mayans also practised moon bathing to appease their lunar goddess and they believed it would grant them cosmic insight, visions and spiritual growth.

In old gardening almanacks, herbalists and gardeners would plant and harvest by the moon rather than the sun. This concept can be traced back to ancient Babylon. This practice is making a comeback with green witches and gardeners alike working with the four main cycles of this celestial orb. Mediaeval documentation believed that water can be drawn deeper into the soil when the moon is waning and when the moon is waxing it encourages the water to be drawn up and out of the earth. Mediaeval writers believed the moon could affect a person's health, hence the word 'Lunacy' and Hildegard, abbess and poet of the 12th century wrote that differing moon phases could determine an individual's personality and prescribed bloodletting during the waning crescent for those who need to release toxins from their body and soul.

Rituals during different phases of the moon can bring about emotional or psychological transformation and even affect physical outcomes of our material world.

There are only three activities in this chapter because there are a plethora of books and online content devoted to Moon Magic. If you are inspired by these three, you can adapt any other moon spell to incorporate poetry and writing rituals into your praxis.

Plant by the New Moon Hymn to Selene

The dark moon after the waning crescent is a phase of new beginnings, potential, gestation, introspection, curiosity and hope. Its frequency is similar to the innocence of the Fool or optimism and renewing energy of the Star card. People born in this phase are youthful souls, light-hearted, enthusiastic for new beginnings and they look at the world with child-like wonderment. This moon phase is all about cosmic resets, planting seeds for new ideas to sprout, starting new projects, creative introspection and listening to your heart for new potential directions.

> *The Astera (stars) hide away their shining for around Selene, when in all her fullness she shines over all the earth"* –Sappho 6th century BCE

> *Queen of the stars, all-wise Goddess, hail! Decked with a graceful robe and amble veil. Come, blessed Goddess, prudent, starry, bright, come, moony-lamp, with chaste and splendid light, shine on these sacred rites with prosperous rays, and pleased accept thy suppliants' mystic praise. –Orphic Hymn 9 to Selene*

> *Hail to thee, thou new moon, Guiding jewel of gentleness! O new moon of the seasons.*

Thou queen-maiden of guidance, Thou queen-maiden of good fortune, Joyful maiden of the graces! – Carmina Gadelica, 19th century

What you need
Jasmine incense
Jasmine oil
Pen and paper
Opal or selenite
8 White tealight candles
Image of Selene
Seeds
Small bowl of water
Small cup of water
Scrying ink
Small pot
Crown

- Wear your crown and light your incense. Anoint your water and candle wax with drops of jasmine oil, you may also wish to anoint your crown too. Plant your seeds in a pot of soil – this represents potential and new growth.
- Place your pot by an image of Selene, create a crescent shape with your eight candles and place your crystals within the crescent.
- Add a few drops of ink into your bowl of water and connect with the shapes and patterns emerging. What do you see in your mind's eye that you wish to bring forth and sprout anew?
- Create a hymn to petition Selene with her bright energy of clarity and let her chart the way.
- Imagine her coming swiftly to you, riding on her horse across the cosmos, carrying your new beginnings on the back of her chariot.

- What qualities do you wish to germinate and bloom right now?
- Once you are happy with your hymn, recite it out loud as you pour the cup of water onto your pot of soil (with seeds buried inside).
- To complete the ritual, you may leave your pot on a sill under the new moon, with the image of Selene and crystals placed at the base to charge and draw down the energy of genesis.

Full Moon Poetry Abundance Spell

The brightest orb in the night sky, this moon phase is all about manifestation and abundance. Its energies are that of the Magician tarot card manifesting desires into reality or the Empress pregnant with the world. People born under this moon are vivacious, bright souls brimming with a creative spark, they have an uncanny ability to manifest their desires into reality. They make waves as they walk their path with their free spirits and wild hearts. This moon phase is all about gratitude, expansion, wealth, fertility, completion and positive affirmations.

You will need:

Money plant or bamboo
Pen and paper
Moonstone
8 silver coins
Cinnamon incense sticks

Write a rhyming poem-spell to attract abundance to you, call in the elements and the moon's energy. Bury it carefully in the soil of your money plant pot (or wrap around your bamboo), place eight silver coins around the plant with the moonstone in the middle (by the trunk of the plant). Leave your abundance manifestation spell there until the next full moon. Notice what you may have manifested over that cycle. Be careful what you wish for, if you manifest it, it might come true!

Example of money manifestation poem-spell:

In the light of the full moon's glow,
Magic dances in a mystical show.
Wealth and abundance, they do bring,
Good health and happiness, they sing.

Under the moon's enchanting spell,
Dreams and wishes, they do swell.
Prosperity and joy abound,
As the moon's energy surrounds.

Embrace the magic of the full moon,
Let your heart and soul commune.
With wealth and health in perfect bundle,
May abundance in your life ever kindle.

To complete the spell, burn cinnamon incense in your home, particularly at your front entrance and near your money plant, cinnamon is meant to be lucky, not only does it ward off unwanted energy but attracts wealth. Visualise abundance coming to you in the breeze, carried on the fragrance of the cinnamon and sprouting from the plant pot.

Optional: Invoke a goddess of luck and prosperity by creating a hymn for her which you can read out daily at your altar.

Ritual of the Balsamic Moon

This is the final sliver before the cycle starts again. Often called the waning crescent, the balsamic moon is cooling and soothing. It is the energies of the Hermit or High Priestess. Individuals born under this moon are solitary and mystical, people are drawn to them but they enjoy leading quiet lives. They have soothing voices and bundles of hidden wisdom. This moon phase is all about tying up loose ends, healing emotional blockages, honouring your shadows, and cleansing your auric field, being at peace with little deaths in life, dream work, shadow work and contemplation.

You will need:

Bath (or shower or container of water)
Labradorite and black obsidian
Tea lights
Herbs and oils for shadow work
Black pen and paper
Black candle
Dark blue candle

Begin by creating a dark sanctuary in your bathroom. If you can, turn the lights down and add tea lights where possible. Burn lavender to cleanse the space and encourage restoration. Run a bath with oils and herbs specific for shadow and dream work such as peru balsam, dark orange, black frankincense, vanilla, salt and rosemary. Soak in the bath to cleanse your mind, body and auric field. Contemplate what needs releasing, can you let it go?

Then once you've spent some time in your incubation chamber, grab a black pen with your crystals and the candles.

Light the two candles side by side, with labradorite placed with the blue candle for reflection and black obsidian with the black candle for release.

On your piece of paper draw a large circle and then write down in a spiral from the top down into the middle everything you've been carrying in your heart that you need to release. You may choose to write this in a prose poem style or as straightforward prose. Once completed you may choose to scribble or paint over all those words to symbolise the waning crescent releasing this emotional debris from you. Fold the paper away from you and place the black obsidian on top.

With another piece of paper do the same but for this time, write in the circle what you're reflecting on? Lessons learned? Feelings that surfaced? How have you grown? You may choose to colour over the text with a royal blue to represent wisdom and serenity illuminated from releasing painful things. Fold this paper towards you and then place the labradorite on top.

Create a personal mantra to chant such as:

> *I am releasing what does not serve my highest good. I am entering this new cycle with a fresh, cleansed and healed perspective of my reality. I vanquish my demons, accept my ghosts and create space from what is now burned to dust.*

Take your release prose poem spell and burn it (safely) with the black candle and you may wish to do the same with your reflection prose poem spell, or keep that one in your grimoire.

To complete the ritual, write in your journal the visions that surfaced during your bath and contemplate what you are thankful for and now you've let go of things, you now have space to attract the new beginnings of the new moon. Fold towards you, add it to a small bag with your two crystals and place it under your pillow to welcome new moon potential.

Tarot Poetry

Poetry and Tarot work really well together as tools to explore abstract and universal concepts. Emotions and the complexities of life can be quite conceptual and difficult to decipher the underlying message and even life lessons. Tarot and poetry can help us communicate things in an accessible and tangible way and assist us with configuring symbolic subtleties through metaphor and universally recognised imagery.

Similarly to bardic epic poems and storytelling of queens and knights and quests, the archetypes of the tarot on the hero's journey are ingrained in our collective unconscious.

Incorporating poetry and tarot together as a way to ritualise your life can be a wonderful combined therapeutic daily practice. You could pull a card of the day and articulate the meaning behind it for you in your morning journaling routine. Or only work with the major arcana archetypes to connect with these characters in your daily life as part of your light and shadow work process, what aspects to these personas do you embody? What messages do these avatars share? How do they inform your strengths and even your shortcomings? Tarot with poetry gives a voice to the visual interpretation of your personal journey.

Five Card Tarot Poetry

You will need:

A tarot deck of choice
Pen and paper

Shuffle your cards and when you are ready pick five cards, it can be shorter than that or longer, it depends on how long you want your narrative to be. Choose cards with intention or let them jump out at you.

Once you have all your cards in a row, turn each of them over and notice the storyline.

With each card, create a sentence. Let the messages come through, consider their general symbolism whilst interpreting codes fitting for you.

For example:

Card one: Five of swords – *Cutting away the hurt of a thousand voices.*

Card two: Four of swords – *I was the soldier in their war but I yield to the sanctuary of serenity when I let go of their demons.*

Card three: Four of wands – *Grace in the form of smiles and stability manifests when I let go.*

Card four: Two of pentacles – *Let those fools juggle with their torment, bite and spite!*

Card five: Eight8 of pentacles – *And I shall rise up in the glory of all my suns and stars.*

Cutting away the hurt of a thousand voices,
I was the soldier in their war but I yield to the sanctuary of serenity,
Grace in the form of smiles and stability manifests when I let go of their demons.
Let those fools juggle with their torment, bite and spite!
And I shall rise up in the glory of all my suns and stars.

The poetic message I saw unfold was of a person who was dragged into a difficult and unhealthy situation, then recognising the need to cut away the hurt created by the voices of these people the protagonist had initially surrounded themselves with. The protagonist recognises they were a soldier in someone else's turbulent narrative but now let's go, to rest and discover healthier and peaceful people. Now as an outsider looking in with wisdom and serenity, the protagonist watches their past friends juggle with the karma they created. To me the eight of pentacles look like solar discs with stars engraved on them so I ended the poem with the protagonist choosing to concentrate on the good things in their life rather than being dragged back into the unhealthy dramas created by others.

Sit with your tarot by your altar. Spend a moment taking deep breaths, holding your deck with your eyes closed and channel inspiration down into your hands. When you're ready, pull out some cards. Begin to write what comes to mind, it is ok if the first draft is 'imperfect', you can format it into a poem that makes sense to you afterwards. From the poem you have created, does it speak to you? Does it feel like a message that resonates with you?

78 Poems of Tarot

Tarot poetry can be incredibly healing. This project is a longer writing ritual than the previous activity but focuses only on one card each time. You may wish to pull one card a day or one per weekend, giving you time to let the energies of that card reverberate and connect with you. This practice can become your weekly oracle messages. Tarot poetry is a wonderful alchemical process that fuses visual imagery with poetry magic, the combination of picture symbolism with wordcraft is a powerful portal to channel messages from the heart or from the threshold. Tarot has been linked to numerology, mysticism, spirituality, occult, astrology, kabbalah, fortune-telling, a psychological journey, therapy, meditation and so on. The list is almost endless. The reason for this eclectic spread of beliefs is because the cards use the language of symbols, and this ensures everyone can relate to them on a personal level.

I would suggest working with the Rider-Waite-Smith deck to begin with and if you enjoyed this process and wish to continue this form of writing ritual, then choose your next deck you wish to work with.

There doesn't have to be a particular order, have all the cards laid out and face down, hover your hand over them and select with intention, which one are you drawn to in that present moment. Don't worry whether your poem is perfect, just explore and play with words that come to you.

Once completed you'll have 78 poems bundled with wisdom and meaning for you. You may wish to write journal entries per card and poem as well to take note of what came up for you. Don't forget to add a date to your entry so you can reread what you thought and felt perhaps a year later to notice what has potentially alchemised and healed.

Important to note: You don't have to follow the literal symbols of the arcana, Death may not mean transformation and new beginnings to you in that moment, the three of wands may not mean study and travel to you. It's so important to tap into *YOUR* intuition and consider your personal journey beyond the typical meanings of the cards.

Ritual of The Empress: An Invocation of Self Love and Abundance

The Empress (Queen of queens) is seated on a lush throne and verdant landscape, wearing luxuriant robes and holding a talisman with the symbol of Venus on it. She is at ease with herself. The Empress is the epitome of grace in turbulence, the Empress endures like water flowing around boulders, extinguishes fire and exudes earthly abundance and pleasure as the Venusian Creatrix.

You will need:

- An image of the Empress Tarot card (Or an image that represents Empress qualities (like queen Cleopatra or pre-Raphaelite painting)
- Rose petals, or flower petals of choice

Rose quartz
Tea light candles
Himalayan salts
Essential oils of your choosing
Dried Rose, lavender, hibiscus, chamomile, passion flower
Honey and Whole milk (optional)
Any other ingredients to make your bathing ritual sumptuous
Pen and Paper
Pouring vessel

You do not need all ingredients; these are suggested ideas to make your herbal ritual bath. If there are items you don't have, you may have a substitute that's perfectly fine.

The best day to do this is a Friday during the full moon. Create a space in the bathroom that feels beautiful and relaxing. Imagine yourself as the Empress, you radiate luxury, beauty, abundance, sensuality – it is flowing from you.

Find a dry spot in the bathroom to create a small altar and place the Empress image there with candles, crystals, flower petals. Prepare your soothing, luxurious bath. You may wish to play music as well.

By the doorway, light two candles across from each other, step through that space as if walking through a portal, imagine yourself shedding negativity and letting go of what no longer serves you.

Make a poem prayer, invoke the Empress qualities within and as an archetype or deity. Aphrodite or Laksmi are wonderful goddesses for a ritual like this. State your intentions clearly, recite the passage with love for oneself.

Here is an example lines from one of my poem-prayers to Aphrodite:

Doused in golden water, I rise and remember,
Between the ancient blue sisters. A soaking. A cosmic ocean chorus.
Wash away the rust and shadow and salt-grit bones.
Glorious lady of the foam, birthed from tectonic fury and swaying grace.
Diamonds and Opals fall from my mouth, I am worthy,
The old self, cast all out to sea.
Aphrodite's Daughter from my poetry book *Aphrodite Fever Dream*

After soaking and focussing on your intentions, use a pouring vessel to pour water over you from your herbal bath. If you do not wish to get your hair wet, simply tie it up and pour down your neck, shoulders and back. Each time you pour these healing waters over you think of the qualities that represent self-love, self-worth, the Empress. If you have your poem-prayer to hand (and you don't mind it getting a little wet), you may decide to recite it again aloud. You can always write it again in your grimoire.

Pour the water over you six times, six is Aphrodite's number. Each time, acknowledge your skin, the curves of your body, your beauty, send love to areas that you've struggled to love such as scars that hold trauma. Cultivate that lush sensuality from within.

Next: Starting at the feet. Give them a massage and then sweep the waters up your body, imagine you are being filled with the abundant energy of Laksmi. As you reach the crown of your head, say "Great Empress! Aphrodite! I invoke you."

When you have completed the rite and you are dry, choose fabric that feels cosy and luxurious. Use your pouring vessel and fill it with some bathwater and sprinkle it around your bedroom using your fingertips, starting in the east – the direction of new beginnings and inspiration.

You may recite your poem-prayer again as you anoint your bedroom space. You may also wish to add your Empress card to an altar by your bedside so it is the first thing you see before you sleep and when you wake to remind you of your worth.

The Queens: A Ritual of Sovereign Reunion

The Queens in the Tarot represent our sovereign sanctuary. The pages denote sovereign study and development, the knights are on a sovereign quest and the queens are the matriarchal leadership who govern their inner and outer sanctuary, whilst the kings' rule over the land and are masters of structure.

The Queens are symbolic of ruling our inner sanctum and personality, governed by the four elements of air, earth, fire and water, each essence depicts the parts of us. Sometimes we can feel a little off balance, are we a bit too fiery tempered and hot headed? Are we a little too complacent and day dreamy or perhaps we're not great at creating boundaries and severing what's no longer needed or maybe we struggle with security and prosperity?

Quick break down:

Queen of Wands: Fire

- Positive traits: Basic instinct, creative spark, courage, vibrant, exudes confidence, strong sense of self.
- Shadow: catty, jealous, vengeful, manipulative, dishonesty, fiery emotions, reactive, self-absorbed, temper tantrums, fickle.
- Lacking: You need to reestablish self-respect and self-confidence. You may be struggling with low self-esteem. Take the time to rebuild your sense of self-worth.

Queen of Swords: Air

- Positive traits: Intellect, sharp wit, and independent judgement, honesty, fairness, and objectivity, cool and diplomatic logic, strong memory.
- Shadow: Critical, aloof but cutting words, barbed tongue, sarcasm, appears unfeeling.
- Lacking: Struggle to speak up, form opinions, speak your truth. Take time to establish boundaries and steer clear of gossip and relationships that can cloud your own core values and identity.

Queen of Pentacles: Earth

- Positive traits: Sensual, lover of all things delicious in life. Practical resourceful, down to earth, abundance, nurturing, generosity, calm, organised, methodical, warm.
- Shadow: Controlling, materialistic, over-indulgence, workaholic, money-obsessed, vain and appearing only to be interested in outer beauty, wealth and material gain.
- Lacking: ungrounded and fickle you struggle to maintain finances or complete projects, debt, irresponsible in day-to-day life. Problems with dependency and possibly lazy attitude. Take time to find your independence.

Queen of Chalices: Water

- Positive traits: nurturing, caring, compassionate and sensitive, intuitive, romantic, emotional depth, gentle, sensitive, empathic.
- Shadow: head in the clouds, disassociation, taken advantage of, detached from the world, avoids conflict, emotional instability, timid, passive, emotionally drained, sulky.

- Lacking: You are perhaps too logical and rigid, struggle to relax, a perfectionist who is hard on themselves and others, selfish and prone to superficiality and suppressed emotions. Taking time to tune into your heart.

We all have many of these qualities and more, we may see where we are struggling or where we might be excessive, notice what could be good for us to work on and simply honour our light and shadow. For me I struggle with self-worth and confidence so I could do with bringing more Queen of Wands energy into my being.

This is a medicinal ritual, tending to your wounds and multifaceted self. Women are often having to fragment themselves to be different smiles to different social settings. This sigil ritual working with all four queens reminds us that every part of us is valid, we are whole and complete as we are.

You will need:

The four Queens from a tarot deck
Pen and paper
Air drying clay
Objects that represent all four elements
Something to carve your sigil into the clay
Healing oil: Rose, Orange, Jasmine, Bergamot
Journal

Take a moment to sit with all four queens with their correlated elemental object. Imagine all the elements are dancing around you. Visualise the wind in your hair, fire in your heart, roses at your feet and rain falling from the skies to replenish you. Imagine each queen coming towards you and saying "I am honoured to be a part of you, I serve you with my sword…my wand…my coins...my cups" Take a moment to consider what each symbol represents to you. You may want to take some time to journal what qualities of each queen you love about yourself, where you feel needs healing and perhaps where there is room for improvement (or not, maybe you like being feisty or a daydreamer). Nothing is invalid here, it's all about witnessing what you associate with ideas of good and bad, are they negative traits or have you been told they are negative? Tune into what you need, where are your wounds, where is your power? Which queen do you feel most attuned to and why? Which queen would you consider your enemy? Would she represent a shadow self you've perhaps repressed or neglected? This is a time for curiosity and self-enquiry.

Create a simple poetic incantation that can be imbued into the clay for each queen, this will anchor your magical words into it as it dries. For each queen write a description of traits that empower you and traits you'd desire more of. You should have four sentences that you can combine to create your incantation.

Once you have your completed incantation you may wish to make a copy in your grimoire. Next read aloud your poetic incantation to the four queens. Then with your piece of paper and a pen, attribute each sentence to a symbol. You can make it up from your imagination or research a multitude of magical alphabet lettering available.

Now you have your four symbols, take your quick drying clay and mould it into two flat disc shapes. Once flat, take your poetic incantation and sandwich it in between the two discs. If you need to fold it up, then go ahead and do that. Seal the edges to keep the paper encased.

Now draw the four symbols onto the clay before it dries. You can choose to keep them separate or bring them together as one flowing and beautiful sigil symbol.

As you draw each symbol, chant the poem associated with it to imbue it with the specific queenly energy.

When the clay sigil is dried, you then anoint it with your healing oil (with herbs associated with each element if you can). Rub this oil around the sealed part and add four drops on the surface.

To activate the sigil hold it in your hands and invoke the queens to assist you. Dip the sigil in water, pass it over flame and smoke, rub some earth onto it for extra potency.

Keep this sigil on your magical home altar or with your travel altar to help you reconnect and cherish all the qualities within you. Know that whilst all of us are here to grow, we are all wonderful in all our multifaceted glory as we are – rain or shine, fire or brimstone. This sigil is to remind you of your worth. You are a Queen of queens!

High Priestess, Keeper of Secrets

The high priestess archetype is one of stillness, she holds wisdom of ancient magical teachings and secret occult knowledge in her scrolls and in her knowing of what is beyond the veil. Her intuition *and* studies guide her path. She is the keeper of memory, the subconscious, the sacred feminine and the mystery of our psyche. Between her are two columns said to represent the columns of King Solomon's temple, painted black and white to symbolise balance of yin and yang asking us to find strength in both our light and dark, what appears to be two opposing paradoxical forces within ourselves, are what actually make us whole and complete – Lady of the in-between, she comfortably straddles betwixt what appear to be superficial contradictions, but are they really? The pomegranates represent the abundance gained from spiritual enlightenment, feminine divinity and connect to the goddess Persephone who travelled to the underworld – a place beyond the veil of our material world. The crown she wears connects her to the goddess Isis, making her an authority figure perhaps of a mystery school and her blue robe represents the flow of a river – the stream of consciousness when channelling divine messages. Enheduanna (from Sumeria), Bulluṭsa-rabi (from Akkadia) and Katebet (from Egypt) were all revered ancient high priestesses and poets of their time who embody the essence of the High Priestess tarot. Needless to say, alongside the Empress and Three of Wands, she is a favourite card!

You will need:

A mirror
A silver candle and black candle
Pen and paper
High Priestess Tarot card
A veil
Cup of water (preferably bathed in moonlight)
Small bell
Incense: Kyphi or Frankincense

This one is a bit tricky and secretive and makes me think of the *Voynich Manuscript* or *The Codex Seraphinianus*. You are going to make your own 'Beyond the Veil' poetic incantation. Keep your mirror veiled or partly veiled if you need it to help you with your task.

First light your silver candle and place it to your left, then light the black candle and place it to your right – they represent your pillars and two being the number of the High Priestess also represents diplomacy and the energy of the iron fist in the velvet glove. She is quiet yet she has a hidden strength for she carries all the memories, wisdom and voices of wise women who came before her (like the Reverend Mother of the Fremen in *Dune*).

Take a moment to intuit a secret you wish to offer to the High Priestess *or* request to gain more wisdom of secret magical knowledge or access information from the akashic records. Let your incantation call upon the High Priestess to ask for her guidance and advice.

Once you've written your draft, learn to write it all backwards to seal it into secrecy so it's harder to decipher unless it is held up to a mirror. *Optional:* write out a second version that translates your original using a magical alphabet of your own choosing but make sure that is also written backwards so that it only makes sense when held up to a mirror.

Whichever draft you choose to use, it will finally be written following a spiral shape that you have drawn on a separate blank piece of paper. Making sure your secret incantation starts at the wider edge of the spiral and works its way inwards to the centre of oblivion. Make sure your spiral is big enough to write your secret spell on it. Take your time with this, it isn't easy writing letters and words backwards!

Now, place the High Priestess card by the mirror and lift the veil from the mirror which represents seeing into another realm, hold up your secret spell in front of the mirror, gaze into the mirror, this is a portal and you are embodying the High Priestess sitting between your temple pillars and holding up your secret scroll.

Visualise any images or symbols that come to you as you gaze into the mirror, what messages are you downloading? What secrets are being whispered to you? Visualise sending your secrets into the portal for the High Priestess to keep safe and hidden.

Chant this twice into the mirror:

My secret is cloaked with the black of night, hidden away from the harsh daylight.
But in the shadows, I'll keep, it's buried so deep, Locked up tight, out of prying eyes sight.
In shadows deep my secret lies, Underneath the moonlit skies, High priestess in the dark,
Persephone, hark, my truth hidden from prying eyes.

Speak to the High Priestess directly and ask her to initiate you into the mysteries. To become a mistress of mysteries, say:

I am the mistress of mysteries; all hidden knowledge will remain within me for no one else to see. I will keep your secrets well.

You may choose to recite your secret spell as well, or not. Perhaps you silently wish its energy to be sent into the portal. Sit in this moment for a while and take a sip of your moon water as part of your initiation. Then ring your small bell as a way to close the portal and banish unwanted energy around you. You may wish to smudge the mirror with your incense of choice before putting the veil over it. Ground yourself in this quiet-dark before blowing out the candles. Journal what information, inspiration, secrets and emotions surfaced for you.

Love Spells

Come, my Soul, swim to me! The water is deep in my love, which carries me to you. I clasp the flowers to my breast, which are naked and dripping with water and the moon makes them bloom like the lotus. Oh my god, my heart yearns to bathe with you. I let you see my beauty in a dress of the finest linen, moist with balsam. I enter the water to be with you. Oh hero, my lover! Come and be with me! –Ancient Egyptian Love Poem-Spell 1540-1087BCE

Love spells and erotic magic date back to around 2200 BCE and found on Cuneiform tablets from the Near East. Priestesses of ancient Sumeria would have been commissioned to perform spells and poetic hymns petitioning Inanna to bless a marriage, soothe unrequited love, concoct love potions or hearten the object of the individual's desire to reciprocate those feelings back.

Humanity has been falling in and out of love for thousands of years. In ancient Egypt some love spells were scratched onto what is called an *Ostracon* which is purposefully broken or found on shards of pottery as a simple tablet to inscribe the spell which would then be buried or offered on an altar to a deity. Broken shards of pottery were cheap and attainable for local citizens whilst larger, well-made tablets written on by scribes would have been commissioned by the elite. An ancient Greek 'fetching' spell called *agōgimon* is archived in the British library, translated into English, the spell instructs the practitioner to take a seashell, write sacred names with the blood of a black donkey, and recite a formula to attract their lover! Another love spell catalogued in the British Library archives is the *philtron* which translates to 'potion'. It describes that the petitioner should acquire a copper nail from a wrecked ship and engrave magical signs (*charaktēres)* with names on a tin lamella, then roll it up with personal material from your crush (hair or fragments of clothing) and then throw it into the sea.

Sanskrit scriptures, considered a sacred language of India for 3,000 years, also includes love poetry, spells and potions! The Hellenistic Greeks performed syncretic magic with the use of a *mágos* conducting ceremony and utilising supernatural forces, astrology and alchemy to bind lovers together, invoke the gods to break up marriages or create love amulets. In Renaissance Europe, clay dolls and written spell scrolls for love were hidden in the altar of churches, even holy candles for mass were inscribed upon and then lit during the ritual!

Many of these spells were documented in scripture and scrolls and cared for by priestesses of a local temple who often had a library attached to the complex. These scrolls held a variety of ceremonies, incantations, charms and spells which would have been performed by a priestess or she'd instruct the person asking for guidance. Two such love spells found on papyrus in Greek petition two goddesses. The first is the *'good drinking cup'* spell. Over a cup, the user should repeat magical words believed to be the sacred names of 'Cypris' (Aphrodite) seven times and then drink from the cup. The petitioner hoped that upon chanting to Aphrodite in the beverage that love would flow to them like water. Another invocation was to Selene, goddess of the moon. For the spell to work you have to address Selene as *'the mistress of the entire world'*, then make offerings to her which consist of a mixture of clay, sulphur and blood of a dappled goat and then pour that concoction into a figurine of the goddess. To finish you must consecrate her shrine with this potion. The shrine must be made of olive wood and should never be sun facing!

With dog slaver, thirst and hunger.
Slap in the face. Rolling eyes.
I have hit you on the head,

I have driven you out of your mind,
set your thinking to my thinking,
set your reason to my reason,
I hold you fast as Ishtar held Dumuzi,
as liquor binds him who drinks it,
I have bound you with my hairy mouth,
My vagina full of wetness,
with my mouth full of saliva,
with my vagina full of wetness,
may no rival come to you,
dog is crouching, pig is crouching,
you too will keep crouching on my thighs.
— Ancient Akkadian Love Spell Poem on a clay tablet, 2,000–1,500 BCE

In this chapter I've added some self-love rituals. We are in the 21st Century and whilst it's lovely to fall in love and be loved, taking time out of our busy lives to give yourself some love is great for wellbeing and de-stressing and it also encourages feelings of self-worth too.

Self-Love Spell

This simple spell will bring feelings of wellness and serenity. Cast this on a Friday because this is Aphrodite's day on a full moon – especially during sunset when the Venusian glow is at its peak. Create an altar dedicated to self-love. You may wish to add a goddess of love (Aphrodite, Venus, Frigg, Hathor) or perhaps Laksmi goddess of self-worth and abundance.

You will need

Red, White and Gold candles
Safety lighter

Small bowl (approx. 7cm)
Spoon
Pan or microwave
Rose tea
A small mirror
Rose quartz or pearls
Shells and feathers
Flower petals
Pen and paper

Ingredients for your self-love body butter
100% organic Rose oil for skin and hair
100% Organic solid carrier oil like coconut or shea butter
Orange essential oil (One drop)
Ylang Ylang essential oil (One drop)

Directions:

- Prepare your rose tea beforehand.
- Cast your circle to create your little love bubble.
- Create an altar of love with objects that represent that loving energy to you. Perhaps a figurine of Aphrodite, love hearts, pictures of yourself now as an adult and pictures of good childhood memories. Anything that represents what you value about yourself, favourite flowers, fruit, friends, animals, things you love to do.
- Set up your altar with the candles, rose quartz, shells, feathers and small mirror.
- Create your luxurious self-love body butter by putting a large solid chunk of shea butter in a microwave safe bowl or pot in the microwave to heat for about ten seconds. Once it is now warm liquid, add two tablespoons of rose oil and mix.

- *(Optional)* Then add ONE drop of orange essential oil and ONE drop of Ylang Ylang, stir again.
- If you feel more shea butter is needed, then add more. It really depends on body sizes and moisturiser preference.
- Enjoy this process, this time is for you. Sing as you stir, chant loving words into your oil.
- Sit with your self-love body oil at your altar. Meditate here and invoke the loving energy of Aphrodite and of mother earth.
- Take a moment to look in the mirror and tell yourself loving words. Speak to yourself with words you perhaps you wished were said to you as a child.
- Take a sip of your rose tea and say "I am deserving of love, I deserve to give myself love, I am able to receive that love."
- Carve a sigil on your white candle that represents your mind. Hold it with loving intention. Know you are deserving of tranquillity, light the candle to manifest this energy. Place on the altar.
- Carve a sigil on your red candle that represents both the heart and the womb. Hold it for a moment to your heart and then to your womb with loving intention. Know that you are deserving of love flowing through your body to these centre points and let go of hurt that has been stuck there. Light the candle to manifest the energy of love here. Place on the altar.
- Carve a sigil on the gold candle that represents your spirit. Hold it up towards the moon for a moment to connect with the celestial spirits around you to invoke love in and around you. Know that you are deserving of love to flow into your spirit. Light the candle to manifest the energy of love here. Place on the altar.

- Call upon goddesses of love: Aphrodite, Venus, Frigg, Hathor and Laksmi (self-worth/prosperity). Sprinkle flower petals on your altar as you call their names.
- Write a love letter to yourself. Include all your light and dark – like Venus as the evening star in the darkest of the cosmos.
- Keep on taking sips of your rose tea whilst imagining all the love you are writing to yourself is being poured into you.
- When you have finished crafting the letter, you may choose to read it out to yourself now or fold it up, wrap a red ribbon around it and place it on the altar for five days and read it out to yourself then.
- Once your tea is finished and your letter complete. Take a bath or shower. Make sure you use your favourite fragrances and bath products.
- After the bath, lavish your body with the body butter that you created with love. Massage your hands, breasts, womb and feet. Nourish your skin with self-love in the body butter you created for yourself.
- Now you are feeling and smelling divine, sit back at your altar and place your hands on your heart. See the light shining in your eyes as you look in the mirror. Say "I love myself".
- Take a moment to thank your deity of love by writing some poetic blessing to her, it doesn't need to be complicated, just a few sentences will do. Leave this on the altar.
- Close the circle with loving intentions.

Poem Spell in a Shell: Ocean Ritual

This is a wonderful simple spell to utilise the ebb and flow of tidal energy. I recommend to do this ritual during the new moon to invoke abundant possibilities, call in more love and set positive intentions as well as let go of what no longer serves.

You will need:

A shell (or mermaid's purse)
Seaweed or biodegradable twine
Pen and paper
Sandalwood incense
Chamomile
Rosemary
Dandelion
Lavender
Basil (Tulsi)
Small bell

Directions:

- On a piece of paper write down what you wish to flow to you and what you wish to let go of.
- On the back draw an eye to represent the all-seeing universe reading your wishes and the 'evil eye' protecting you from any negativity. You want good things to flow your way and ward off ill intent. Write your name in the eye.
- Fold up your piece of paper towards you and then tuck it into the shell
- Add a pinch of Chamomile for self-love, Rosemary for forgiveness and remembrance, Dandelion for letting go of the past, Lavender for serenity and Basil for prosperity.
- Add sea salt as an offering to the ocean spirits, to give thanks for accepting the spell.
- Bind everything so it doesn't fall out by wrapping seaweed or twine around it.

- Hold in the palm of your hand over the smoke of Sandalwood (Often used to exorcise demons and evil energy, conjure beneficial spirits, and promote spiritual awareness, great for blessings, abundance and prosperity). As you hold the shell over the smoke, make a circle widdershins to draw the abundance to you and speak out loud what you wish to manifest. Then clockwise to request what you wish to let go of.
- Go to the beach, face the ocean. Imagine the tides bringing abundance towards you and carrying away all you wish to let go of. Meditate here for a moment and remind yourself of your self-worth, that you are deserving of peace, love and joy.
- Hold the shell in your palm and whisper words of love and joy into the shell.
- Invoke the ocean spirits, ask permission to throw the shell into the water, visualise a being giving you permission and taking the magical shell for you into the sea. Notice what creature comes forward in your mind's eye.
- When you're ready, cast the shell out to sea.
- Ring the small bell to produce a divine resonance sending out good intentions with each tidal pull to end the ritual.

Couples Love Poem and Potion Spell

I worked this spell with my now fiancé. I asked permission to perform it and if he'd like to join me. He said yes! Inspired by Egyptian love poem-spells I created this ritual for you and your partner to deepen your love for each other. Best time to perform this spell is during the waxing crescent on the Friday closest to the full moon. Strongest time of year to perform this spell with your partner is during the month of Libra or Taurus (both months are ruled by Venus) or perhaps this could be a wonderful spell for Valentine's Day!

You will need:

Items that represent you and your partner to create a small love altar
Pen and paper x2
Red candle for love and passion
Blue candle for loyalty
Yellow candle for joy
Orange candle for friendship
Pink or red ribbon for love
Gold ribbon for prosperity and joy
White ribbon for peace and harmony
Blue ribbon for devotion
Green ribbon for fertility and abundance
Water in a bowl with small spoon
Small bell
(*Optional:* Choose 5 ribbons that represent your relationship instead)

Herbs:

Vervain
Rose
Meadow sweet

To cast your spell

- Firstly, add the dried herbs of Vervain, Rose and Meadow sweet together to make a cup of tea for you and your partner. Vervain was considered a sacred herb used in temples dedicated to Venus, it represents how sacred your love for each other is, Rose for romance and unconditional love and Meadow sweet brings peace, brings cheer to the heart and represents matrimony and loyalty.

- Gather all your ribbons together, make sure they are quite lengthy! Knot them together and braid them, it doesn't have to be perfect! Optional: thread charms on this braid that represents your love for each other. Once completed, what you've made is a small handfasting cord, a devotional love braid to gently bind your hands together.
- Sit together and enjoy creating your love altar. Play romantic or soothing music.
- Sit together holding hands, looking deep into each other's eyes (it's ok to giggle too!) and really take in each other's wholeness.
- Place a hand on each other's chest, foreheads touching and your other hand over the top of your partner's hand (that is placed on your chest) so you're creating a circuit for the loving energy to flow. Close your eyes and imagine the energies rippling through you both and expanding with every heartbeat. Stay here for about a minute.
- In this moment whisper sweet nothings to each other.
- Grab the love potion tea each, and again whisper loving words into the cup. Hand the cup imbued with love over to your partner and have a drink.
- Take a pause here and write a poem-hymn to your lover (if you're unsure and need examples, do an internet search for ancient love poems for inspiration!)
- When you're both ready, recite the poems to each other.
- Light the candles to ignite this love and the deepening qualities between you both.
- Now take your braided ribbons and gently wrap them around your joined hands. Take in five deep breaths together, be in this moment of sweet devotion for each other. Say out loud "I love you" to your partner.
- Finish with gently sprinkling water over your altar and each other five times (the number associated with

Venus, representing perfection of the five senses, the nuptial number of love and union) – you are blessing and bringing both your five senses together as one.

- Ring the small bell to invoke a resonance of joy and positivity to complete the spell.

Love Spell in an Orange

A simple spell for attracting the right person to you or if you are already in a relationship this is a wonderful little spell to attract more joy, zest and playfulness into your romance.

You will need:

A small orange
3 pins
Paper and pen

Write a love poem to your beloved on a piece of paper. Here is an example poem for inspiration:

My love for you is so true
As deep as the ocean's blue
Like the orange it is joyful
And like the strawberry so sweet and bountiful
I call on Aphrodite to bless it with all that is beautiful
This is my everlasting devotion oh (name), that I have for you

Cut a chunk out of the orange and insert the paper into its flesh. Take three pins and pierce them through the paper and into the orange to bind your spell to its flesh. After three days being placed on your altar, take the pins out, keep the poem with you and feed the orange to creatures in your local woods as an offering to nature to attract the abundance of positivity into your love life.

Sacred Heart declaration of love ritual

She looks like the star-goddess, rising
at the start of the good New Year.
Perfect and bright, shining skin,
seductive in her eyes when she glances,
her hair is true lapis,
her arm gathers gold,
her fingers are like lotus flowers,
She has stolen my heart with her embrace,
and she is seen going outside
like That Goddess, the One Goddess
Ancient Egyptian Love Hymn, Ramesside Period

This is a love letter to yourself or to another with the inclusion of candle magic and sacred oil anointing. The Celtic bard, Gwerful Mechain, recited bawdy devotional poems to the 'fine bright cunt' as the highest blessing to be saved by God. The Sumerian high priestess Enheduanna wrote devotional and sometimes erotic poetry to represent the sexual appetite of the goddess Inanna, she chants:

> *Peg my vulva, my star-sketched horn of the dipper! Moor my slender boat of heaven, my new moon crescent cunt beauty.*

Priestesses of Egypt chanted love hymns to Isis, Bes and Hathor with ritual oils during fertility festivities. Many of these priestesses were trained chantresses and Myrrhophores. A Myrrhophore was a woman from the ancient near east whose duty was to create and store anointing oils as well as carry out important rituals with these oils, whether funerary rites, fertility ceremonies, marriages and invocation of deities. Popular ceremonial oils from antiquity were:

- Blue lotus
- Spikenard
- Rose of Sharon
- Cassia
- Myrrh
- Jasmine
- Neroli
- Orange Blossom
- Amber
- Cinnamon
- Kyphi in particular was a complex aromatic blend used in temples for meditation and divine rituals as well as for medicinal purposes.

I encourage you to connect with this energy as you perform this ritual of sacred sensuality and love.

You will need:

Paper
Two pink wax candle figurines
Scraps of text from old books and newspapers
Anointing oil of rose, Jasmine and Orange
Magenta and deep purple ribbon
Dried rose petals
Honey

If this ritual is to honour yourself you only need one candle figurine, or you may choose to use the second one to represent your chosen deity to devote yourself to.

- Create a love altar however you desire, anoint it every day with oils or rose water for five days (five being the number of Venus). This is to take time to consecrate the space.

- The best moon phase to work this ritual is during the strawberry full moon or when there is a full moon in Libra.
- Sit by your altar and stand the two wax figurines on a patera facing each other. Play classical music that feels romantic and soft.
- Take the magenta and deep purple ribbons and braid them together. Magenta symbolises resonance and romantic harmony, and deep purple represents devotion and a deep loyal bond.
- Once braided into one long ribbon, anoint with your love oil and call in your love goddess as you wrap the ribbon around the figures and tie them together gently.
- Put a few drops of your love oil in the palm of your hands, rub your hands together and then bring them gently over your face, take in a deep inhale and exhale – breathe in the fragrance of love. Then place your hands on your chest and be still for a moment to connect to your heart before massaging your feet with a few more oil drops or rose water to encourage a state of sensuality and groundedness.
- Now with your pen, paper and scraps of text begin to create a collaged love-prayer prose poem, it can be as simple or as wild as you like. This is a devotional prayer brimming with prose poetry! Draw down inspiration from nature and the heavens! Or sensual quotes from a favourite erotic novel. Feel free to tea stain it to look old or maybe use pink card paper? Once you feel it is completed, drip your love oil and honey onto the prayer. Let the sensuality of both potions be fed to your words on the paper! Glue dried rose petals around your words and any other decorative symbols you wish to add.

- As it dries, recite it out loud to the two figurines burning with love and to your altar. Offer this prayer up to the goddess to conjure and activate the lushness of desire and love wherever you wish to direct it (to yourself, your body, a beloved, as an offering to the goddess?)
- Take a sip of honey for yourself, feel its sensual sweetness delight your tongue and drip down into your heart centre and all the way into your womb.
- Close the ritual by chanting *"Good goddess, lady with the largest heart, lady of the stars and the wild, I pray that love flows freely to and from my heart, for the highest good of all, harming none."*

You may wish to complete the ritual by doing something luxurious and sensual for yourself, or if your partner has joined you in this ritual, making love is a great option!

Shadowlands & the Twilight Path

But, O Goddess, the fact that Mahisha, having seen (your face) angry, terrible, with knitted brows, in hue like the rising moon, did not immediately give up his life is exceedingly wondrous – for who can live, having seen Death enraged?
–Devi Mahatmya, 4.12, 6th century CE

The *Egyptian Book of the Dead* is a collection of scrolls containing spells and hymns as well as practical funerary rites to help a soul journey through into the afterlife. There are spells to help you control your body, spells so you don't decay, spells so you don't lose your heart and even incantations so you remember to breathe, eat and drink. The scarab figurines found in their tombs are usually engraved with funerary prayers.

There are many references in Old English, Germanic and Norse texts that describe the haliorunna, helliruna, helrune, as "witches" "necromancers" and "sorceresses" who had oracular powers, in touch with the earth and spirits of the dead. These priestesses chanted and sang over tombs and barrows to appease or commune with the dead for messages. The name of these wise women are believed to be derived from the word "rune" which means "magical secret counsel" or "what is spoken softly and solemnly", The word Rune can also be translated as, *"mysteries of the burial mound"*; or a *"tomb epitaph, burial song"*, and thus Hell-Runa women can be interpreted as those *"having knowledge of the secrets of the dead''*, *"those skilled in the mysteries of hell"* or *"hell-whisperers"* – Hell being a Nordic goddess of the 'Afterlife' the personification of the underworld.

In Russia, there is a ceremony celebrating the *Maslenitsa*, the butter lady, who is the spirit of Spring and forgiveness. Maslenitsa was also a chance for people to *'warm their dead'* by including their ancestors in the festivities, visiting their graves, and eating traditional funeral foods. And in Poland, on the first day of spring, people would make an effigy of Marzanna, goddess of winter and death, set it on fire, and then drown it in a river. In China on the 4th April, the Qingming Tomb sweeping day is when Chinese families visit the tombs of their ancestors to clean the gravesites and make ritual offerings to their ancestors. And in Ireland there is a Gaelic Celtic tradition called 'Keening' which is a vocal wailing lament for the dead.

And night vigils by graves over candle light on the 'Day of the Dead' festival in Mexico is a beautiful celebration to honour and remember ancestors. The ancient Pictish river goddess-mermaid, Nessa, would be sometimes seen singing sad songs of grief and loss, offerings were made in the loch to appease her.

Grief rituals are a great restorative way of accepting the end of something and even processing difficult emotions that come up, whether it is a literal death of a loved one or the death of an aspect of your daily life. Here we can combine shadow work with spirit work to heal and comfort us in times of in-between and transition. We can also honour what has passed, as we mourn, we can write our memories via ceremony, poetry, journaling and more. The pen becomes our guiding light helping us move through the shadows so we don't remain in perpetual state of limbo and darkness.

Poetry rituals are an incredibly potent healing methodology for grief. It can help you express your emotions and release any hurt that is stuck.

Hekate can assist you as a gentle guide walking through your underworld of sorrow, or perhaps Rhiannon a comforting presence? Both are wonderful goddesses for shadow work, death work, walking between the crossroads and for lighting the way as you walk through your grief.

Another goddess you can work with is Seshat who is an Egyptian funerary goddess. She is also, interestingly, a goddess of writing and books! In ancient text she is described as 'being pregnant with the deceased' and her responsibility involved keeping the memory of the dead alive by writing down accounts of their life. With her energy we can be inspired to write letters to our ancestors to keep their memory alive in our hearts.

We can also tap into this beautiful yet poignant archetype of Seshat – letting her dedication to the dead inspire us to create our own poetic eulogies. Perhaps you wish to call in the poetess Al-Khansa too? She wrote elegies of remembrance for those who died and performed these poems in rituals for her tribe.

I used to write letters and poems to my grandmother when she passed, I'd slip them in the back of her picture frame like a letterbox mailing them straight to her.

> *When I lost my mother and also at the same time I separated from a lover, I was overwhelmed by grief. And with grief you cry like a child, you cry like a beast, you also rise up because you realise, all of a sudden in extreme pain or situations of extreme danger or despair, you rise up to become who you are. Your spirit is your answer, your choices by that ache define you. I brought everything that I was feeling, that grief, that longing also for hope to the table. I accepted I was naive but I am a poet and through creating poetry I like to make sense of life with magic. I like to 'abracadabra', using a prayer poem as a way to transform. I connected with the archangel Michael when my mother died and I wrote songs to him and I dress up as him in my performances. I like to believe in that magic, because if I don't believe in that then my life is meaningless.*
> – Héloïse Letissier, aka Rahim Redcar

In this chapter are also rituals for embracing your shadows, cutting cords and allowing the past to die away. Life is not all love and light. To truly accept all aspects of nature and ourselves, we must embrace the darkness and acknowledge the shadows in order to be truly balanced. The act of death births life and taking the time to mourn and accept loss creates space for new life to sprout. The energy of the dark moon can sometimes bring a gentle release and other times it can feel like the Tower Tarot card, an utter fall from grace or harsh crisis that creates a very traumatic ending. But it is in these moments, in the deep dark soil, that creates nutrients for us to grow and transcend to become wiser, patient, compassionate beings. Threshold life experiences can be: a break up, grieving a death, severed friendship, loss of job, moving from one place to another or loss of any kind. They are in-between times, spaces between the past and the future. Here are some death and shadow rituals you may wish to try to support your cross over.

Letters to the Dead

This can also be a letter to Death itself, a goddess of the liminal, an ancestor, a recently deceased loved one or even a relationship that was brutally severed? Perhaps you wish to commune with a parent or ex-friend for closure (of course, don't send them the letter!)

You may wish to keep them in a journal, or burn or bury them. Writing a letter, pulls the grief in your heart out onto the paper rather than being stuck in the body.

You will need:

A picture of them or something that represents them
Pen and paper
5 white candles

You may choose to place the photo and items in the middle of the candle circle. Meditate on memories of this loved one, visualise them appearing in the room with you.

The first candle you light represent grief. As you light it, say out loud:

The pain of losing you is intense. It reminds me of the depth of my love for you.

The second candle you light represent courage, light it and say:

I gently want to confront my sorrow, to comfort myself during this shadowy time, to acknowledge this has changed my life.

The third candle represents your memory, light it and say:

I remember the times we laughed, the times we cried, the times we were angry with each other, the silly things you did, the joy you brought to my life and the love we gave each other.

The fourth candle represents the light of love, light it and say:

Life is like the seasons; you were like a warm summer's day in my life and now it feels like winter without you. But I cherish those memories of you in my heart, my warm summer's day in a chamber that will always be reserved for you. I am thankful for the gift of your living that you shared with me.

The fifth candle represents hope, light it and say:

I know you now walk with me in spirit, I cannot see you in the body but you are my guiding light and I hope the winter of my grief falls away into spring and new beginnings so I may smile again, celebrate your life well lived, to honour your joy by creating more joy in my own life. I miss you and I love you.

Tears may arise as you chant these five incantations, allowing any emotion to rise up and out of you. There are no rules for grief.

After reading these verses and feeling the presence of your loved one near, begin to craft a letter to them, gaze into the candle flames to help you channel the otherworlds. Sometimes the grief of losing someone is more complex, perhaps they hurt you, can things be forgiven? Know it is ok not to want to resolve things, maybe you feel them haunting you and you want to let them know you're ok and they can leave? Speak your truth and honour feelings that surface.

Optional: write a psalm of lament to say goodbye to them. Psalms are based on Hebrew poetry. Typically, a psalm of lament follows this structure: open with an invocation to a particular deity or spirit, followed by the lament itself and pleas for help/ message, and often ending with an expression of confidence and then wisdom you have gained.

When you feel the ritual is complete, keep the candles burning if you like and move into the energy of reflection and ground yourself back into the present moment. Perhaps you want to share a meal, have a cup of tea, go for a walk and bury your letter, dance to their favourite song or be in silence and let the tears continue to fall.

Beyond the Veil Automatic Writing

A multipurpose simple ritual, focused on automatic writing with the aid of a scrying mirror to channel inspiration through our ancestors, from beyond the veil.

It can be performed to evoke free-flowing drawing, automatic writing or to call for inspiration for automatic poetry, during a dark moon is the optimum time.

Connect with Water Beforehand:

Perhaps prepare yourself a long ritual bath with candles, olfactory elements & auditory input or maybe enjoy wild/sea swimming or visit a lake, stream, spring or river and simply dip your hands to connect with the water.

It's important to get in 'touch' with the element of water, in some way, prior to the ritual, as the depths of water connect us symbolically to our subconscious (so in turn to the spiritual realms) meaning when we later submerge ourselves into a trance state, it will feel an intuitive transition.

Preparation and Items needed:

You will need your chosen offerings for your ancestors, a scrying mirror, a long white candle, loose sheets of paper, a pen (plus spares, in case the first runs out of ink), black fabric to cover the mirror and Incense of your choice.

Set ritual intent beforehand – decide in advance if you'd like to write poetry or do freehand automatic writing/drawing.

Setting up for the Ritual:

Put in place any protective measures before you begin. Place your mirror facing you (but just off to the side of you, so it's not your visual focal point) with the candle and the incense placed between you and the mirror's face, the pens and papers should be ready at your fingertips.

Place offerings around the mirror and call to your ancestors, by first welcoming them and then stating your ritual intent (asking your ancestors to gift you with poetic inspiration, for example) then be seated, light the candle and incense and hold the pen very gently in your hand.

Induce trance in your usual manner, if you do feel any resistance, remember how the water flowed and felt on your skin, as a (now vivid) sensory reminder that reaching beyond the veil is just as effortless as submerging oneself under water.

The Ritual Process:

Once relaxed into your gentle trance, feel the creative energy flowing through the mirror from your ancestors, then hold your pen over the paper and allow whatever you hear, feel or see in your mind's eye, to flow through your pen, onto the paper, without trying to control it at all.

Allow yourself to scribble everything, even if it makes no 'logical' sense at that time. You may find that you write inspirational prompts/scribble key words, already fully formed verses of poetry, snippets of sentences (which may serve as tiny inspirational seeds, that grow into poetic works later) or find yourself scrawling images, pictorials or symbols.

Often automatic writing which makes no 'sense' at the time, becomes clearer after we have 'slept on it', to allow our minds to process the jumble of words/images or ideas gathered from behind the veil.

To Close Channels:

Once the inspiration dwindles, or you feel ready to end this session, place down your pen on the paper, turn to face the mirror and offer thanks to your ancestors for their inspirational gifts, wisdom and insight.

Bid them farewell, cover the mirror with the black fabric and blow out the candle to close the channels. Carefully discard ritual offerings the morning after.

This ritual is by Jade who is an artist, mirror maker, witch & Scrying practitioner. She is also the creatrix and shop owner of 'Urania's Magick Mirror' on etsy and Instagram @uraniasmagickmirror

Swords & Roses Cord Cutting Ceremony

This is a four-part ceremony I have created for letting go of a friendship or a relationship that became malignant whilst also creating boundaries and reminds you of your self-worth. As a hybrid ceremony I have also included options for shadow work journaling to consider karmic lessons learned from the friendship, self-reflection, to be guided by your inner realms alchemising and transmuting the pain in order to bloom from the ache of separation and any malicious intent bestowed upon you.

A good time to do this spell can be during the Balsamic waning moon. *'Balsam'* means 'to soothe' and it is a releasing moon, or during the new moon for new beginnings.

What you need:

Picture of frenemy
Black string
Yellow and black rose petals
Rose thorns
Intact red rose with thorns
Black candle
Lilac candle
Cord cutting anointing oil (sandalwood, lemon, chamomile)
Tarot Cards:

- Ace of Swords
- Eight of Wands
- Queen of Swords
- Justice
- Strength

Pen and paper
Ribbon and scissors

Part one

First, take the photo of your ex-friend and bind it with black string, the black string represents all their negative energy being bound back to them. Then stick the bound photo in the freezer for nine days, nine is the number of letting go, nine is the energy that asks us to explore the space that any endings in our life will bring.

After nine days, take it out of the freezer. I encourage you next to create a small altar with the inclusion of the tarot cards suggested. The swords in tarot are swift and sharp and they represent the element of air. The Ace of Swords symbolises cutting through the nonsense to provide searing clarity and the honest truth and cuts away with boldness and integrity, the eight of wands aims this energy outward swiftly, a high-level energy that propels forward to reach your desired destination at a *very* fast pace. The Queen of swords is a lady of clear insight, quick thinking and an ability to pierce through the noise of slander and gossip, there is a detached logic to her that keeps your heart guarded, she will shield you from hurt.

With these three cards, you can include items on your small altar that represent letting go such as black obsidian, Apache's tear, dirt, dust, small items or letters of said ex friend, anything you like. Inscribe their name onto the wax of the black candle and yours onto the lilac candle (which represents inner peace), stand them apart but facing each other and tie the black string gently around them, tethering them together, then light them. This represents your energetic bond, the black candle representing the energy of your ex-friend you wish to be rid of like a scab or dead skin.

Sit for a moment by this altar, allow all emotions about this friendship to surface – good and bad. You may wish to journal what comes up.

Write a cord cutting poem incantation that you will recite nine times.

Examples:

There once was a friendship so grand
But it crumbled like castles of sand
You turned on me with such spite
I'll sever ties, take flight
Goodbye, I'll leave you where you stand

Or

There once was a friendship so dear
But now it's turned to dust, I fear
I send hate back to you
Goodbye, we are through
Like a rose with thorns, I sever you clear.

Part Two

Now take the photo of your ex-friend and rip it into small shreds. Add these shreds to a container with the yellow and black rose petals as well as the thorns (or something that resembles that sharpness – pencil shavings perhaps). Mix it all together and anoint it with your banishing oil. Put this to one side until later.

Now gaze into the flames of the black candle, begin to visualise this ex-friend in your mind's eye, imagine a golden cord stretching from your heart to theirs, watch the golden light dim until the cord is completely dull, take all the time you need for this part, an array of memories may come up for you. In your mind's eye, see yourself as the Queen of Swords gracefully holding up her sword and when you're ready, swiftly sever the cord and notice your ex-friend's half of the cord propel away from you, back towards them. As you see this, take some scissors and cut the string that tethers your candles. The cord is cut. You are no longer bound to each other's hearts energetically. Focus now on your lilac candle to conjure a sense of inner calm and individuality as the bond is broken.

You may wish to chant your poetic spell to end this part here. Chant nine times and then blow out the candles.

Part Three

The next day, take your bowl containing the shredded photo, petals and thorns out for a walk in the woods, preferably somewhere hilly, best results are when it's windy.

Away from people and animals for safety. Again, chant your banishing spell into the bowl nine times.

When you are ready, simply LET GO. Let go of any bitterness or resentment, let go of their power over you, let go of it all, shake it off! Take the contents into your hands and blow them away. Yellow rose petals are symbolic of friendship and black are symbolic of endings. The thorns represent a karmic force, sending their insults, slander and malice back to them.

Let them go with love in the wind, wish them well, wish for them to sort out their own karmic rubbish, let it all go. You do not have to carry this hurt in your heart anymore. Their spite is blown back to them with the momentum of the energy of the eight of wands. Visualise it all leaving your energetic field and your life.

Part Four

Come home and take out the tarot cards Strength and Justice. Hold them close to your heart with an intact red rose. These qualities represent you right now, making peace with your own light and dark, your softness and your thorns, finding balance in the chaos of that friendship that you needed to sever.

Often when a friend betrays us or causes extreme emotional harm, we can end up having low self-worth, there's confusion, grief and questioning our own identity for a long time because of malicious things said about you and the slandering you've perhaps endured. After your cord cutting rituals, this is a good time to do shadow work journalling. You may wish to self-reflect on your part played in this broken friendship, or go inwards to heal your wounds. Keep the rose on your altar with Strength and Justice cards for as long as you desire. You'll swiftly begin to notice feelings of peace and lightness of being, as if a heaviness has been lifted from your life and heart. Newly empowered, you are your own hero giving yourself the rose, your thorns are strong enough now to create strong boundaries, you can get rid of what no longer brings happiness, your self-worth will bloom once again. Let that person *learn* to receive their own thorns, hypocrisy, hate and karmic descent whilst you walk away with peace and clarity.

I hope this ceremony creates space in your life for new beginnings, now there is space in your heart for healthier friendships to bloom.

Candle Grief Ceremony

Grief manifests in a variety of ways. This ritual is a death ceremony for anything you've struggled to let crossover or a time in your life when there was the energy of death that you may not have been able to heal or let go of and it haunts you? Perhaps you lost a job? A friendship ended? Divorce? Loss of financial security? Things that end are difficult to fathom but we can create rituals that soothe the ache, allow you to mourn, then transform and release it.

You will need:

1 white candle (healing, strength, peace)

1 pink candle (spiritual healing, emotional healing, friendship, healing if it's someone you loved dearly)
1 black candle (Protection, grounding, allowing the grief to surface)
Rose Quartz, Apache's Tear, Jet, Rainbow Obsidian
Matches/lighter
An item that belonged to them or that symbolises your relationship to them
A toothpick
A comforting beverage
A card or a blank piece of paper
A pen or pencil

*You can substitute any of these for what you feel is right.

Directions:

1. Pick a day that was important to either of you such as their birthday or the day they died to do this ritual.
2. Take your candles and carefully carve their name into them before lighting the candles. Then place a black crystal by each candle.
3. Place a photo in the middle with the rose quartz on top.
4. Gently grab your item that reminds you of them or belonged to them and hold it as you watch the candles for a few moments. Think of some of the happy memories you had together and focus on things that you loved about them.
5. Whenever you are comfortable, continue to allow the candles to burn down and make yourself a relaxing beverage of choice.
6. Prepare yourself mentally and emotionally to write a poem or a small note to them. It can be as long or as short

as you want. Also, you can write whatever you want to them as long as it's what you truly feel.

7. As memories and emotions come to the surface- let words flow out of you. write the poem while drinking your beverage and let the candles burn out.
8. Read the poem out loud so that if their spirit is listening, they can hear it in your voice.
9. Once finished, store your poem in a safe place where you are able to take it out and look at it from time to time. If you are able and feel comfortable doing so, take the poem to their gravestone.
10. If you're not comfortable keeping the letter somewhere, you can also burn it using the lit candles in a fire safe bowl or cauldron. Then you can deliver it straight to them wherever they are in the world around us. You can even save the ashes to make black salt if you'd like.
11. Close the space with a few words of love and closure. *What would your words of closure look like? Will it explore forgiveness? Saying goodbye? Will it honour your pain?*

Jar of Grief Spell

You will need:

A Jar
Cypress
Dirt from the earth
Salt
Hyacinth
Marjoram
Lavender and/or sage Incense
Black Candle
Paper and pen

Black feather

Instructions:

- Take a jar and add any of the ingredients if you wish:
- Cypress, Hyacinth, and Marjoram for grief. Salt for purification of grief. Dirt from the earth for power and grounding. Burn some lavender incense and add the residue into the jar for healing.
- Write out your grief onto a piece of paper. Write down everything that you are feeling. All your pain, all your sadness, etc. You may wish to scrunch up the paper to add in the jar or burn it (preferable with a black candle, but not necessary) and add the ashes to the jar as well. Add tears if able.
- Shake the jar as hard as you can to release your sadness or any other difficult emotions that arise.
- Write a short poem-prayer for letting go, recite it out loud whenever you come back to your jar to add more ingredients.
- Repeat this process as needed. After each session of doing this, do something that will calm your nerves, like taking a bath with bergamot and rose oil or listen to soothing music.
- You may bury the jar if you wish as this may help you bury your grief like a funerary rite or keep it on an altar space or if you burn the contents, you can include the ashes as a ritual to Rhiannon during the waning moon, she will guide you through your grief.

Walking the Liminal Path with Hekate

It is said Hekate originated in ancient Thrace which is modern day Bulgaria, Turkey and Greece as a goddess of the wilderness and childbirth. She later evolved into a Hellenic deity of the crossroads, underworld as well as the sea, earth and sky.

This spell is to invoke Hekate to help clear your path, gather up the old dust and guide you through the liminal to find clarity and move past what has been stuck or hurtful. The best time to work this spell is during the balsamic waning moon – that liminal sliver of light as the birth of the new moon comes into being. This represents the threshold between death and rebirth. Balsam means 'soothing' so connecting with that energy allows for Hekate with her torch to shine a light on which paths you wish to take.

For Your Altar You Will Need:

A key
3 gold candles
Pen and biodegradable paper
Objects to represent Hekate
Crystals: Obsidian, Jet, Lapis Lazuli, Labradorite
Anything to represent the deep sea, dark earth and the stars/moon
(She walks between these realms with ease as well as the realms of spirits)

Offerings for Her Deipnon

Sweets (Like cake and honey)
Dandelion for persistence
Mint for alleviating mood and digesting stuck energy
Garlic for protection
Mugwort for dreamwork/walking the threshold
Lavender for clarity

Unwanted items:

Dust, dirt, old bits of rag (biodegradable), Hair and fingernails,
Anything from your past you wish to let go of.

Instructions:

Arrange your altar with the candles being placed in an inverted triangle. Sprinkle some of the herbs around the base of your candles and keep some later as an offering at a crossroads in nature.

Take a piece of paper and draw a personal sigil that means something to you and then place it in the centre of the triangle, then position the key over the top of it – giving you permission to open portals.

Sit here a while and write a devotional poem to her to invite her in, before lighting each candle. As you write and recite this poem, contemplate what has been holding you back, what hurt and blockages are keeping you from seeing your path clearly, what do you need to let go of? What needs to 'die' and be sent into the shadow realms to transmute into light?

Light the first candle and say:

Hekate Enodia, lady of the crossroads, I call on you to help me! Open my roads, clear my path of hurt and misfortune. Purify my blockages, gather up my ghosts. Guardian of the many paths and portals, show me the way, show me the right path.

Light the second candle and say:

Hekate Dadophoros (Torch Bearer), shine your gentle flame upon me, shine it far into my night to see the path of prosperity. Lead me from misguided roads, walk with me and lead me to my truth. Hekate whose flames burn with knowledge, luminous lady – burn away the ghosts, illuminate my road to victory.

Light the third candle and say:

Hekate Kleidoukhos, keeper of the keys, please may the doors of opportunity and abundance open up to me? May I be granted good fortune and keys to clarity and success as I walk the road you guide me down. Hekate, queen of thresholds, may my key unlock doors that are right for me and lock those that no longer serve.

Write a short letter to Hekate on the biodegradable paper as the candles burn, express to her what hurt and hardships have come up for you in the past months or year, tell her your sorrows and pain or struggles. Ask for her assistance as a soothing guide and to take away what no longer serves. Perhaps a friendship ended? Perhaps you wish to leave a disappointing job and desire a new opportunity to present itself? Perhaps a health struggle feels stagnant and you're praying for a second opinion? Maybe you need to create boundaries in one area of life but open up another? Petition Hekate to open the right doors in the labyrinth of life.

Gather up the rest of your herbs, dust, dirt and unwanted items with your sweets and place them on the paper. The dust and dirt are physical representations of what no longer serves you. Fold up the letter with the herbs and dust inside.

You may leave this little bundle on your altar for the day if you wish or place it under the waning crescent for a night.

Next day go to your local green space with your offering bundle and find a crossroads. You may choose to leave it on the ground or bury it between the crossroads.

Chant:

> *Hekate! Lady of the three-formed path of earth, seas and heavens. Hear my prayer. I honour you with my offerings. Cleanse my pathways and unlock fortuitous doors. Oh bright queen I invoke you, work my spell with all your divine grace and magic.*

After your heartfelt prayer to Hekate thanking her for guidance, walk away and don't look back so as not to look back at the past she is taking from you.

Embracing the Shadows: A Ritual for Grieving and Shadow Work

Here's a ritual that combines elements of witchcraft, introspection, and honouring the memory of a loved one:

You will need:

1. A quiet, sacred space where you feel comfortable and safe.
2. A black candle to represent the shadow self and the mourning process.
3. A white candle to symbolise healing, light, the presence of your loved one's spirit.
4. A small mirror to reflect upon your inner self and confront your shadows.
5. A journal and pen for self -reflection and processing emotions.
6. Optional: Any additional items that hold personal significance to you or the loved one you're grieving [photographs, mementos, favourite flowers].

Preparation:

1. Set up your sacred space by clearing the area of clutter and distractions. You may choose to cleanse the space with sage, palo santo, or your preferred method of purification.
2. Arrange your materials in a way that feels intuitive and meaningful to you.
3. Take a few deep breaths to centre yourself and set your intention for the ritual. This could be seeking healing, understanding, or acceptance of your grief and shadows.

Ritual Steps:

1. Invocation: Light the white candle and say a simple invocation or prayer to invite the presence and guidance of your loved one's spirit. Speak from the heart, expressing your desire for their support and comfort during this ritual.
2. Acknowledgment of Grief: Light the black candle and place it next to the white candle. As you do so, visualise the shadows of your grief and pain being illuminated by the light of the white candle. Take a moment to silently acknowledge and honour your feelings of loss, sadness, anger, or any other emotions that arise.
3. Mirror Meditation: Sit comfortably in front of the mirror and gaze into your own eyes. Allow yourself to see beyond the physical reflection and into the depths of your soul. As you confront your own shadows and vulnerabilities, remember that they are a natural part of being human. Take as much time as you need to sit with these feelings without judgement.
4. Automatic writing Journaling: Take your journal and pen, and write down any thoughts, memories, or

emotions that surfaced during the mirror meditation. Use this space to explore your grief and shadows further, allowing yourself to express whatever comes to mind without censorship.

5. Release and Letting Go: When you feel ready, take a deep breath and visualise releasing your grief and shadows into the flame of the black candle. Imagine them transforming into smoke and dissipating into the air, leaving you feeling lighter and more at peace.
6. Gratitude and Remembrance: Close the ritual by expressing gratitude to your loved one for their presence and support, both in life and in spirit. Take a moment to remember and honour their memory, perhaps sharing a fond memory or saying a few words of thanks.
7. Closing: Extinguish the candles in reverse order (black candle first, then white candle) as you thank your loved one and any spiritual guides or entities you invoked for their presence and assistance. Ground yourself by connecting with the earth beneath you, feeling its stability and support.
8. Integration: Reflect on your experience and any insights gained during the ritual. Consider how you can carry this sense of healing and acceptance forward in your journey through grief and shadow work.

Remember, this ritual is just a framework, and you can adapt it to suit your personal beliefs, preferences, and needs. Trust your intuition and allow yourself to be guided by your emotions as you navigate the complexities of grief and the shadows within.

A poppet can be a powerful addition to this ritual, serving as a tangible representation of the person you're grieving or aspects of yourself that you're working to heal and integrate. Here's how you can incorporate a poppet into the ritual:

Using a Poppet

1. Creation: Before beginning the ritual, create or obtain a poppet that represents either the loved one you're grieving or aspects of yourself that you're working to heal. You can make the poppet out of fabric, clay, or any other material that feels significant to you. Customise it to resemble the person or embody the qualities you wish to address during the ritual.
2. Anointing: Once you've created the poppet, you may choose to anoint it with oils, herbs, or symbols that hold personal significance. This could be a healing oil for comfort and support, lavender for peace and relaxation, or any other herbs or essences that resonate with your intentions.
3. Integration: During the ritual, place the poppet on your altar or hold it in your hands as you meditate, journal, and engage in introspection. Use it as a focal point to connect with the energy and essence of the person or aspects you're working with, allowing it to serve as a conduit for healing and transformation. You may wish to write a letter to your loved one who has passed over.
4. Release: Toward the end of the ritual, you may choose to incorporate the poppet into the release and letting go process. This could involve speaking words of release and forgiveness, visualising the transfer of energy from the poppet into the flames of the black candle, or any other method that feels appropriate to you.
5. Closure: After the ritual, you can choose to keep the poppet on your altar (or in a box as a peaceful resting place for them with your letters to them, dried flowers, bay leaves, crystals and trinkets of theirs) as a reminder of the healing work you've done and the connection you've made, or you may decide to bury or otherwise

respectfully dispose of it as a symbol of closure and completion.

Remember that the poppet is a tool for focus and intention, and its use should feel meaningful and empowering to you. Trust your instincts and allow the poppet to guide you in your journey through grief and shadow work.

Self-Care Note

After completing this ritual, it's natural to feel a range of emotions, including tiredness or overwhelm. Shadow work can stir up deep-seated feelings and memories, and it's essential to prioritise self-care in the aftermath.

Take time to rest and replenish your energy. Drink plenty of water and nourish your body with nutritious food. Allow yourself to indulge in activities that bring you comfort and relaxation, whether it's taking a warm bath, spending time in nature, or curling up with a good book.

Be gentle with yourself and honour the process you've undergone. It's okay to feel emotionally drained or vulnerable after engaging in shadow work. Give yourself permission to process your feelings at your own pace and reach out to supportive friends, family members, or professionals if you need additional support.

Remember that healing is a journey, and taking care of yourself along the way is crucial for your well-being and growth.

This ritual was created by Wendy Rivera in honour of her grandmother. Wendy is an Artist and Witch from Texas, USA.

Healing Rituals

One of the earliest spells for healing comes from ancient Sumeria and is known as the Marduk-Ea incantation, recited in exorcistic healing rituals – alongside physical examinations and operations to expel the actual sickness, they'd also exorcise the malevolent entity associated with the illness. The incantation also involved what is known as incubation rituals for dreamwork, the priestess-doctor would go on vision quests into the higher realms to see if there was anything stuck in a person's aura in the etheric sphere causing them continued ill health or if all was clear. An ancient Egyptian spell to invoke Hetepet, an aspect of Hathor, as goddess of drunkenness is recited during the drinking of beer and is said the spell needs to be spat up with the beer to prevent a hangover and *wurmsegen* spells of mediaeval Germany are pre-Christian pagan poems containing magical words for casting out the "Nesso" worm causing the affliction! In Tenerife, the cave of *Santo Hermano* is a small grotto dedicated to a hermit saint, votive offerings surround the cave with thousands of petitions and prayers on scraps of paper folded into the rock crevices for blessings and healing. Votive rags and prayers can also be found on the wishing tree of the *Agia Solomoni* catacombs in Cyprus requesting for cures and good health blessings and a wall in Verona is caked in letters petitioning Juliet, asking her to bless new love or soothe the ache of heartbreak.

After the storm and our tower has fallen, we often feel depleted and our energetic battery runs on low. It is hard to transmute pain into healing, it is hard navigating life when things have been cloudy, it is difficult to find peace and boost our self-worth in moments of darkness.

After death comes a rebirth and the journey of healing blooms, like nature after the long dark winter. We too can thrive and see the light again. These rituals are for rest, recuperation, building self-worth back up and invoking healing through nature. Soothe the ache with tree magic, conjure your self-worth with power words and utilise the protective healing qualities of pomanders to ward away harm.

Foraging Ritual and Cleansing Tea

This healing ritual involves making your own cleansing tea, that includes gathering your own ingredients, picking them with an intention and treating the infusion as a very potent potion that benefits your body and soul.

You will Need:

Basket
Scissors
Rubber gloves (for picking nettles)
Stinging nettles (Utica dioica)
Cleavers (Galium aparine)
Teapot
Tea light or candles
Honey (optional)
Paper and Pen

Foraging rituals are the set of practices and behaviours that we engage in when searching for and gathering food and medicine from the surrounding natural environment. It's crucial to gather your herbs at a specific time of the day. I pick my herbs on dry days. If I need flowers I would always venture out when the sun is out. Herbs for our cleansing tea, can be picked in the morning. I truly believe that mornings are the best as the energy is flowing in the plants.

As part of your ritual, take time to ask Mother Nature if you're allowed to pick the plants and give thanks to the sustenance you are gathering, you may opt to leave bird seeds as an offering to nature in some way.

I encourage you to connect with the number four as it represents inner strength and the four elements. Find four nettle plants (and four Cleavers as an added option) and cut them carefully. For me, *four* helps to restore homeostasis in the body and is often associated with stability and balance in Greek mythology. That's a perfect example where numbers are used symbolically to convey deeper meaning of plants.

Deepen your connection to the land by paying attention and I encourage you to saunter with a relaxed way of being. Give yourself permission to slow down, be inspired by your surroundings. In this moment I encourage you to sit somewhere comfortable and journal about how nature makes you feel, recall nature memories of your childhood, how do these joyful memories soothe you?

Foraging by the moon is an important and common practice in multiple cultures. Connecting to Selene goddess of the moon will bring that extra hint of magic to your time in nature. You may wish to create a poem to her which you can chant as you hold your tea later.

Moon Phases for Foraging:

- New Moon: for new beginnings and growth. Foragers scout new locations, plan upcoming harvests and gather roots and tubers that thrive underground.
- Waxing Moon: is increasing in size; plant growth is stimulated. Focus on harvesting leafy greens, herbs and fruit as they are at their peak flavour.
- Full Moon: The full moon is often associated with abundance and fertility. Foragers prioritise harvesting wild edibles and herbs that are believed to be more potent during this phase.

- Waning Moon: Good time for preservation and storage. Time to reflect and cherish nature's abundance. It's perfect timing for drying, storing and preserving.
- Dark Moon: Introspection and rest. This is a time of reflection and giving thanks to Mother Earth. And also giving her time to rest and restore too before we forage from her once more by the new moon. The dark moon is a very quiet and healing moon, a perfect time for your healing tea!

Tea ceremony:

1. Be ready with your teapot and teacups.
2. You may want to light the candles to make the atmosphere even more special.
3. When using herbs for making tea, try not to use boiling water. Boil it and let it cool down for about five minutes, then use for brewing.
4. Place your fresh herbs in the teapot.
5. Add hot water: Pour a required amount and let it steep for at least 12 minutes.
6. Invoke the soothing properties of Nettle to take away the *'stings'* of life. You may wish to chant your poem to Selene into the cup for added healing energies.
7. Serve the tea to yourself or people who share the ceremony with you.
8. Drink it with all its goodness in mind.
9. Clean and dry the tea utensils after the ceremony.

This healing ritual was created by the wonderful Joanna Ruminska, Green Witch, expert forager and nutritional therapist. She facilitates foraging walks across Devon & Cornwall www.incredibleedibleuk.co.uk

Infinity Symbol Rebirth & Self Worth Spell

The Infinity Symbol or the sleeping 8, is an ancient Greek alchemical symbol that represents boundlessness and endlessness. Life is a loop of ups and downs. The number eight represents the balance between the spiritual and material worlds with its middle acting like a gateway between the two – when the veil is thin and the two holes represent the eyes of the eternal universe or supreme being.

We can harness the energy of the infinity symbol by recognising our own boundlessness – you matter because you are made of matter that came from the heavens. This can be very healing to know you are worthy of wielding this power for it is innate in and around you.

With a piece of paper or card, draw and cut out the infinity sign, big enough so that you may write your magical intentions on it. Let this symbol hold your power words on it. What are you wishing to invoke more of? Self-confidence? Attracting prosperity? Healing creative blockages? Letting go of something so you may heal and grow?

Keep a small bowl or glass tray close by and light a white candle for healing and cleansing. Helping you to let go of what no longer serves whilst shining light on invoking a new beginning of self-worth, a rebirth from the struggle.

Hold your infinity symbol with your power words over the candle and call in the elements, then recite your power words into the flame. Allow the paper to burn slowly to ignite your intention, alchemising your words as an act of manifestation out into the aether. Put the flaming paper into the bowl and let it completely burn into ash. (Avoid Glossy or Coloured Paper as they may have chemicals that have harmful fumes. Use biodegradable or untreated paper and keep some water with you to quench the flame for safety.) Once burned right through you may wish to use the ash to draw the infinity sign on your third eye or heart centre to attract the potent energies even more towards you. The best time to do this spell is waning crescent because this is a time for introspection and reflection.

The Power of a Name-Self-worth Ritual

> *Language shows us that naming an experience doesn't give the experience more power, it gives us the power of understanding and meaning* –Brene Brown, Atlas of the Heart

I find the etymology of names fascinating. Just by discovering the root meaning of syllables can gain access to their hidden power. For example, take my name Katie Ness. Katie, which is short for Katherine, derives from the ancient Greek *Aikaterine* or *Hekaterine* as variants of the goddess Hekate. In the early Christian era, the name was later changed to *Katheros* to mean 'pure' to cleanse it of its pagan origins – which I don't care for one bit!

My surname is Scottish and my father's family tree extends quite far back, with ancestors from Fife that were Pictish in origin (which is stated on a Heraldry site). Ness is a Pictish word which has two possible meanings, either 'headland' for settling on a peak or named after the Pictish river goddess Nessa.

> *"Ness was first used as a surname by descendants of the Pictish people of ancient Scotland"* –House of Names.com/family crests

Knowing this gives me not only a sense of pride but also personal power, knowing the hidden meaning behind my name is possibly the names of two goddesses!

As we know, words have power, knowing the power of our names can act as a protective charm against insults, name calling, slandering. For me I can chant:

I embody the words of the goddess, her energy is imbued in my names, your hurtful words have no power over me, I know my power, I know my name.

It is almost like a protection spell!

Your name will be completely different – perhaps its power is that of the earth? A skill? An element? A myth? A flower? My fiancé's power name is essentially 'Rock Marigold' which suits him perfectly because he's a lovely balance of masculinity and femininity or solid foundations with cheerful softness. To speak your name and know its meaning can give it power and encourage you to know thyself.

When you research your name, try to find its syllabic root. If you don't want to use your birth name and to empower yourself with a magical name or pen name then this is valid too.

You will need:

Quick dry clay
Image of the goddess Saraswati
Stick for inscribing
A small bell
Daisies or yellow flowers

Saraswati in her avatar as *Vāc* is the personification of divine speech. She inspires poets and visionaries and assists them to express their words with authority and grace.

Create a small altar to Saraswati, dress it however you like.

Sit in a comfortable position before commencing mantra chanting. The mantra for Saraswati is "Om Aim Saraswatiye Namaha." (transliteration: Om eye-mmm Saras-wat-yay Nama-ha), chant nine times. As you do this, sprinkle white or yellow flowers over her altar as an offering. Ring the bell to protect the space.

Take a chunk of quick dry clay and mould it into a palm sized clay disc. On the surface you may write symbols using the stick, engrave these power symbols associated with your name into the clay. Example: For me, Hekate is associated with the moon and Nessa is a river goddess. I can engrave a moon symbol with flowing lines underneath to represent a river. It's as simple as that. Chant your magical words associated with your name into the clay: Example if your name is Victoria, then your power word might be 'Victory' or 'Hazel' to imbue you with the power of trees and nature.

Allow your talisman to dry and anoint it with your own sacred oil or incense of choice.

Knowing the meaning behind our names and nicknames can be a powerful self-worth ritual and protective self-affirming word-charm.

Close the ritual space by ringing the bell and chanting *om shanti shanti shanti oooommmm.*

Conjuring Your Magical Motto

Maude Gonne, Moina Bergson, Annie Horniman and Florence Farr were women of the Hermetic Order of the Golden Dawn. Which was founded in London in 1888 by three Rosicrucian Masons. It was a secret society devoted to the study and practice of occult Hermeticism, metaphysics and spiritual development during the late 19th and early 20th centuries. All four women performed a variety of rituals and ceremonies dedicated to goddesses, became initiated priestesses and rebelled against social norms of Victorian society. In the public eye they were actresses, playwrights, theatre managers, activists and writers among other talents. Within the Golden Dawn they weaved magic, cast incantations, visual journeyed and invoked deity through various ceremonial practices.

Each woman chose a motto to define her personal search for meaning and her link to the divine. This motto became her magical name, in naming herself with these magical words encouraging her to bring these principles to life within and around her. Through these mottos we glimpse the inner myths through which these women breathed life into and embodied.

- Florence Farr's Magical Motto was: *Sapientia Sapienti Dono Data* which means "Wisdom is given as a gift to the Wise".
- Annie Horniman's Magical personality was: *Fortiter Et Recte* which translates to "Bravely and Justly".
- Moina Bergson was known Magically as: *Vestigia Nulla Retrosum* which means "I leave no trace behind".
- And finally, Maude Gonne's motto was *Per Ignum Ad Lucem* which translates to "Through the Fire and Light".

You may wish to have a magical motto. What would you choose for yourself to express your own inner myth and power? To feel radiant and brimming with self-worth and to heal any low confidence struggles. What do you feel is your central principle or belief about oneself and of living life? Wisdom, Peace, Joy, Justice, Unity, Strength? Spiritual quest? To learn? Is it symbolised by your heart? Or the heavens and the stars? Or perhaps what a specific tarot card stands for? Or the symbolism of the natural world? Or the attributes of a deity you wish to embody more? You don't have to be fluent in Latin, your personal motto can come to you in your mother tongue and you may wish to translate into Latin at a later point.

Ritual Meditation to Bring Forth your Power Motto

Sit in a relaxed position in a low-lit room with minimal sound or interruptions. Place a purple candle in front of you, purple is the colour of intuition and the third eye. And keep a pen and paper with you. This is a meditative automatic writing activity to go deep into your psyche to retrieve your motto from the subconscious realms.

Candle gazing known as *Trataka* in Sanskrit is an ancient yogic technique that helps you quiet the mind and focus.

Cleanse the area first with sage because you are essentially opening a portal.

Take your attention to the candle flame, draw in a long, slow breath through your nose. let go of all worries that may have been troubling you this day and breathe deep down into your belly. Keep your focus on the candle's flame and keep your gaze soft. Allow words to come up in your mind's eye or if you see them in the flicker of the flame. Write them all down, contemplate what is important to you, how do you want to live your life? What are your personal morals and beliefs? Let the power words rise up out of your subconscious, from your inner you.

After a while, close your eyes and rest here in deep relaxation. When you're ready, open your eyes and have a look at what words you have written, do they make sense to you? Can you form a motto? If nothing came up for you this time, that's ok, you can come back to this practice whenever you want.

If you feel you have found your power motto read it out loud to activate it.

Close the portal by giving thanks and blowing out the candle. Leave a few drops of lavender oil around the space to add protection as the portal closes. Have something to eat to ground you back to reality.

Invoking Your Power Words

A poetry-spell to invoke feelings of self-worth.

You will need:

Tigers eye (courage and resilience), Citrine (Positive Thinking) or Garnet (remove blockages)
Red, black and purple candles

Frankincense incense
Any other symbols that represent feeling powerful to you
Salt
Tea light candles
Matches/lighter
Paper and pen
Bell

Set the space by creating a circle of tea lights for you to sit inside. This is your power circle, to invoke your inner power. Sprinkle salt for purification and protection inside the circle.

Set up your small altar with the three colour candles in a triangle formation inside the candle circle, and choose a crystal to be placed by each candle. Light your incense. Sit with the strength of the triple goddess and gently ring the bell to invoke clarity.

Begin to list ten words that feel potent and powerful to you. This could be favourite colours, flowers, trees, an animal, a weather system, an emotion or specific quality you'd like to experience.

With each word that comes through, meditate on it, spend some time repeating the word aloud or whisper to yourself. Say each word slowly and with intention. If a word comes through that doesn't feel quite right, then let it go and allow another one through.

As you write down each word, notice what feelings come up and how your body reacts, is there a temperature change? Does the word resonate with a particular organ of the body or a memory, a dream? Write it all down.

Notice if there are images that come through or perhaps other sensations? Write these associations too.

For example, one of my power words is 'waterfall'. Associated words or prose that came through for me are:

Pearl-silk, foam, royal, lush, enchanting, raw, brave blue, resplendent, vast, fresh, feral, rejuvenated, holy skin, spirited, reborn, defiance, sapphire fire, willow, awakening, tranquil hush.

And already you can see here is the beginnings of a potential poem about a waterfall being a symbol of freedom and inner power.

Once you have your ten power words plus their associated words. Take some time to either write ten short poem-spells or an epic poem incantation using all your words!

Use your power poems whenever you need them and/or you can petition and dedicate your poem to a goddess who symbolises power to you.

Ritual Dedicated to Nemetona

Nemetona in her primary aspect is the Lady of Sanctuary, of Sacred Groves and Sacred Spaces. She is present within the home, within our sacred groves, invoked at sacred sites as protectress of important locations; whether that's home, temple or land.

As the guardian of sacred groves, Nemetona embodies the spirit of nature and oversees the preservation and sanctity of these holy sites. Her presence emanates a profound sense of tranquillity and reverence, infusing the groves with an atmosphere of divine intrinsic energy.

Devotees seek her protection, guidance, and wisdom within these hallowed groves, understanding her role as a facilitator of spiritual connection between our realm and that of the nature spirits and also the liminal realms.

Immersing oneself in these sacred spaces allows for a deep connection with Nemetona's divine essence and the elemental forces of nature, fostering personal growth, healing, and a greater understanding of the interconnectedness of all life.

This ritual is inspired by the ancient Wistman's wood and Upland Oak wood in Dartmoor which reminds me so much of Nemetona. Both are considered temperate rainforests and are important for their fragile mosses, liverwort and lichens and carpeted by bluebells. In these places, I have felt what I imagine Nemetona's presence to embody as a sacred, loving energy reverberating throughout the forest.

- **Purpose:** To seek oneness with nature and the goddess at a deep level. It is especially good for soul healing or clarifying one's path.
- **Need:** Woody essential oils like rosewood, sandalwood, petitgrain or cedarwood, leaf or fern from ritual site (be respectful when taking), solar-infused hawthorn tea, musical instrument like shamanic drum or kalimba You will also need scrap (biodegradable paper) and journal with pen.
- **Prep:** Wear earthy tones and adorn hair with hawthorn flowers (if desired); choose a ritual spot near an ancient tree. Make hawthorn tea to bring with you. Carry with you a small altar to set up by a tree.

Ritual Outline:

1. This ritual is best performed amongst an ancient grove of trees. The natural setting is important in this ritual, as Nemetona's presence is said to be especially strong in these areas.
2. Calm your mind for a moment and meditate on your intent in this ritual.
3. Purify with leaf or fern (or another piece of vegetation from ritual site).
4. Cast circle with twig or wooden wand / invoke elements and Nemetona.

5. Light candles (or a lantern) and set up your altar.
6. Sit or stand leaning your back against the ancient tree. Do a tree meditation, first imagining yourself growing roots, then rising up into the sky, and then coming back to your centre. Feel the life essence and ancient, healing energy of the tree.
7. Open yourself to the forest around you. What does it have to tell you? Does Nemetona have a message for you? What do you feel? Take as long as you need for this.
8. Hum or chant (or play an instrument like a drum or kalimba) to raise energy and when you are ready, feel the forest's energy cascade gently upon you, infusing your body and soul with healing, wisdom-filled energy. Invite Nemetona into your heart space.
9. Ground by drinking Hawthorn tea, offer some to the earth.
10. Perform a self-blessing with your woody essential oil of choosing.
11. Take a moment to write down on a scrap of paper a message you wish to offer to the Nematon. Perhaps you're asking for her wisdom, maybe you're dedicating a short poem to her, perhaps you're releasing something back to the earth? Asking for direction in one's soul path? Once you've written this piece you can bury it in the earth by the roots of a tree.
12. Give thanks and spend some time connecting to the energies all around you before closing the circle by leaving a small gift – perhaps a pebble? A small corn dollie? Seeds or plant a tree?
13. Sit for a while and write about what came up for you during this ritual, journal your thoughts, feelings and visions.

In modern Paganism, Nemetona represents a conduit to ancient Celtic traditions and beliefs. As practitioners seek to reconnect with their ancestral roots, Nemetona serves as a guide, offering wisdom and inspiration. Her role as the guardian of sacred spaces and nature aligns with the reverence for the Earth and its cycles which is an important practice to have, not just for our own wellbeing reconnecting and remembering our relationship to mother earth but also re-building our relationship to the trees, plants, seasons and eco-systems in order to protect our haven, our heaven in the vastness of space, for this is our earthly sanctuary.

The Healing Ritual with a Tree

Write down a wish that you desire, or a blessing you wish to send to someone. Wrap this blessing around a coin or trinket and take this bundle with some seeds and water out to your local woodland or park. Find an ash tree or apple tree and kneel by it. Scatter the seeds at the base as an offering to the birds and chant sacred words letting the tree know that you are offering sustenance and wish for abundance in return. You may pour the water around the tree soon after and chant a similar verse but with reference to offering the water and quenching the tree's thirst and asking for blessings in return. Bury your spell coin by the tree before standing up to put both hands on the trunk, chant three times:

> *May rain fall for you to quench your thirst, may wind blow and scatter your seeds, may sun shine so you may feel warmth and may your branches continue to grow so you may continue to thrive…Grant me (or someone you love) the same healing and blessings in return.*

Walk away visualising healing and love coming towards you, feeling nourished by the tree's energy.

After three days return to the tree and see if there is anything lying on top of where you buried your wish – could be a feather or an acorn or small stone. This is the tree's receipt to let you know your wish has been granted. Carry this item in your good luck bag for luck.

You can do the same by a river. Instead of a coin, wrap your wish or blessing around a pebble and bind it with a red thread. Chant your magical words and throw the trinket into the waters. Come back three days later to see if anything was left for you, keep it as a good luck and healing charm.

Pomanders and Poetry

Pomanders were once protection amulets carried or worn by a person, their style evolved from round balls into a variety of shapes like skulls, hearts, books and ships! In the mediaeval period they were used as religious keepsakes and in the 16th century they were used to hold liquid perfumes, blended with powder and absorbed on a sponge or piece of cotton. A version of the pomander with oranges, cloves, oils, and a golden ribbon may be used as a recovery charm in witchcraft. The use of Pomanders has devolved as an archaic Christmas craft decoration but it can be utilised as a wonderful and simple healing spell.

Take a moment to create a short poetic incantation to invoke protection and healing for within the home. Take time to contemplate your verse and use of powerful words of healing.

Once you feel your poem-spell is complete, choose a healthy grapefruit or orange.

Carefully pierce holes in the top layer of rind and not the underlying fruit. As you pierce holes, try to form the rune word Uruz into the skin of the fruit. Then stick cloves into each hole.

Focus on your desire to ward off ill intent and illness from entering the home as you add clove into these holes. Once finished you'll better see the word Uruz become apparent due to the darker tones of the cloves against the orangey skin.

Now, take your poem for healing and protecting the home and recite it into this pomander. Murmur your sacred verses and blessings.

Add drops of cinnamon oil and lemon balm to the pomander and onto the paper your poem is written on.

You may wish to roll up your poem into a scroll and tie it up with the pomander using a red ribbon by your front door to repel and remove illness, ward off bad intentions and encourage healing.

Daisy Magic for healing and joy

Daisy flowers blossom in abundance from spring to autumn and carry energies of joy, light-heartedness, and playfulness. They are also great for connecting to your inner child. You may remember interactions with daisies from your younger years, like playing on fields and lawns where they blossom, picking flowers, creating flower garlands and wreaths, and using a daisy blossom to answer specific questions, like *"he/she loves me – he/she loves me not"* while picking off a petal at a time. For hundreds of years daisies were known as the 'wound-healer' that heals bleeding, coughs, bronchitis, wounds, and many other conditions and a scientific study published in 2012 has confirmed this with results showing wounds healed very well with the aid of daisies and left no scarring.

Daisies are a flower of healing and joy, in times that are hard it is comforting to sit in a meadow of daisies to connect with our inner child and soothe the aches of life.

Below are some activities to connect to daisy flowers and create spells to call in a sense of joy and playfulness.

Sitting with the daisies:

You will need:

Paper and pens
A blanket or something to sit on
A jar or a tub for collecting flowers

Find a place where daisies grow. Sit down with them for a while if it's comfortable.

Take some deep breaths, a moment to ground yourself and become present in the moment. Then spend a little time connecting to the daisies, giving your full attention to your surroundings and the flowers. Maybe you would like to introduce yourself (this could be done verbally or quietly through thoughts). Example: "Hello, beautiful daisies. My name is (name), I am grateful to be here and spend some time with you, to be present and to connect to your energies of joy and light-heartedness". (You can use this or reframe it into your own words.)

You may also want to spend some time writing down some of your thoughts and what you are experiencing, allow their sweet, playful and healing energy wash over you. Spend some time resting in contemplation, writing and drawing what is being invoked within you. If there are plenty of daisies around, you might like to pick some to take home and dry. I always like to ask permission to pick plants and feel for a moment; if you feel it is okay to collect, go ahead and pick some, making sure you also leave plenty around.

Drying flowers and Making Little Spell Cards

Materials:

- For drying flowers: Flower press or books, non-stick paper
- For making spell cards: Card or thick paper, glue stick/ PVA, pens
- Optional: Watercolour paint

If you collect some daisies, dry them as soon as possible. You might have a flower press, or you can use books. Use non-stick paper to place the flowers in and then press them in a press or in a book, with extra books on top to add weight. Then give it a few days or longer to leave the flowers to dry.

Making daisy spell cards:

Cut some card paper or watercolour paper, into smaller pieces, with enough space to write your spell and some space to decorate with flowers or drawings. I like to use coloured card or paint my own watercolour backgrounds. Then I write my spell and decorate the card with the dried flowers or draw on some daisies, symbols, and decorations. Allow yourself to be creative when creating your spell cards.

If you use dried flowers, handle them carefully with tweezers and use a glue stick or a small amount of PVA to add them to your spell cards.

Below you can find some example spells. Feel free to use any of these or create your own:

- "This little card is intended to bring a connection to the spirit of daisies and shall bring joy and light-heartedness to its beholder."
- "May the daisies help you find joy and playfulness."
- "Like a daisy in the grass, I remember to be joyful and playful."
- "Dancing daisies remind me to be abundant with joy, helping me to release my pain to the wind with softness and gentleness."
- "I invoke the daisy meadow to gently soothe my ache and help me see the light."

You can keep any card you make for yourself, and you could also make some to share as gifts. Write your own mantra or incantation that you can chant with these cards that you make, so when you hold these cards, you chant the mantra to bring you peace. You may keep it in a precious place, like an altar or somewhere you can see it often. Whenever you would like a moment to connect to your spell or intention, you can sit with your card for a moment, take a few deep breaths, and while you hold the card, connect to the energies of your spell and your intentions.

Spell by Jodie Hansen, Yoga Teacher, Artist and Kitchen/Green witch who works with plant and animal folk, esoteric wisdom and feminine spirituality.

Protection Spells

Protection spells also known as *Apotropaic* magic come in various forms. They are intended to repel or banish negativity and misfortune from your life and protect you from further harm. Protection spells to ward off evil are found in the Greek Magical Papyri and mediaeval manuscripts. Some of the earliest known protection spells repel Lilith demons from attacking the home and protecting babies, many protection spells are found woven into textiles or worn as amulets. Banishing and protection spells can create boundaries against malicious intent, hexes, negative enchantment, psychic attack and even trauma dumping. Some traditions utilise animal figurines as guardians of the home like the Chinese *Fu* dogs, the *Duk Koor* guardian of the Romany, Elegba head of the Yoruba religion, or invoking Durga or Kali by chanting mantras to them. There is a Cypriot and Greek folk tradition of baking and then throwing *"loukoumades"* (a donut-like dessert filled with syrup) and sausages on your roof, and singing a specific song to deter a creature called *kallikantzaros* from entering your home, you can also leave a pair of old, smelly shoes outside your front door during the 12 days of Christmas to ward them off too!

Another fascinating spell invokes an Egyptian spirit called Mafdet who can be summoned to protect you from demons, poltergeists or bad energy sent to you. This spirit manifests as a large wild cat. Minced meat is moulded into a phallic shape, your enemy's name is to be inscribed on it with a toothpick as you chant their names out loud. Then feed this meat to feral, hungry cats. Mafdet is said to devour the ill intent of evil entities causing you harm as the cats devour the meat! *Kupala,* the Slavic spirit of water and botanicals can also be involved for protective blessings. The Ostracon of ancient Greece was a broken piece of pottery used for writing love spells and even curses on, potentially to ostracise the individual the magic was aimed at, hence where the word *Ostracism* originates from.

'*Resasay*' is an Iraqi-Jewish traditional ceremony meant to clear the person of the Evil Eye. you heat up a spoon with olive oil and lead, and once the lead has melted on the spoon, you hold the pan consisting of water, salt, bread and a sprig of Rosemary over someone's head and drop the lead inside the pan, as you chant a Hebrew-Arabic blessing saying *'Expel the evil eye!'*. The lead will hiss loudly inside the water, once cooled down, remove the lead and inspect its shape to see how badly someone has been affected.

The *Lares* of the ancient Romans were guardian quasi ancestor-deities for the home, hearth, boundaries and fields. A shrine for the Lares was built in the vestibulum of which offerings were given such as honey cakes, honeycomb, wine, fruits, grains and incense, plus any food that fell to the floor during a banquet was also theirs. These statues were present during family meals and even weddings and poetry evenings. A cave along the shores of Gibraltar is said to have been the home of Medusa, an icon of her head among other offerings was found here, she was considered a protectress of sailors, the weather and seas, her name actually means "Guardian" and "Protectress". A massive upside-down head of Medusa was also discovered in an ancient reservoir called the *Basilica Cistern* in Massine, Istanbul, again petitioning her as a protectress of water and in Malta, sailors for 13,000 years still paint the symbol of eyes on the front of their boats for luck and protection. The remnants of ancient rites to the *Mater Larum,* surviving as folk-magic among women during a festival called Feralia: involves an old woman sewing up a fish-head, smearing it with pitch then pierces and roasts it to bind hostile tongues to silence: she thus invokes *Dea Tacita* 'The silent goddess', goddess of the dead, she had an oracular insight and she could be invoked to destroy a hated person!

Humans have been petitioning for protection for thousands of years. Magical borders may help ward off what is causing you disharmony so you may retrieve your peace once again.

Mugwort Protection Bag

Place Mugwort, Saint John's Wort, Bay leaves, Peppercorn and Marjoram into your small protection bag. Add one silver charm, one gold charm and one iron charm into the bag. You can also include a small tumbled Carnelian stone.

Create an incantation on a piece of paper and roll it up like a small scroll towards you, wrap white and blue string around the scroll four times each. In your scroll you may petition a spirit guardian, deity or even a saint. For example:

I call upon Saint Lucy,
Who watches over me truly,
With eyes bright and clear,
She'd ward off all fear,
Protecting me from harm, unruly.

Hold your bag over Amber or Myrrh incense and leave it on your altar or by a window to soak up the rays of the new moon.

Carry for protection in your purse, pocket, bag or even stitch into the inside of a coat jacket.

Soul-Door Technique

A protective spell to observe, understand and set your boundaries the way your soul needs them to be set.

This ritual, or rather a technique, was revealed to me in a dream, May 2024. In the dream, I was visited by a vampire, who was trying to get closer and closer to me, approaching from different directions, wearing different faces and different moods. To protect myself from this being, that concluded all I did not wish to enter my personal energy field, I drew a door to my soul, and, around them, several protective portals to not to be passed by anything unwanted or evil.

You will need:

- A sheet of white paper
- A pen, pencil or anything you feel comfortable to write with
- A candle in a colour that means protection of the soul to you, it can be white, black, purple, or any other colour
- An incense or incense blend that you connect with protective abilities, e.g. white sage, lavender, mugwort, frankincense, palo santo etc.

Instructions:
Sit down with the pen and paper at a place that feels safe to you. The best option would be by an altar or in the bedroom of your home, but it may also be a quiet corner of your living room, garden, or even a forest.

If it is safe, light the candle and incense to help you focus on your goal and its wording. If you are in an environment where a candle or an incense could draw attention or create damage (e.g. forest in the times of drought), you may exclude these tools from the spell.

Draw a door to the middle of the paper. You may choose its size and design; just keep in mind you are going to need a bit of space to draw and write also around it. If you wish, you may write the word 'soul', 'self', your name or some significant number on the door. On the door, right around it, or under it, write to whom you are willing to open your soul and let them look at you in your natural beauty.

Add several portals around the door, creating a rainbow. Each of these portals will represent a guardian of your soul-door. Fill these guardians with purpose: write between the lines, what is each portal for. You may create as many portals, with as short or as detailed descriptions, as you feel are needed for the door to your soul to be protected, but still able to open to the people, who love you and are here for you.

Keep the soul-door somewhere you can often see it, so it reminds you, what kind of energy are you open to, and what, on the other side, is not allowed to reach to your inner harmony. You may adjust or recreate the door and portals as required by your current situation and life experience.

You may change spell-tools to your liking, add gemstones and crystals to your door to enhance the goal, place other items of power, protection or soul-work in front of the drawing etc.

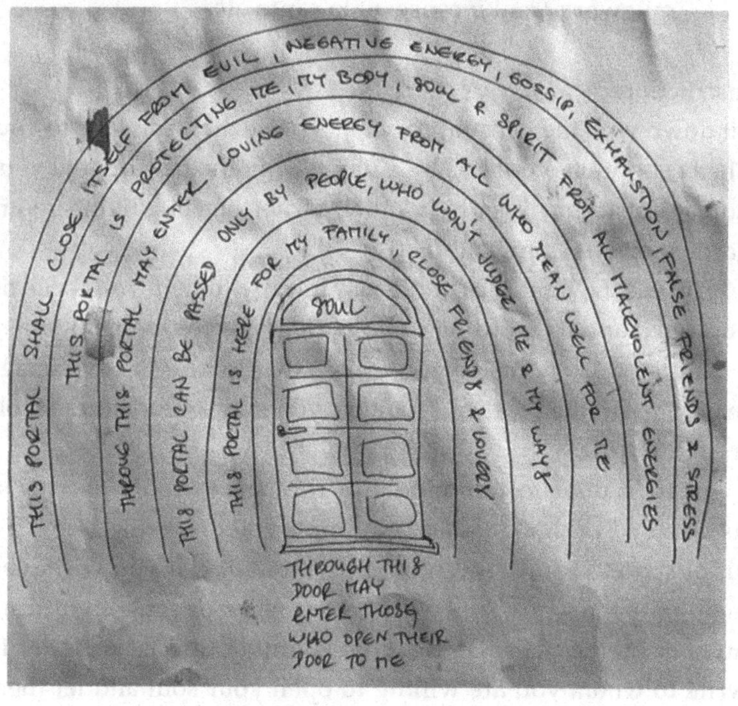

This spell is by Johana Coreyemmah Reuter, *practitioner of liminal witchcraft with love for Czech, German and Irish myths, and editor at Femme Occulte Magazine*

Egg Shell Banishing Spell

A simple spell to ward off those with ill intent. Take an egg from your kitchen, crack it open carefully and cook the egg or dispose of it. Gently clean the egg shell halves by rinsing under tap water. Leave to dry.

Once dry add salt, honey, sage, dill and lavender inside the shell. Alongside stinging nettle and st John's wort and a small piece of Iron. You want to write on a small piece of paper a short banishing rhyming poem such as these examples:

Devil mouth, be gone, I send your words back,
Your venomous lies, I will attack,
With strength and with grace,
I'll put you in your place,
No more will your evil ways stack.

There once was a devil so sly,
With a mouth full of deceit and lies.
But I won't be their prey,
I send their words astray,
Back to where they shall reside.

The cracked egg full of honey acts as a decoy to deter the negativity from you and your home as it appears vulnerable and sweet with honey, but the herbs are all potent banishing energies with the nettle for added sting! And the Iron is associated with the God Mars who will create a strong boundary. Your poem activates the spell.

Bury in your front garden during the dark moon and chant your magical words for extra strength.

Animal Protection Jar Spell

I have always had a strong connection to animals and wildlife. I was always the child petting the various cats on the walk to school or scooping up bumble bees so they wouldn't get stood on. Artio has always intrigued me because of this. The Goddess of animals and protector of the natural world. I admire her as she is easy to connect with, she embraces nature and all living beings, protecting them at all costs. I have always felt this desire and passion to be each creature's voice and to protect and help them flourish and survive in this world.

With this in mind, I have created an animal protection jar along with a spell to perform a ritual. This can be to protect all animals within nature, or alternatively it can be more personal to a family pet for instance. Combining this with the four elements (Earth, Fire, Water and Air) the ritual can be carried out within nature, for example, the beach, woodland, a field or simply just your pet's favourite place.

You will need:

A glass jar or potion bottle (cleansed beforehand with a sage incense stick)
Sea or pink salt (half a tsp)
Dried sage (half a tsp)
Dried rosemary (half a tsp)
Cinnamon (half a tsp)
Lavender, can be fresh or dried (half a tsp or a sprig)
A piece of fur, a feather or nail clipping if specific to a pet
A brown, white or pink candle to seal the bottle or jar
Moon water
Matches or a lighter
Petition of intent (a small piece of paper folded up with the words "protect all the animals here or insert name of pet"
The hand written blessing on paper (see below)

Instructions:

First, cleanse the bottle or jar with your sage incense stick, then add all of the above ingredients including your petition of intent. Melt the candle for the wax so you can seal your bottle or jar. Using the moon water to soften the earth, dig a hole to bury your protection jar. Once covered, recite the following blessing/ spell from paper and ink

By Earth may your body be healthy, by air may your mind be at ease, By fire
may your spirit be strong and by water may you be full of peace. No harm will
come your way dear one, blessings to you every day, so mote it be.

Repeat three times. Or you may opt to create your own blessing protection spell that is specific to your pet or wildlife's needs. Once recited, use a match or lighter to burn the blessing and allow the wind to carry its ashes away to settle within nature.

The conclusion is that with the help and guidance of Artio and Mother Nature, the spell will protect all living beings. As said previously, this can also be used for a more specific blessing to a sick or injured pet perhaps.

Artio's feast day is October 21st. This ritual can be carried out on any day, but it is best to honour her and thank her on this particular day. Crystals can also be used to honour her, axinite and brown jasper are significant.

This spell was created by Lizzie Claridge, Nature Witch who works a lot with animal spirits and she is the owner of Mooch Pooch, Dog walking business.

Purple Candle Banishing Spell

This is a simple spell to banish someone causing harm in your life. You can also use a black candle if you prefer.

You will need:

Brown paper and a pen
A purple candle
Banishing oil
Bowl or dish

Write the name of the person causing harm and whom you wish to protect yourself from on the square brown paper. Write a short sharp banishing chant, e.g.:

There once was a pain in my chest
That put me to the ultimate test
Farewell to the hurt,
I bury it in the dirt,
So now I am free,
I banish thee,
And finally, I can rest.

Underneath your banishing chant write the person's name on the paper and then write your name over theirs to essentially cross them out to take back your power. Say these words out loud:

I cover you; I cross you; I command you; I compel you [Name]
BE GONE! Get out of my life!

- Dress the candle in banishing oil. The oil can include herbs like: Angelica, St John's Wort, Rosemary, Dill, Garlic, Thyme and others. Most of these you can find in your kitchen.

- Place the paper on the dish and stand the purple candle on top of it.
- Burn the candle and chant those words again.
- Once the candle has melted and burned right down to the paper.
- Option You can add menstrual blood for more potency because it will encourage the energy of releasing and cleansing.
- Collect what is left and bury it. Best time to do this spell is during the waning or dark moon.

Trapped in a Bottle Banishing Spell

This spell is fantastic not only as a banishing spell but will also bind whoever you're banishing to their own negativity and karma. Perform this during the dark moon and for added potency, call in Hekate or Soteria (epithet of Persephone) whose name means 'deliverance' or 'safety'.

You will need:

A glass jar or bottle
9 rose thorns
Rose petals
Salted water
Dark fabric
Garlic
Red chilli pepper
Nettles
Pen and paper
Something that reminds you of them

Put the item that reminds you of the person you wish to banish into the bottle. This item could be a photo you have of them, something small they gave you, a letter they wrote, anything that has their energy.

Draw the Evil Eye on a piece of paper and then write the person's name somewhere in the eye. On the back of the paper write a small limerick banishing poem that includes their name, for example:

There once was a lady named Nic,
Whose words were harsh as bricks,
And I desperately wanted to get rid,
Her evil intent towards me I forbid!
I tried to be kind,
But she had a mean mind,
So, to her own karma I shall bind,
The dark moon is upon me, I need to be quick,
Banishing her to her own demons will do the trick!

Your poetry doesn't always need to be serious or perfect, you can have a giggle with it to lighten your mood a little!

Once you've written their name and poem on the paper, fold the paper away from you and bind it with a wax red seal or red string.

Put the folded paper into the bottle with all the herbs listed and then drop nine rose thorns into the bottle and say:

Evil Presence I banish you! This rose now knows her thorns! I will protect myself!

Next drop 13 rose petals into the bottle as a symbol of love, that you don't wish this person any harm from you and the only harm they will know is what they created and sent back to them three-fold, you have bound them to their own karma. Add some salt water into the bottle, close the lid and shake it a little so everything mixes and binds together.

Leave the bottle open under the dark moon to draw the individual's energy into the bottle, directing it away from you and trapping their own negative energy inside and thus within themselves. Before sunrise, seal the lid shut and leave the bottle in a dark place for nine days.

Wrap the jar or bottle in a dark fabric, wrap it with red thread and then bury it very far away.

Abundance and Prosperity

In antiquity and the mediaeval period, many abundance and prosperity rituals were in the form of petitioning for good grain and harvest and invoking weather or earth deities hoping for a prosperous year for the community's sustenance. In Ukraine, one folk custom called the *vrozhaini obriady* involves the village elder taking off their hat, turning it towards the sun and uttering an incantation to the fields (grain spirits), asking to share the harvest. A woman reputed to be lucky cuts the first sheaf of grain and other women reapers then roll around on a cleared patch of the field with the purpose of absorbing strength from the soil. Later, the first sheaf would be placed in the icon corner of the elder's home where it was to stand until the end of the harvesting.

On the first day of Chinese New Year, Chinese families and businesses roll oranges and coins over the threshold of their front door, to ensure that prosperity will flow into the building all year long – petitioning to quite literally roll in abundance! In Singapore, if you buy a new home, you roll a pineapple into the house whilst chanting "huat ah!" – a Hokkien phrase meaning "to prosper".

Vietnamese prosperity bowls called Bagong Taon involve placing cotton inside a clear bowl to encourage a lightness of being in life, easy money and success, then place Malagkit rice in the bowl over the cotton, this is for good harvest, good family bonding, business prosperity and good friends. Next you place 12 eggs around the bowl for new beginnings, love, abundance and opportunities. Cleansed 12 gold and silver combined coins are added in between the eggs, soon after that 12 rolled up paper bills wrapped in red ribbon to attract wealth are placed in front of the coins, 12 gold foiled chocolate coins to attract sweetness in relationships are placed in a circle, laurel leaves considered a 'wish leaf' are placed along the outer rim of the bowl, three sticks of cinnamon are added in a triangle formation near the rolled up paper bills for protection and abundance, and finally an orange is placed in the centre of the chocolate coin circle for good health, wealth and prosperity. Ten wishes on a piece of paper are written down, folded towards the person and then placed in a red envelope before putting it in the bowl.

Priestesses of the ancient near East would have been called upon to chant hymns and sacred dances to bring good harvest to the community whilst the medicine man/woman of Indigenous Americans perform rainmaker dance rituals to invoke rain for bountiful crops. We've been wishing for wealth and prosperity in an abundance of forms for a very long time!

Apple Prosperity Spell

The most effective day to work this simple spell is on a Wednesday which represents Mercury's influence or Thursday when the expansive energy of Jupiter is strongest. Perform this *prosperity spell* during the waxing crescent moon to harness the potent manifesting energies of this *moon phase.*

Go for a walk in nature with an apple, a toothpick, pen and paper and small altar with nine crystals (the number nine is associated with abundance, generosity, and humanitarian pursuits). It is believed that by sharing wealth and resources, individuals can attract more abundance into their lives.

The crystals I recommend are:

- Tigers eye for finances.
- Jade for good luck.
- Rose Quartz which helps attract what you desire.
- Green Aventurine celebrated for its ability to attract success and money.
- Citrine to attract positive material and emotional wealth.

- Tree Agate to ground your desires into reality and sprout into being.
- Clear Quartz for clarity and amplifying dreams.
- Lapis Lazuli imbued with flecks of gold to attract wealth and enhance your intuition to grasp good opportunities in finance and work.
- Opal for peace and harnesses the energy of Venus as a bountiful frequency of attraction.

Close your eyes and visualise prosperity coming towards you as you're sitting with the trees and flowers. Perhaps prosperity is coming to you on the wings of a bird or butterflies? Is it raining down on you like golden rain? Now open your eyes and imagine energy beaming from your crystals into your apple, their light is energising the apple. Take the apple and cut it in two. Make sure the core is visible to represent the seeds of potential. In some apples you can see the star of Venus in their cores – another symbol denoting attracting abundance. If you don't, feel free to draw a star around the core of your apple with your tooth pick. After that, draw the rune symbol Fehu on one apple half. This word represents material gain, good fortune and wealth. On the other half, draw the rune symbol Uruz which is symbolic of strength, health, potential and flow of energy – encouraging a balance of wealth and health so you may enjoy your fruits in both external and internal aspects of your life.

Now eat the parts of the apple with the rune words on them. As you eat, imagine that glorious, abundant energy flowing through your body. Feel strength and confidence that you will achieve anything you want. But don't forget to express gratitude for all you are abundant with now.

Next take the remaining parts of the apple and give it to nature. You may wish to chop it up a little more and leave on tree branches for birds and squirrels to nibble on. This is a gift of sharing your abundance and as it degrades, it nourishes the soil – you are offering a gift to mother nature as a thank you for assisting in bringing a flow of wealth and blossoming opportunities into your life.

Once the spell is complete, take a moment in contemplation in nature to reflect on this present moment, how you're feeling and what you wish to manifest. You may wish to journal about it later.

Wealth Charm for the Home

This simple charm will encourage the energy of money to flow to you, best time to do this is during the new moon.

You will need:

- Clay
- Green candle
- A small piece of parchment paper and pen
- Cinnamon powder
- Basil
- Nutmeg powder
- Something gold
- Chamomile
- Bergamot Oil
- Bowl of rice
- Citrine Crystals
- Cinnamon incense
- Journal

Write out your petition on a small piece of parchment paper alongside the mantra *aim hrim shrim paramalakshmai namaha* to call in the goddess Lakshmi. As you do this, light a green candle because green attracts wealth, growth and success and is also the colour of the heart chakra associated with love, sharing and abundance.

Take a moment to hold your petition in your hands and place on your heart and imagine wealth and prosperity is flowing to you, be specific with what you desire, write it down in your journal what wealth means to you, what do you wish to be abundant with and what are you grateful to be abundant with in your present moment?

Mix all your herb ingredients together. Then take your clay and form it into a flat pebble shape the size of your palm, then with a toothpick inscribe the rune Fehu (which is symbolic for wealth) into the middle. Take a pinch of your herb blend and mix into the clay and anoint it with Bergamot oil (eight drops to represent the infinity symbol for prosperity being in continuous flow). Take your written petition and fold it towards you and then place in the middle of your clay pebble before folding the clay over it and pinching the sides to seal it.

When the clay seal is completely dry you can put it on top of a bowl of uncooked rice. Treat it like a small money altar. You can place citrine around the seal and add cinnamon or patchouli incense sticks in the rice. Place this offering bowl near the entrance of your home or living room.

Handkerchief Prosperity Spell

Although this spell was initially intended for the planting of seeds for an abundant harvest, it can be easily adapted to any prosperity and abundance ritual. This is a great spell to do for Beltane in the hope we will be bountiful by Lughnasadh.

You will need:

7 seeds of wheat, barley, or rice.
7 coins.
A white handkerchief.
A felt pen.
Cornucopia charm.

Needle and thread (optional).
Pen and paper.
Peony plant or seeds.

Begin by writing your intention out on your handkerchief. You can also stitch a symbol like an acorn, leaf or lotus flower onto the handkerchief as an extra sigil to bring in the energies of prosperity. Then, place seven coins and seven seeds in the handkerchief. Add the Cornucopia charm in the middle with a pinch of ginger and thyme. Spend as long as you need crafting a simple limerick to attract wealth by invoking Cornucopia. For example:

Queen Cornucopia of wealth I sow,
Seeds of bountiful harvest do grow,
Bringing in riches and health,
In abundance and stealth,
In the land where good fortunes flow.
A bountiful harvest we reap,
As joy and prosperity, we keep,
Bringing us wealth and good health in tow,
Mistress of all that is lush doth glow.

Then wrap the seeds, coins and charm inside. Tie the handkerchief with green string or twine.

Go outside during a new moon. Bury the bundle in a plant pot near your front door and plant Marigolds over the top. Marigolds are hardy, grow very fast and easily, they represent abundance and they will draw down the abundant rays of the sun and rain water into your handkerchief charm to activate the energies of prosperity from the flow of nature.

Zodiac Poetry

This is a fun, playful chapter based on ancient mystics and wise women predicting the skies and charting people's lives in conjunction to the trajectories of planets and stars. Priests and priestesses of antiquity did worship and personify the heavens, there are myths associated with each zodiac and there are hymns and blessings to some of them such as canticles to Venus as the morning and evening star, songs to Astraea (goddess who became the constellation Virgo), sailors petitioning the Dioscuri (Gemini constellation) for safe voyages, Dea Artio (She-Bear of Ursa Major and Minor) was worshipped by Gallo-Roman people for abundance and transformation, Orion (Osiris) was often invoked for rebirth and resurrection and Asteria, the goddess of falling stars was invoked for nighttime divination, dreamwork and astrology.

The ancients probably didn't create zodiac poetry as a way to intuit an individual's weekly forecast; however, we can play pretend!

Creating Zodiac Blackout Poem Spells

A fun activity utilising blackout poetry as a form of divination to describe and forecast each star sign.

You will need:

A black marker
A pencil
An old book (or newspaper)

Start with making a poem about your own star sign. Skim the passage and keep your eye out for that eye-catching word that will guide the theme of your poem Use the pencil to lightly outline words you like on a page of text. When you are happy with this, go over your pencil outlines with the marker and then completely black out the majority of the page, leaving your chosen words standing out. Start a new page for the next star sign. Soon you'll have 12 poems as horoscope messages to each zodiac sign.

Perform this during the new moon. This phase begins the moon's cycle and harnesses a quiet, restful energy. It is a time to tap into your creative thinking. You can also choose to channel a deity, Enheduanna or other spirit guide to help you with messages and clear thinking.

Speak the words out loud. When you read the words out loud, the poem becomes a living, breathing thing. The energy changes around the words, as you release the words into the universe.

Keep a journal of your musings or stick your magical black-out poetry in your Grimoire. You can create black-out poetry as daily oracle messages too.

Bibliomancy Zodiac Predictions

Bibliomancy is a form of divination originating from mediaeval early Christian Europe and was codified in the 11th-century *Divinatory Psalter* of the Orthodox Slavs. Eventually the practice was condemned by high official Christian leaders, this magical praxis continued to be in use in secret regardless.

Traditionally bibliomancy involved using the Bible for spiritual messages and oracular prophecy, even the 90's band *'Destiny's Child'* used this technique to choose their band name!

Simply choose a book or a few books, (I personally prefer poetry books because you're guaranteed more whimsical results!) Hold the book with both hands, have a question in your mind's eye, direct that question to the book and then fan the pages. Similar to pulling a tarot card out of the deck, listen to your intuition and you'll know which page to stop on. Then take note of the first sentence at the top of the page. Does it answer your question? Is it obscure or does it make sense?

Does it bring clarity? You may choose to find other sentences on the same page or flip through other pages and note the top sentence for each in order to form a small paragraph. Or opt for the *bookshelf method*: meditate by your bookshelf, pull one book, flip through it, stop at a page, write down the first sentence at the top of the page and put the book back before grabbing the second book to repeat the process again and again for a third, fourth, fifth time until you feel the message is complete.

Essentially what you will have conjured are little prophetic poems for each sign and for you to interpret the hidden essence. You can incorporate this activity into your journaling and even shadow work since you are working with the liminal realms to channel messages.

Example of my own poetry I created from random books I picked off my shelf

Gemini – Beauty does not need a concrete meaning. Be challenged to walk through the heart-gate, our feelings are much more sacred than we can ever grasp in the vastness of stars.

Capricorn – Take a slow breath, never are you for a moment left alone. But think twice before the climb, Pause before the mountain, a holy humbling.

Pisces – Dragon of the bitter waters look to the moon, you can rewrite your story, face your fears with courage. Retreat into your own world for renewal wherever you want.

Zodiac Haiku

Haiku poetry began in 13th century Japan as part of a longer poem style called Renga. By the 16th century it broke away to become its own style. Haiku is often utilised to express the sacredness of nature, encourages a sense of contemplation and invokes a tranquil beauty inspired by zen Buddhism and Shintoism.

Haiku consists of three lines, the first line is structured with five syllables, the second with seven and the third with the final five.

You can divine your own Haiku for weekly zodiac forecasts, predictions or full moon manifesting. I have created three of my own as an example to describe the general characteristics of their sun sign qualities. You can also chant them in a ritual or specific spell devoted to your desired outcome (e.g./ qualities of Libra for fairness, qualities of Aries for assertiveness, qualities of Cancer for healing and so on).

Libra
Rose red soft, sweet smile,
voice tamed the beast's cruel heart,
tore her pain to shreds.

Scorpio
Medusa queen,
venom incubated ache,
The bite, the bitter rage.

Aquarius
Chimera gryphon
Wide-eyed curious soul.
A reckless wreckage.

Postcard Poems for the Star Signs

This one is a little crafty. You can make your own with card paper and mixed media to design the front or buy some from online sites like Etsy. I had a San Franciscan friend I met in Morocco, who during his retirement years enjoyed making postcard poems and sending them to friends around the world including me. I looked forward to finding one among piles of bills. He'd often print his own photography and collages onto card paper and leave a poetic and meaningful message on the back. I have kept all of them in my keepsake box.

Postcard poems are prose poems embroidered with sensory detailing and memories. They are meaningful and pull us into feelings of joyful nostalgia as well as closeness to each other. Quicker than writing a letter with a playful energy, these are great little time capsules that hold on to someone's personality through their notes of *sweet nothings*. Create and send to your witchy friends for them to add in their grimoire or on their altar.

Example

> *Leo* – A vivacious forest nymph, so daring and dazzling that she sizzled in the sunlight. Daughter of the sun, she smiles up at that radiant mirror. She knows she is the glitter on the ocean, the shimmer of a beetle wing and the warmth of a summer morning's kiss.
>
> *Aries* – The battle scars are my stars charting maps many fear to tread. At the end of days, I'll be there, sword and strategy ready. Behind this combusting courage is a heart so true, even the goddess Aphrodite would fall to her knees.
>
> *Taurus* – The morning star beckons me to lounge in a field of daisies, so I succumb to the sumptuous pleasures of eating strawberries and cream under a willow tree and making love during the balmy friction of a heady thunderstorm's groan.

Poetry Magic with Art-Craft

> The word artist did not appear in the English language until after the mediaeval period. In the mediaeval period manuscript artists were often called *'Limners'*, the word is an altered form of *'Luminer'* meaning *'illuminator'*, from the Latin *lumen* meaning *'light'*. Artists were – in a literal sense – bringers of light. –Mary Wellesley Author of *Hidden Hands: The lives of Manuscripts and their Makers*

In 2009, artist Kirstie Macleod began 'The Red Dress' global embroidery project providing an artistic platform for women around the world. The project travelled the globe so women could embroider their stories and culture onto the dress. Embroiders included refugees from Palestine and Syria and women seeking asylum in the UK from Iraq, Kosovo, Nigeria and Rwanda. As well as Afghanistan, Kenya, Pakistan and more. The project wanted to generate a sense of community without borders, a merging of cultures and freedom of creative expression. Up close and sewn on the panels, you see women's voices surrounded by flowers and patterns, words of hope, love, Sesterstvi (sisterhood), peace, friendship, life and joy – powerful words to conjure positivity and healing. You can also see bird totems with incantations on them and a 'darkness to light' sigil. The power of words and symbols woven into cloth!

Poppets are an old form of folk magic created by many cultures globally. Poppets are sometimes contained in a vessel with the spell included on a tablet or parchment and some dolls have had the sigil or written incantation sewn into it with specific herbs and oils for healing or as a blessing. One such poppet is called a 'Peg figurine' from ancient Sumeria, that are frequently carved with poetic spells and hymns, then hammered into the ground by the foundations of temples, buried as guardians of the complex.

The combination of artisan craft with spells and invocation is a fascinating topic to research and it seems to be a popular magical practice even today. As a gift for a friend's pagan wedding, I created a flower wreath that included two sealed bottles that were suspended and hung from the wreath with ribbons. Inside the bottles were sand and shells (because they were from Cyprus) and two blessing spell-poems on little scrolls. The first was based on an old Celtic marriage blessing and the second was petitioning Aphrodite and Hera for a loving and happy marriage.

In this fun chapter I wanted to include handicraft with poetry. Often many ancient and mediaeval poem-spells and incantations are incorporated with an object. Whether a protective sigil is sewn into a poppet or stitched onto textiles, included in good luck charm bags, hung on trees with blessing rags, added into decorative jars for the home or inscribed on clay or metal appliances as every day sympathetic magic, humans have been combining art with poems as a way to conjure magic for centuries.

As historian Mary Wellesley states, Artists were called *Lumineers,* which means 'illuminator' during the mediaeval period. In this section of the book, I encourage you to be playful as you make things with your hands. Become a bringer of light!

Good Luck Talismans

Although I've written in this book the importance and power of speech and words, often we take our words for granted. Throughout history many cultures around the world have creation myths that tell of gods uttering our existence into being with the word. And we know that utilising the correct name of a person or thing imbues it with power. Writing across the ancient world was a sacred tool as well as a means to communicate. There is a resonance that reverberates through specific letters, words and sentences that are potent and attributed to the innate power of a primordial energy deity or essence.

Talismans make use of writing, symbolic lettering, and names like a circuit board or conductor of that energy and harness it for attracting good fortune or repelling negative intent. They can be etched on stones, inscribed on parchment, sewn into textiles, added inside handmade poppets and so on. This chapter focuses on art with magical words to create potent talismans.

Making your own Talisman and Blessing Holder

Spend some time contemplating which word, symbol or image is best for your chosen purpose. Be clear about what you want, make sure it is personal to you. Carefully draw the symbol or words (magical sentence using runes for example) on clean paper with a pen. Keep in mind the energy you want your talisman to bring about.

As you consider what energy you manifest – whether it be love, letting go, protection, wealth. Find colours, herbs and oils associated with that energy. Add your magical word talisman into a small bag with relevant herbs, colours and oil drops with salt for preservation and binding all these qualities together, you may wish to add a crystal or charm too. If you can make or embellish your own little pouch bag then all the better because you've made something for the purpose of this talisman. If not, a small jewellery bag will do and you can sew little charms onto this bag for extra magical potency.

Place three lighted candles in a triangle shape of your altar space. Put incense to the left and a small bowl of water with a few drops of your oil of choice plus a pinch of salt sprinkled into the water to your right. Place your talisman in the middle of the triangle of light.

Imagine you are in the middle of this golden light as it expands out like a giant pyramid conducting and transmuting the energies of your talisman. Pick up the talisman and pass it three times over the flame of the middle candle, then three times over the incense smoke and finally sprinkle three times from the water of your bowl. As you're doing this, utter your magical intent, call on your guardians and the four directions and the elements to bring power to your talisman. If you have a deity you work with, call on them too to imbue it with their wisdom and protection to help you bring to life exactly what you want to utilise this talisman for.

With one final thank you to the elements and higher powers charging your talisman with their resonance you can choose to wear the bag holding your talisman, sew it into an item of clothing or keep it in your purse to have with you at all times.

- **Blessing holder for Love** – Write a short love poem-spell to yourself or a loved one. Collect some rose petals and leaves, three apple and pomegranate seeds as well as a rose quartz or Rhodochrosite. Include a heart shaped charm or stone plus feathers from a dove/pigeon. Tie the leaves and feathers together with a red chord. Place all items together inside your blessing bag. Perfume it with rose and ylang ylang oils for love and joy.
- **Blessing holder for Health** – Gather sprigs of motherwort, St John's wort and Oregano with a leaf from an Oak for longevity and a pebble or crystal that is round and has an orange-reddish hue. Include a charm that represents good health to you and inscribe the runes Uruz (for healing), Laguz (for the element of water as purification) and Perthro (feminine motherly energy). Place everything together in a small bag and tie that bag with a braided cord of red, green and white. Perfume with a few drops of sandalwood and frankincense.
- **Blessing holder for protection** – Gather some leaves from the Rowan tree as well as the herbs rosemary,

> Angelica and Lavender. Include Hekate's wheel, the Hamsa hand or eye of Ra as charms to ward off evil. You may also include a shard of a black mirror to reflect back negativity against you. Add the crystal rainbow obsidian to shelter you from harm – specifically ill intent and emotional attack. You may wish to add a cat's claw (naturally fallen off), a metal nail or small crab pincer for extra bite! Sprinkle everything with salt. Write a short magical rhyming poem to banish what wishes you harm. Place everything together in a black bag tied together with a silver ribbon. Perfume with Sage and Bergamot.

Another option for a blessing bag is a Pomander. I mention Pomanders in a previous chapter regarding healing through the use of sticking cloves into an orange fruit. But did you know Pomanders were once bag-like round scented containers that people carried on their person? Similar to a blessing bag, you could put charms and poem-spells inside them with specific magical sigils, herbs and oils as protective amulets which I find rather quirky and delightful! Potentially first used as an early form of aromatherapy, they soon became a sort of magical fashion accessory. The 16th century Pouncet round carrier box was created to be hollow inside with a clasp to open it and put things inside it. You could make your own with a tennis ball covered in soft leather and embellishments. Add your poem-spell, herbs, oils, charms, shells and more inside it, depending on what you desire this pomander to be specifically for?

Incantation Clay Bowl Protection Spell

Across what is now known as Iran and Iraq, archaeologists have unearthed bountiful artefacts known as incantation bowls that were created during late antiquity from the sixth to eighth centuries, particularly in Upper Mesopotamia and Syria as a form of sympathetic folk magic. The bowls are usually inscribed with an incantation from the top of the rim and down into the middle in a spiral. Sometimes a crude drawing of a demon – usually Liliths (Night wind demons), are drawn in the middle as though they are trapped and contained by the magical words. These bowls would be buried upside down to capture all sorts of demons, preventing them from entering people's homes. They were also buried near to thresholds such as cemeteries, courtyards and even in the corner of homes of the recently deceased. Most of the 2000 bowls found were inscribed in Babylonian Aramaic. One Bowl discovered had an incantation for Kuktan Pruk during her pregnancy for a safe birth, and another bowel to protect Anush Busai and his family against bad luck, both bowls from southern Mesopotamia (200-600 CE).

To perform your protection spell you will need:

Air drying clay
Marker pen
Pen and Paper
4 black candles
Cinnamon
Sage
Rosemary
Black sea salt
Banishing oil of choice

This spell is best done during the waning crescent. First you need to make your bowl, the size is up to you and it doesn't have to be perfect – it will be buried anyway. Air drying clay is easy to work with, easily accessible and affordable from most craft stores. Let your clay bowl dry and set once you are happy with your overall shape. Take your herbs and sea salt and mix them altogether in a separate pot. Cinnamon shields the home from negative energy, Sage purifies and cleanses, Rosemary wards off evil spirits and bad energy and Black Sea salt absorbs negative energy and drives away evil spirits.

As you are waiting for your clay bowl to dry, take a moment to write your banishing spell on a piece of paper. Often these incantation bowls are repetitive in style similar to Mantra. You want to produce something simple yet strong, something you can remember to chant easily on repeat. You may choose for it to rhyme.

Once you feel you are happy with your spell, you can then inscribe it on the bowl using the marker. Remember to start at the top of the rim and work your way down in a spiral motion until you reach the middle – you may wish to draw a demon or goblin-like creature for added effect.

Now when everything is ready. Set up four black candles in a square. Anoint them with banishing oil. Light them up and call in the four directions to assist in this protection spell to banish ill intent from your life. Four in numerology represents structure and creates a boundary like a strong fortress. Chant your incantation four times as you grab your herb mixture and sprinkle or rub onto the bowl widdershins to encourage the herbs to help cast out demons. Add your bowl into the middle of the square formed by the candles and chant your incantation again.

Optional: You may wish to add a few drops of peppermint oil (or purposefully made Banishing Oil made from Lemon, Basil, Angelica, Wormwood and Rue) and sprinkle sharp shards to further dispel bad energy from lurking.

Once all this is done, hold the bowl over some sandalwood incense and chant your incantation four times more. Call in your guardians to help activate the spell.

When you're ready, pick a spot near your home that has the energy of a crossroads, dig a hole and first tip the herb mixture into the hole before placing the bowl over the top, upside down before burying it.

Creating your own 'Duk Rak' Protective Seal

My grandfather was half Romanichal (Angloromani) and half French. His mother, my great grandmother, who was a Tasseographer fortune teller, taught him the Roma way and he was even fluent in Romany. I remember his crudely hand painted 'EUREKA' sign above his door which in Greek means "I have found it", he told me that it was symbolic for a few things, particularly for his hoarded treasures in his small flat and the gold and money he'd hidden in floorboards that nobody would find but him! He also made what is called a 'Duk Rak' which are small protection seals you can leave at the gate or door of your home. This is a form of barrier magic to keep negativity away. A traditional Duk Rak involves five or more stakes made from 'holy' wood such as Oak, Ash, Yew etc. Sometimes stones are used. Then dip your hand in red paint (a colour for power and passion) and wrap your painted palm around the stake to create a handprint, as you do this, focus all your intention into your hand, you want to direct your boundary energy into a palm print to protect your place, once you're done, ground these stakes around your property in a circle.

You can make your Duk Rak from air drying clay by creating five palm sized pebbles and make them extra potent by writing a sigil or charmed words on a piece of paper to banish negativity, roll up the paper away from you and before the clay sets you can place the paper on the surface of the clay and fold the clay over it to seal it inside like a clam. Light a red candle and burn some dragon's blood. When the clay pebbles are set with the paper spell inside you can then paint them red – add your thumb print or 'witch mark' or symbol of choice with black paint or marker pen. Hold the Duk Rak over the flame of the candle and incense smoke to seal the spell and then walk out of your home, starting at the main gate, walk clockwise around your boundary and plant your seals around each corner and chant *"I place you here to protect all that I have and all that I love forever."*

Imagine a force field around your home, encircling your property before going back inside and having a cup of tea.

Stitching Spells

Sewing magical symbols onto cloth

Across the world people have been sewing protective sigils and fertility symbols into textiles for hundreds, if not thousands of years, infusing the cloth with meaning and power for the wearer. Proverbs are added to the bottom of the East African khanga, the marguerite star of Venus is embroidered on to traditional Lefkara Cypriot lace to petition the goddess of love and *Amazigh* Berber women would paint, tattoo or weave their traditional symbols onto pottery, clothing and skin for protective and votive meaning often associated with fertility, life force, courage, happiness and warding off evil.

You will need:

Piece of cloth
Needle and thread
Paper and pen

Stitching and sewing doesn't need to be perfect for the spell to take effect, have fun with this, be playful! Take some time to sit in contemplation, perhaps in nature with your pen and paper and think about what word, phrase or symbol has meaning to you? Or perhaps you wish to create something as a blessing for a loved one? Perhaps you want more kindness in your life and simply sewing the word kindness is all that's needed? Maybe you want to embroider an eye onto the cloth, a protective sigil to keep negativity at bay? Perhaps you're pretty good at sewing and wish to sew a powerful phrase onto the cloth.

Once you've decided on what you're going to sew, take some time to work the cloth and visualise the energy you are invoking, imagine this energy being drawn down through your hands and into the cloth.

Once completed, anoint your cloth with blessing oil (rose, spikenard, orange, lemon, sandalwood) and say a personal prayer as you hold the cloth.

You may wish to go for a walk in nature and connect with a tree, ask permission to tie the cloth to its branches, perhaps leave some seeds as a thankyou offering before you leave.

You may wish to do a similar thing with clothing, perhaps you wish to sew a protective word or symbol hidden somewhere underneath by the hem or stitch onto a poppet or perhaps a biodegradable ribbon to tie on a blessing tree.

Clay Grief Jar

I saw this simple activity in a workshop at a women's festival once and thought it was a powerful way of letting go of something painful. Ritualising grief and death with our hands and words provides us with a sense of personal power to walk through a challenging time, process emotions and gently put things to rest or perhaps you want to banish your ex! In ancient Greece from around 375 BCE, a Funerary *Lekythos* jar was discovered, this is a small terracotta Vessel engraved with a young woman that carried funerary oils and in Egypt round burial containers resembling wombs or eggs were excavated. Archaeologists believed these symbolic funerary pots facilitated the process of rebirth after death, petitioning great mother earth to birth the spirits into the afterlife.

All you need is some quick drying clay, pen and paper and anything small like an old earring, shell fragments, hair, dried flowers, pebbles, charms, ripped up photographs – anything you like. Perform this spell during the dark moon or during Samhain.

Firstly, make your clay pot with the quick drying clay, it doesn't have to be perfect but make something about the size of the palm of your hands. You may wish to scratch 'witch marks' inside or outside your pot whilst it is still malleable. Let it dry.

As it's drying, light a black candle and write out your incantation. Do you want this poetic spell to rhyme or are you petitioning a deity like Kali or Persephone, Seshat or Ker? Channel your energy of letting go into the poem. What are you letting go of? Is this a funerary pot? A banishing jar? Maybe you just want to write a letter to someone who recently passed away?

Once you've written your piece, fold or roll it up and tie it with a black ribbon, or you may wish to burn it to ash and place the ash into your clay pot.

Include all your collected items in the pot as well as dirt plus a few drops of oil. If it's a funerary jar add some oils such as lavender, yarrow and sandalwood. For banishing unwanted energies or people, consider frankincense, sage, peppermint.

Once everything is in the jar, you may wish to create a lid with clay or cloth, seal it with wax or string and find a place you consider a good location to bury it. As you bury it, treat your clay pot like an urn, the energy inside it is energy you wish to let go, and put in the ground to say goodbye to. If this represents the passing of someone you loved or perhaps a pet, this could be a very emotional experience, or perhaps anger may come up as you banish what no longer serves, all is valid in this death ceremony.

Once you've conducted your burial, take some time to reflect and write in your journal what thoughts and emotions surfaced for you.

As you fill in the dugout hole with your urn inside, chant a few words of letting go, for example:

In the stillness of the night, I release you with love
Goodbye whispered softly, sent on wings above

Our time together now a memory to hold dear
As I let you go, my heart sheds a silent tear

Fly away now on wings of fate's design
I release you with love in this moment divine
Goodbye for now but not forevermore
Our paths may cross again on some distant shore

The sanctuary of Aphrodite is a Byzantine church of *Agia Paraskevi* (the milk-giving virgin) in the village of *Yeroskipou* (sacred garden). Along the walls of this church are crude infant effigies people can purchase to petition for healthy pregnancy and birth. The ancient Egyptians created wax idols for funerary rites and life sized, realistic waxworks are being created by Tibetan Buddhist monks to continue honouring the life of deceased Buddhist Masters which is a brand-new votive offering in present day Tibet.

Sometimes written spells can be folded up and sewn into poppets or wax effigies.

If you have a mould in your desired shape, you can add your written spell into the melted wax before it cools and hardens. Or simply place the paper in the back or head of the fabric poppet with stuffing before it is sewn up.

Wax Baby Effigy Blessing Spell

You can purchase wax moulds online and from Amazon. There is a lovely silicone mould baby footprint and also moulds in the shape of a new born baby.

You will need:

Pan and stove
Silicone mould of desired shape
White candle

Bag of white candle wax flakes
Pen and paper
Blessing oils: lemon balm, chamomile, baby's breath
Herbs: rosehips, rose, tulsi
Daisy flower heads or petals
Cloth and white ribbon

Light the white candle, sit in meditation, call in your guides and angels as you write a blessing prayer for the baby or pregnant mother. Pour out love and well wishes as you hold them dear in your heart, keep it short and sweet. Petition a preferred deity, perhaps Eileithyia, Greek goddess of childbirth or Brigid the Celtic goddess of midwifery, motherhood and poetry?

Heat your stove and place your bag of wax into the pan to melt on a low heat. Once it has melted and kept in the melted state on a very low heat, add three drops of lemon balm, three drops of chamomile and three drops of baby's breath. The number three represents a safe and positive journey and encourages a loving space for new beginnings. The Empress in the tarot who is fertile and abundant is associated with the number three too so it is a very potent number for pregnancy. Then add a pinch of rosehips, rose and tulsi (if you can't attain tulsi 'holy basil', ordinary basil will do) and then daisy heads (or petals).

Pour the mixture carefully into your mould and as it cools (before it sets), roll or fold up your blessing prayer and place into the mould. Once set, take the baby effigy out of the mould and wrap it up in a bundle of cloth (if you know the gender you may choose a specific colour) and gently tie with a white ribbon. Optional: add a little charm or bell to the ribbon for added protection and blessings.

You may gift this to your expecting friend who might want to put it on her altar or if your friend is not a practitioner, keep it on your altar with the white candle lit so you may continue to send love and well wishes. Always blow out the candle when not in prayer.

Note: I chose white candle wax because white represents new beginnings and innocence. However, this is your spell to adapt how you wish, if you wish to create a baby effigy of a different colour then please do so.

Releasing Anger: Invocation of Sekhmet

Sekhmet, whose name means 'She who is Powerful' is the ancient Egyptian lioness goddess of the fiery desert sun, transformation, medicine and healing.

Anger can be a difficult emotion to process, some of us struggle to express it which leads to bottling it up, and others tend to be hot headed,

This is a spell for anger transformation and release involving a Sekhmet doll or cat mummy poppet.

You will need:

- Material to create your poppet, options: clay, cloth or needle felting
- Red and orange candle
- Pen and paper

Begin by creating or acquiring a Sekhmet doll or cat mummy poppet. This can be a small figurine or representation of Sekhmet. Options: Make her from polymer clay or papier mache.

Find a quiet and sacred space where you can perform your spell without interruption. Light a red or orange candle to invoke the fiery energy of Sekhmet, symbolising transformation and passion.

Hold the Sekhmet doll or cat mummy poppet in your hands and close your eyes. Take a few deep breaths to centre yourself. Visualise the anger or negative emotions you wish to release.

Imagine this energy as dark clouds swirling around you. Feel their weight and intensity. With each exhale, imagine sending these clouds of anger into the Sekhmet doll or poppet.

Whisper your prayers and intentions for transformation and release into the doll, asking Sekhmet for guidance and assistance in letting go of this anger. Ask her to be the fierce vessel of which she will transmute and dissolve your pain to make space for healing. You may write your own incantation invocation to accompany your Sekhmet doll which you may choose to tea stain and roll up like a scroll and place it with her on your altar or perhaps you may wish to burn it to ignite further metamorphosis.

Chant this incantation out loud:

Divine Sekhmet, fierce and mighty, Keeper of flames burning bright,
In the depths of my soul's night, I call upon your sacred light.
Grant me strength to face my fire, to quell the flames of the raging fire.
Transform my anger into power, in this transformative hour.
From darkness, let growth arise, through your wisdom, let me realise,
that within the depths of my despair, lies the seed of growth ripe and rare.
Guide me through this sacred dance, as I confront my own circumstance,
may your fierce grace lead the way, turning night to the light of day.
Sekhmet, lady of transformation, in your name, I seek salvation,
Help me embrace the path I tread, as I journey from anger to growth ahead.
With every step, with every breath, guide me through this inner depth,

Let your presence be my guiding flame, as I rise from darkness, never the same.
Hail Sekhmet, fierce and true, In your grace, I find my breakthrough,
Transform my anger, heal my pain, Let growth and transformation reign.

As you continue to breathe deeply, envision Sekhmet's fierce energy surrounding you, enveloping you in her protective embrace. Feel her strength and wisdom empowering you to face and transform your anger.

Once you feel a sense of release and transformation, extinguish the candle, symbolising the completion of the spell. Thank Sekhmet for her guidance and assistance in your journey towards healing and transformation.

Keep the Sekhmet doll or poppet in a safe place as a reminder of your commitment to releasing anger and embracing transformation. You can revisit it whenever you feel the need to reconnect with Sekhmet's energy and continue your journey of healing.

Ritual Activity Created by Wendy Rivera, American Vietnamese Artist and Witch from Texas, USA.

The Dreaming Space

The Gipar was the living quarters for Enheduanna and her priestesses at the Ningal temple of Ur in ancient Sumeria. The root meaning of the word *'Gipar'* means 'Storehouse' and this is because the harvest was considered sacred and needed to be housed next door to the temple so that the priestesses could sanctify and keep watch over the grain. Later the complex expanded to become a home for the priestesses which included a medical centre (birthing hut), ritual washing bath house with waterproof sunken floor, library, menstruation room, small ceremonial spaces with altars, herb garden and mantic room with a ritual couch for the incubation of dreaming, oracular visions and eliciting divine response.

The Oracle of Delphi of ancient Greece also utilised a dark cavern-like space for clairvoyance and prophecy. The ancient Greek Eleusinian Mysteries would often include *Kykeon* which is a type of beverage to induce a state of wakeful dreaming during ritual consisting of water, barley, honey, pennyroyal and wine and the ancient Cypriots would export Opium to the Egyptian temples in bilbil juglets (they look like inverted poppies) so that the priestesses could create a concoction of opium and blue lotus for a transcendental state to commune with the gods during special ceremonies. In central America tribes meditate with Cacao and in Japan, their tea ceremonies invoke a sense of serenity in the present moment. In European herbalism, Mugwort tea is perfect for healthy dreaming and feelings of waking tranquillity. Mugwort has been used for centuries to promote vivid and lucid dreams, as well as improve dream recall and overall sleep quality. In present day Druid training, there is a practice at the end of the Bardic stage called 'The Cell of Song' of which the student enters into sensory deprivation for several hours to channel inspiration from *Orbis alius* (Otherworld) and from within themselves to produce Bardic poetry and/or wisdom.

I am a lover and advocate for daydreaming and spending hours contemplating life over a cup of tea whilst watching the rain. I can spend an entire day going inwards and allowing myself to be a channel for whatever flows through me from the gods or from the dream time. I am also a lucid dreamer and will have a dream journal by my bed to write down what I witnessed in my dreams upon waking because perhaps the dream world has a message for me? As a child I was prone to dream-like states of consciousness to expand my imagination, it gave me a feeling of enchantment and inner alchemical play. Being in a meditative state whilst walking in nature or whilst in prayer at your altar, not only allows your mind to rest but it creates space for inspiration to strike.

We live in a busy world that can clog our brains with a lot of static. What if you took time to quiet the noise and allow yourself to be transported to your inner world? To make sure this practice stays healthy and not maladaptive, I stay grounded with a cup of tea (and honey on toast) or if I go for a walk, I sit for a while by a tree and be present with the elements, the birds, dandelions and woodland creatures – touching the earth with my bare feet keeps me rooted. Being tethered to the present moment keeps you centred so you can expand your consciousness and saunter through portals. My best work has come from this realm. I am a pilgrim wandering through my portals!

This chapter provides visual journey and dreamy yoga nidra scripts to encourage a state of consciousness between waking and sleeping. In this state images and words may flow to you. Keep a notebook and pen just in case. This is all about free writing, perhaps you birth a poem? Perhaps it inspires a painting? Perhaps you journal about the journey and want to decipher the symbols presented to you. Whatever manifests, it's all valid. Ask a friend to read the scripts out to you, use them in your own circle sharings, record your voice reciting the script and play it back to yourself, enjoy connecting to the otherworlds over your favourite beverage.

The Dreaming Priestess visual journey

The Dreaming Priestess, also known as the Dreaming Goddess or the Sleeping Lady is a figurine dated to be around 3200-2500 BC and she was found in the "oracle" room of an underground labyrinth called the Hal Saflieni Hypogeum on the island of Malta. The Hypogeum is an underground temple and tomb dating back to the Neolithic, and is dedicated to the incubation of dreaming. Due to its connection to the dead, it was considered a liminal space where numinous powers of the divine could be channelled to attain messages from the otherworlds through the practice of dreaming. This complex became a hybrid dream-healing temple and entrance to the underworld. Scholar and historian Cristina Biaggi considers this reclining beauty to be a priestess engaged in dream incubation who would have also given oracles, interpreted dreams or utilised mantic practice for suggesting cures.

Upon learning about this figurine and ancient dream temple, it inspired me to create a visual journey for you. Keep a pen and your journal ready for any messages from the threshold!

First, brew yourself a pot of mugwort and chamomile tea. Gentle instrumental music is optional to add to the sensory experience if you wish.

Mugwort is wonderful for wakeful dreaming and chamomile is a soothing herb to create feelings of peace. Find a comfortable resting spot, either laying down with blankets or in a sitting position and relax.

Close your eyes, and bring your attention towards your beating heart, away from external noises, away from the thoughts floating around your mind, and into the presence of your body. Connect with your breathing. Inhale feelings of peace, exhale worry and stress. Imagine your blood circulation ebbing and flowing like the ocean, moving golden light towards the shore of your heart and releasing negative debris out beyond the horizon as you exhale.

Breathe in.....

Breathe out.....

Pause...

Feel your whole body relaxing, let your face soften, your jaw untighten, your shoulders drop and your spine loosen.

Breathe in....

Breathe out....

And sink deeper into relaxation.

Pause...

If your tea is cool enough, take a few sips at this moment and feel free to sip your beverage whenever you want throughout this guided visual journey.

Let the noise of the world disappear so you can walk through this inner realm, your dream state.

Standing in your heart chamber you see the walls are a lovely soft red hue, it's cosy in here, isn't it? This is your safe, sacred space where all your love is stored. But you see a door on the other side of this room and there is a light glowing around its frame. Curious, you walk towards the door you notice a symbol decorated on the wooden surface. Make a mental note of this symbol and consider what it means to you or its message it brings.

Grabbing the handle, you open the door and step into a quaint and quiet town, with cobbled paths and full glorious sun.

As you walk up the cobbled path, people stop you with smiling faces and point to where you need to go. They tell you "She's waiting for you".

Take a moment to picture their faces with clarity, who are these people to you? Do you feel a connection? Are they ancestors or perhaps beings from another realm? One of them hands you a note...

Holding it in your hands you open it and read it....

What does it say?

Walking down the hill you finally come to the entrance to a stone cave. The smell of incense wafts through the air and feels inviting. Birds are chirping in the trees and flower petals appear to be falling from the sky. This cave feels welcoming and familiar and you walk closer. The sandstone gently gleams in the sunlight.

As you stand at the entrance of this place, a woman opens the door. Her robes are radiant and silky and she is holding a juglet of the finest oils which smells so divine.

She tells you to come in, make yourself at home, take your shoes off.

She brings you to a chamber for a soothing meditative bath. Dressing you in a white gown, you enter the pool and float there for some time. As your body floats, you begin to have visions. These visions are so clear at the forefront of your mind. Breathe here and take note what images come up for you....

Pause for about two minutes

After bathing and cleansing yourself in the waters, you dry yourself and the lady then asks you to sit on a cushion in front of an altar carved into the rock. She provides you with some fruit and chocolate and begins to anoint your hair and skin with this lush fragrant oil. Dressing you in a fine silk robe she tells you "My lady is ready to see you now" and ushers you to another door leading into a subterranean walkway lit by tea lights.

Finally at the bottom of the stairs you walk into a snug chamber aglow with lanterns on the walls and figurines dotted along a stone shelf. A lady reclining on a bed of cushions is waiting with a warm smile and a patera of water sits in front of her.

Take a moment to visualise what this lady looks like to you in your mind's eye, her hair, her eyes, what she is wearing, her physique and personality....

She says "Come, look...peer into the water...what do you see?" and you kneel in front of her to glance into the rippling mirror. Take a moment here to bring what you see in the water into your mind's eye. What are you seeing? Is this a relevant message for you? Can you decipher the symbols? Is what you are seeing a memory? A flower? Words forming a poem? A weather system or another body of water? A place or person? What comes to you at this moment....

Pause for two minutes

The dreaming priestess places a cloth over the patera and gazes into your eyes. She tells you to join her in the dreaming world, that the use of water is a wonderful scrying technique but that we can attain messages from other realms from wakeful dreaming.

Imagine yourself now lying down on cushions in this mantic cave, get comfortable and close your eyes. Imagine the priestess chanting an ancient lullaby – hymn to help you deepen your dreaming journey.

Here you fall into a state of wakeful dreaming and you can travel through any and all portals. You have absolute freedom to explore where you go and who you meet...Keep on breathing deeply and calmly and stay connected to your heart beat to keep you grounded...

Long Pause for Dreaming (Five Minutes or More)

You've been journeying for some time now. You have been given the message you need. It is time to go back.

Slowly you begin to drift out of the portal and into the cave with the priestess, she is sat cheerily upright pouring you a new cup of tea. She watches you waking up...

You stretch and open your eyes and you feel serene.

You chat with her for a while before hugging her goodbye and you head back up the stairs lit by candles.

The lady by the altar is awaiting you and she gives you a gift before you leave, note what it is that she hands to you.

You hug her goodbye and walk out gently into the bright light and warmth of the full sun and follow the cobbled path back up the hill, waving goodbye to the town's people.

You come to the door with the symbol on it and walk through it, back into your heart chamber.

Sitting back in this space, you begin to have awareness again of your present moment, of your breathing and heartbeat.

Keep on noticing your breath, guiding you back into your room.

Inhale....

Exhale....

And when you are ready.... Open your eyes.

Take a pause here to orientate yourself, take a few sips of tea to ground you.

After a spell, spend some time writing down what you experienced and the images and symbols that were invoked on this dream journey. Once you've scribbled down the bare bones of it, you can then craft it into a prose poem or short story. Let your poem or prose become the vessel of the energy summoned from your meeting with the dreaming priestess.

Meeting a Tree Spirit inside the realms of your heart

The Druid path communes with trees and all of nature, whether physically or in the subtle realms. Many bards were druids and as I stated earlier were known as 'carpenters of song', perhaps this epithet is in reference to their connection with the natural world and their inspiration to channel words for poetry and song comes from their relationship with tree spirits? Find a comfortable and quiet place, feel free to play relaxing music and take a few deep breaths.

Relax your body, rest your active mind. See yourself on the sofa just resting.

Breathe into the centre, coming to rest, bring your focus into your inner light.

Find your glowing heart, here you'll see a door, open that door and walk through.

And from here you enter a natural landscape. There is a meadow, your feet are bare, have a look around at this lush place.

At the horizon you see a mountain, this is a vast and regal mountain, you feel its energy. Contemplate any thoughts and messages that come up for you from this mountain.

This mountain is the guardian of this place.

Close by there is also a river and you walk alongside it.

With every step you feel lighter and more in tune with this sacred space.

To your left there is a grove of trees, it's a vast forest. And walking through the forest you feel pulled to go a certain direction...Follow it with curiosity.

In the distance you see a very old tree, which you approach with respect and presence. Connect with her beauty and her wisdom, in your mind's eye picture what kind of tree she is. She has been here for aeons! She is the guardian of this forest within your heart space. Standing in front of her, and say hello and be in gratitude in meeting her.

Ask permission to enter her portal, to be given access to her wisdom with you.

Here you may see a sign that tells you this tree welcomes you – a soft gust of wind, a butterfly? Perhaps her leaves fall on you? This signals that you may enter, but first you give an offering of sage, sweetgrass or perhaps a flower, a poem, clootie or pebble. And then a door opens at the trunk of the tree. Inside the tree as you step in. Looks so much bigger!

Inside it is dark and cosy like a womb space and you see another door on the other side.

This door opens by itself and we come out of the back of the tree into a landscape not of this earth, it is not the earthly plane. It is radiant and golden. Its frequency feels lighter, softer, warmer. I invite you to look around, what do you see and feel? It is a sacred place of beauty.

Sitting at the trunk of the tree, lean back and feel held in this space.

Take a deep breath, close your eyes, become one with this tree.

She nurtures you with life force. With love.

Notice some of your negative thoughts and worries are being transformed by her presence. Her knowledge is so vast because her roots go deep and entwine with the energies of mother earth and her branches reach so high up to the cosmos within and around you.

You feel your worries being released from you, transformed into flowers and blown away.

With every breath you feel one with this tree and its spirit, you are rooting and being held by the earth. Feel the soil, the ley lines, the quartz- the heart centre of the earth. You feel more centred here. Feel this energy rise up through you like a kundalini spirit, through your spine, your chakras, into your heart and third eye. Feel the energy of this tree soothe your womb space. This grandmother tree asks you to consider your sacred path and invites you to have compassion for yourself and others which may have caused pain throughout your life.

Love it and let go. Do not let all these dark experiences darken your light.

Hug the hurt dearly, tell it you love it and let go. There is no blame or shame. There are things that happened to you but it is not yours, do not hold it in your body, womb or heart. Like this tree, shed your pain like the falling leaves. Feel it fall away from you softly. Whilst you are contemplating these thoughts, you begin to hear a shaman drumming and chanting which calls to your imagination, this is your poetry portal. This is a soul connection. Now there is an energy coming towards you. Perhaps a sparkle. A different colour. It turns into another portal in front of you. This is going deep into your heart space. This is your sacred origin. It is a bridge that opens. Paint this bridge in your mind's eye- is it golden? A rainbow bridge? A bridge made of chocolate? This is your place. Take a moment to breathe and create this space, notice any words that flow through this portal to you.

As you step through you see a presence coming towards you. Who or what is it? Notice who or what is coming forward? Take in their energy. They offer a hand; they are smiling at you with love. Is this presence old, young, feminine, masculine, is it human, motherly, playful, serious, wild, regal, stoic? This being now sits in front of you, welcoming you to join them Feel this energy from the ancestral realms. of the cosmic dimensions.

Allow yourself to meet this archetype within your heart. Golden fibres flow from you to them, creating a sacred connection. Allow their medicine to flow through to your heart space. Be reminded in this present moment of the sacredness of life itself and that you are part of this great big cosmic dance. Know that you are invited to deepen and strengthen your relationship with this being who will guide you and love you on your journey. Imagine the medicine feeding your heart. Know that you can share this love with the grandmother tree. Everything around you start to connect with this golden fibre, it is overflowing and pulsating with your heart beat. As you connect, give thanks and gratitude.

What messages are being shared with you from this being? What do you need to hear today? What gifts are being exchanged? The connection has been established. There is now a sacred bond between your heart and the heart of this being. The being hugs you goodbye and offers you a gift, and walks back over the bridge. The fibres slowly disappear. The portal closes. And you walk through the grandmother tree – giving thanks to her and this sacred place. Walking through the door and out the other side. You come back to the grove. For a moment you stand, holding the gift given to you. You open the box to see what it is, what do you see? What are you bringing back with you? Walking along the river, looking back at the majestic mountain, you bow in its presence. As you continue walking, the grove disappears and you come back to your centre. Back to the room you are in, back to your breath. Inhale all the love you've shared at this moment. Exhale out love for others and the planet. Take a deep breath and when you are ready open your eyes.

Once you feel centred back in your room, brew yourself a cup of tea and treat yourself perhaps to some cake to ground you and when you're ready, journal what came up for you? What allegorical symbols presented themselves in your heart space? Consider their meaning for you. You may choose to leave this activity as a journaling exercise or create a poem inspired by this visual journey.

Heart Alchemy Visual Journey for the Heart Chakra

The ancient yogis believed that there was an actual centre of spiritual consciousness, called the "lotus of the heart", situated between the abdomen and the thorax. It is said that it had the form of a lotus flower and that it shone with an inner light, it was beyond sorrow. If the body is thought of as a busy and noisy city, then we can imagine that, in the middle of this city resides a shrine, and that, within this shrine, the Atman, our real nature, is present. As Rabia of Basra says "In my soul, there is a temple, a shrine, a mosque, a church that dissolves, that dissolves in God."

In Eastern tradition, the secret chamber of the heart is described as an eight petaled lotus or chakra called Ananda-Kanda "The root of bliss". And within this sanctuary abides your divine spark, your light, your union with spirit.

With eyes closed, take some deep breaths and keep your attention from all outer circumstances. Each time you exhale, consciously release your tensions and worries. Now centre all of your energy and attention on your heart chakra, feel the music pulse with your heart. See in your mind's eye the intensity of the sun and transfer that globe of light to the centre of your chest. You are aware of nothing else but this sphere of light. Take another deep breath and as you exhale, visualise yourself gently descending into the sphere of light, energy and consciousness, that is your radiant heart chakra.

You are entering it entirely, moving further away from the limiting dimensions of time and space. Allow the golden light to pull you towards it. Travelling deeper and closer to this light you come to the heart gate, the door to your temple. Your heart-door has been waiting for you to let in some light. Visualise yourself walking to this gate as though you would enter a temple, paint a picture in your mind's eye of what your shrine or temple looks like, what offerings can you picture in your hand, are these offerings personal to you? In your mind's eye, decorate the door? What material is it made of? What is its shape, colour and size? This is your temple, play with your imagination, it can be as down to earth or as magical as you like. Begin to feel the divine stillness of perfect love and compassion.

This is an inner experience, you are one with the cosmos, you see Devi or goddess standing at the gate waiting for you, Devi is you, your higher self, for Devi is a Sanskrit word meaning "she who shines"'. Take a moment to visualise what Devi (or Deva) represents to you, how are they dressed, how do they smell? Are they accompanied by an animal, flower or gift for you? what are their features, their age, size? Are they human? Do they have a message for you? Do you have a message or heartfelt prayer for them? When you meet this inner you, does it feel like coming home? Or is this wonderfully new? What emotions are coming up? Take a moment to be with Devi. Devi directs your attention to the sacred flame. Your divine spark that burns at the centre of the altar. This is the place you go for alteration- for transformation, for alchemy.

It is here we leave behind an outworn portion of ourselves, like leaving our shoes outside the temple before we enter it. Visualise yourself shedding layers of your aura that are ready to be discarded. See them fall to the ground for mama earth to take or burn them away in your sacred flame. Fold your hands at the centre of your chest. Feel the beating of your heart and see your divine flame on the altar of your heartgate. Picture the flame with three parts, give them different colours, the first represents divine power, the second embodies divine wisdom and the third radiates with divine love.

First chamber: *Walking through the heartgate, passing the garden and into the first chamber. Visualise a room fruitful with nature, in your mind's eye describe the plants that you see, touch and smell- notice what flowers or plants you are drawn to? Pick that flower and hold it lovingly to your chest. Picture the sky- is it day or night or maybe twilight or dawn? Really tune in and feel, use all your senses to bring the elements to life. Is it hot, cold, raining, muddy, foggy, humid, quiet, noisy with bird song? This is your earth space, where the elements roam. In the centre of this chamber is a bonfire, walk to it and picture how it looks- is it burning brightly or flickering gently? Are you alone or perhaps another is sat by the fire? This fire is where you will set your summer solstice intentions? Write down your intentions on a piece of paper, fold this paper up, say a prayer and when you are ready, throw this intention into the fire. Releasing your magic into the great cosmos.*

Second Chamber: *Stepping away from the bonfire and walking though the field or jungle, you see another door, open it and walk through... Inside the second chamber is a minimal room with boxes of numerous sizes all about you, of different shades and textures. One particular box grabs your attention, notice its appearance and its function, what energy does it give off? Walk to it and open it. Peer inside. This is a gift for you but this is also a gift from you. Your gift to the world. What is this gift? What is the object you are now holding in your hands? What does this object mean to you? What are your gifts? Do you want to share with the world or keep as a keepsake? What feelings come up as you hold this object that represents a special gift?*

Third Chamber: *Putting your flower from the first chamber into the box with your gift, you walk to the back of the room to another door* *and into the third chamber. Here you stand by a giant waterfall and lake, take a moment to breathe in the silky taste of the air and cooling energy of the water, perhaps you dive in and go for a swim? Really tap into how the water flows and feelings....*

I guide you to walk behind the waterfall and into a cave covered in crystals, they shimmer all around you. From the back of the cave a shadow slowly comes towards you, you are not afraid because it feels familiar and you coax this being to come into the light. Slowly you start to see its features, it is an animal of some kind. The closer it gets to you the easier it is to discover this is your power animal. With your mind's eye begin to truly see this animal as it stands by your side. Notice its patterns and its body language, how is this animal responding to you? be receptive and free of preconceptions. It may or may not be the animal you were anticipating, or it may be more than one animal. It may even be a mythological animal. Once you see the animal, watch it carefully to see what it does. Open your spiritual ears to any and all messages, whether they are feelings or words, colours, sounds or something else entirely. Notice.

Fourth Chamber: *Walking to the back of the cave you notice the final door and walk through it. Notice if your power animal walks with you or remains in the cave also. This final chamber is covered in letters and scrolls. These are all good memories or words of love you have stored inside your heart since the day you were born. Take in the smell and texture of the paper. On a chair you notice a person sitting there waiting for you, who are they? Perhaps a loving relative who has passed, a guide, an ancestor, an angelic being. You feel their love for you radiate and envelop you so you run to them to embrace them. You've missed them so much! Spend a few moments taking their image in, smiling at you with so much love. Holding your hands they say "I have a message for you" and they hand you a scroll tied with a ribbon. Gently opening it you read out the short message or word. This message comes directly from your heart and from source. This is* *the message you will take with you out into the world and everyday life. Hold on to those words, what do they mean to you?*

It is time to go now, so you say goodbye to your loved one, put your scroll inside your box with your flower and your gift. And all the chambers begin to gently fade away until you are back outside of your temple, closing your heart gate, or perhaps you keep it open? Or slightly ajar? Devi is there smiling, waiting to greet you. She holds you close and reminds you of your beauty, your strength, your courage, your love. Everything you need is already within you and whenever you feel as though life is too much, you can come back to your temple residing in your heart and visit your chambers. This is home, this is your sanctuary. You are a scientist of the spirit; you are an alchemist on a hero's journey. What you create every day can be a new expression of love, compassion, mercy, patience, devotion and forgiveness...If you want it to be, if you want to open up your heart door and let in the light and allow for the magic to manifest.

You may wish to listen to this visual journey on my SoundCloud for *FREE*: https://soundcloud.com/katie-wild-yogi

Part III

"She who knows the secret of sound, knows the mystery of the whole universe."

— Hazrat Inayat Khan

Closing the Circle

Wander, Weave and Write with Freedom
Blessing & Healing Prayer

This is what I know. Poetry, like thread on a loom, weaves the intangible into tangible textured patterns. Writing conjures and calls forth energies we can wield, alchemise and transmute.

Poetry and writing are a codex for sharing – whether in women's healing and goddess circles or covens, or sharing as part of a solitary ritual to goddess. The ancient priestesses understood the power of poetry, chanting votive hymns to invoke deity in fragrant temples and the witchy wise women of old understood the importance of canticles, charms and casting as they cackle under the moonlight, warning us *'Be careful what you wish for!'*

Sometimes this energy pops, cracks and sizzles with the tumultuous frenzy of a storm and the collapse of our Towers, other times it is like a river cascading from pen to paper, pouring onto parchment with Ace of Cups abandon. I believe in the potency of poetry-magic and word-craft to spellcast and ritualise our lives.

The murmuring frequencies of grief, lullaby prayers of birth and the arduous hymns of life flow through us with the alchemy of Temperance and The Star's grace – always shimmering, and orbiting currents of shadows and light, towards a new trajectory on numerous horizons as a way to cultivate, generate, articulate or excavate something alive, something holy yet intrinsic as we navigate our pilgrim's path to *psyche* in communion with the *Anima Mundi*.

To close the circle, we will call in Brigid, Celtic goddess of women, wisdom, poetry, water, alchemical force of fire, traditional craft and skills, knowledge, healing and much more. Brigid is the mistress that embodies the perfect balance of water and fire (yin and yang, Ida and Pingala, masculine and feminine) Her origins are said to have spread from Southern Germany to Turkey, Spain and finally Britain and Europe, thus making her a woman of the world. A woman who represents *all* women and our abilities for craft, skills and healing.

Described as the 'Exalted One', she is patroness of poets, healers, midwives, newborns and craftspeople. Known to be the inventor of Keening (lamenting the dead) makes her not only a goddess of life and birth, but also of death. Minerva, Athena and Saraswati are said to have similar qualities to her. *Brigid's Way Celtic Pilgrimage*, is Ireland's version of the Camino de Santiago trail. The Brigid Pilgrimage is a nine-day route from her fire temple in Faughart, Louth to her Wells in Kildare.

I wanted to close this space with a blessing spell working with Brigid as sister-goddess to Minerva, whom I opened the book with because both are two faces of many sides of The Goddess and the many facets of women. You may wish to perform this ritual at one of Brigid's sacred sites in Ireland, how lovely would that be? Or wherever you like. This is a blessing for everyone and wishing for world peace.

You will need:

Pen and paper
Blue candle
Blue Ribbon
Cup of water

Begin by lighting the candle and bringing your hands to your heart. Call in Brigid's loving and healing presence. Ask her to send warmth and feelings of safety and sanctuary to those in need. Ask her to send clean water and abundance for those who are struggling. Ask her to send out healing, resilience and protection to women and children surviving in places of conflict, war, violence and poverty and as a result are experiencing grief, loss, fear, displacement, unsafety, lack of sustenance insecurity and more. May Brigid's healing light flow through to these women suffering under regime's, dictatorship, communism and patriarchy. May sons be born who pave the way for peace, who respect and care for women. To bring balance of the masculine and feminine back to our global community.

Think of these women now, these voiceless faces and pray that one day they will be liberated to speak and chant and sing and write with absolute freedom. May they one day cast poem spells to the mountains and embody their words to weave new worlds of love, safety, sovereignty and serenity.

Take out your pen and paper and write a prayer to Brigid, petition her to protect and bless those in our lives and in the world who do not have a voice, who are disempowered and in pain. Ask for her sacred waters to be a cool healing balm to cease fiery conflict and ask her gentle flame to create a loving, warm hearth. Direct energies of compassion and kindness to these women and children now.

Notice Brigid's presence with you now, imagine her blue cloak and open arms holding those in need of sanctuary and healing.

Use the technique of candle gazing to divinate words, visualise Brigid or invoke the faces of those struggling. You may call on your ancestors as well, those who came before you and whose struggles have passed but live on through you. You can be a breaker of chains and heal ancestral wounds right now in this prayer-poem. Connect with your heart and send out love on the wings of a giant dove.

When you feel you have completed the prayer, read it out softly into the flame and water. You may wish to roll it up like a scroll or fold it up and put it in a sacred place.

Take your blue ribbon and hold it over the candle to imbue it with Brigid's flame (be safe, don't set it on fire). And then dip the ribbon in the water to bathe it in her healing waters.

Take the ribbon outside and hang it on your door or window sill. In Celtic tradition it is believed the ribbon will be touched by St Brigid on her travels, imbuing the fabric with protective energy that will ripple out on the wind towards humans and animals who are in need of healing.

You may keep your ribbon in the sacred place with your prayer to use again for invoking healing. *Optional:* it can be sewn into clothing as a protective talisman for the wearer or added to a flower wreath and you can continue adding Brigid healing ribbons to your wreath every time you perform this blessing ritual. Or create wreaths with Brigid ribbons to give to loved ones, perhaps during Imbolc?

With words we summon our sovereign magical voices and awaken the voices of the women who have gone unheard and silenced, their magic choked and defamed. Priestesses have watched their temples crumble as monotheism squats on ruined goddess sanctuaries, their scriptures and libraries burned to the ground. And our wise women tortured and slain upon the rise of the witch trials, left neglected in unmarked graves on haunted hillsides – their grimoires disappear from historical records and anchorite's preferring devotional solitude so they can write prayers and mystical journals in communion with the divine, undisturbed by the patriarchal constraint.

May we now remember and honour those priestesses, poetesses and mystical women who shaped their spells through poetry and divinatory writings which were almost, or have been lost to obscurity. May we honour our sisters and raise each other up. May all of us honour our words, speak and write with intention, integrity, kindness and truth.

May we honour our own voices, may our word magic reverberate across the sands of time.

May all of us one day be completely free to embody the energy of the word. May we all feel free to wander and roam, free to write what we Will into being and weave our worlds with words.

Extra Poetry/Writing Prompts

For inspiration. Simple creative writing prompts if you're stuck with writer's block or have never tried word-craft before.

Have a journal to hand, these are just exercises to help you practice writing with intention.

- The longer I live, the more I realise that…
- Thank your physical body for all it does for you.
- Write some prose describing the rain.
- Honour a country you have visited, describe the location, the weather, the memory.
- Gratitude poem: Describe the last time you walked barefoot on the grass; how can you express your gratitude to the earth?
- Write an ode to something or someone…
- Heartbreak has taught me…
- Write a poem about a sacred site you visited, describe the landscape, the weather, flora and fauna and how you travelled there.
- Write a letter to someone you want to forgive. You don't have to send it.
- Journal about the greatest lesson a mentor has taught you.
- Revisit your last nightmare, describe it and bring its shadows to the light.
- Concentrate on an area of your body you struggle to like, write a poem about it to see its sacred beauty.
- Connect with a tarot card you feel most resembles you right now, journal about what comes up for you then write a poem about those energies and feelings.

- Write a poetic prayer to a deity of your choice, consider what feelings come up for you as you think of words to describe their energy and your emotions.
- Concentrate on a part of your body, let an organ or feature speak to you, what does it say? What feelings are coming up?
- If you were in a room with everyone you've ever met, who comes to mind instantly? Who would be the one you'd look for?
- If you had the chance to relive one day of your life, what day would that be? Describe it.
- If your future self-sent you a letter, what advice or insight would you hope to read? Write it!
- If someone gave you a box of everything you've ever loved (and also lost), what is the first thing you'd look for? Describe your feelings at that moment.
- What energy do you wish to leave on this earth, what propels you forward and brings joy and purpose? Journal how that influences your daily life.
- If you could revisit a dream you had, what would it be? Dedicate a poem to it.
- If you could revisit a moment of your past, what moment would you choose and why? Would you change it or leave it?

Journal your thoughts...

Bibliography

All these books, articles and videos listed were part of my research for this book. I've separated them into sub-categories in case there's a particular topic of interest to you.

Non-Fiction books

Fantastic books I highly recommend to continue your word witchery journey

Beyer, T., Hemphill, D. and White, L. (2023). *Poetry as Spellcasting*. North Atlantic Books.

Herne, R. (2012). *Bard Song*. John Hunt Publishing.

Lisa Marie Basile (2020). *The Magical Writing Grimoire*. Fair Winds Press.

Tinker, F. (2012). *Pagan Portals – Pathworking Through Poetry*. John Hunt Publishing.

Pagan Portals Books that furthered my general research

Patterson, R. (2023). *Pagan Portals – Gods & Goddesses of England*. John Hunt Publishing.

Jhenah Telyndru (2018). *Pagan Portals – Rhiannon*. John Hunt Publishing.

Joanna (2014). *Pagan Portals – The Awen Alone*. John Hunt Publishing.

Lucya Starza (2018). *Pagan Portals – Poppets and Magical Dolls*. Moon Books.

Teixeira, J. (2021). *Pagan Portals – Temple of the Bones*. John Hunt Publishing.

Brannen, C. (2019). *Keeping Her Keys*. John Hunt Publishing.

History books related to the topics of goddess worship or the importance of magical writing and poetry

Bogin, M. (1980). *The women troubadours*. New York: Norton.

Bowden, H. (2010). *Mystery cults of the ancient world.* London: Thames & Hudson.

Crerar, B. and British Museum (2022). *Feminine power: the divine to the demonic.* London: The British Museum Press.

Dashu, M. (2016). *Witches and Pagans: Women in European Folk religion, 700-1100.* Richmond, Ca: Velona Press.

Enheduanna and De, B. (2006). *Inanna, Lady of Largest Heart: poems of the Sumerian high priestess Enheduanna.* Austin: University Of Texas Press.

Graves, R. (2000). *The white goddess: a historical grammar of poetica myth.* New York: Noonday Press.

Greer, M.K. (1996). *Women of the Golden Dawn.* Park Street Press.

Hammer, J. and Taya Shere (2015). *The Hebrew priestess: ancient and new visions of Jewish women's spiritual leadership.* Teaneck, New Jersey: Ben Yehuda Press.

Haynes, N. (2022). *Pandora's jar: women in Greek myths.* New York, NY: Harper Perennial.

Hughes, B. (2019). *Venus and Aphrodite.* Hachette UK.

Rao, A. and Mahesh, S. (2024). *How to Love in Sanskrit.* Harper Collins.

Sorita d'Este and Rankine, D. (2009). *Hekate liminal rites: a study of rituals, magic and symbols of the torch-bearing triple goddess of the crossroads.* London: Avalonia.

Tikva Simone Frymer-Kensky (1992). *In the Wake of the Goddesses.* Random House Publishing Group (10 Feb. 1993).

Wellesley, M. (2022). *HIDDEN HANDS: the lives of manuscripts and their makers.* S.L.: Riverrun.

Wilkinson, T.H. (2016). *Writings from ancient Egypt.* London UK: Penguin Books.

Watterson, M. (2018). *The Divine Feminine Oracle.* Hay House.

Poetry Books

Bly, R., Mīrābāī and Hirshfield, J. (2004). *Mirabai: ecstatic poems.* Boston, Mass: Beacon Press.

Carmichael, A. (1971). *Carmina Gadelica: Hymns and Incantations.* Edinburgh: Scottish Acad. Press.

Ceisiwr Serith (2020). *The Big Book of Pagan Prayer and Ritual.* Weiser Books.

Christina Georgina Rossetti (2017). *Goblin Market and Other Poems.* London, UK Penguin Classics an Imprint of Penguin Books.

Davis, D. (2021). *The mirror of my heart: a thousand years of Persian poetry by women.* New York: Penguin Books.

Dickinson, E. (2013). *The Gorgeous Nothings.* New York: New Directions.

Gwerful Mechain and Gramich, K. (2018). *The Works of Gwerful Mechain.* Peterborough, Ontario, Canada: Broadview Press.

Lallācārya (1993). *Naked Song.* 2nd ed. Maypop Books.

Matthews, J. (2022). *Book of Celtic Verse.* National Geographic Books.

Rayor, D.J. (2023). *Sappho: A New Translation of the Complete Works.* Cambridge University Press; 2nd Edition.

Sappho (2009). *If Not, Winter.* Translated by Anne Carson. Vintage.

Shin, S. and Tamás, R. (2018). *Spells: 21st-century occult poetry.* Ignota Books.

Swami Satyananda Saraswati and Maa, S. (2018). *Devi Gita.* Temple of the Divine Mother, Inc.

Various and Ladinsky, D. (2002). *Love Poems from God.* Penguin.

Articles

Altuntas, L. and Buyukyildirim, O. (2024). *Love and hate in ancient times: Exploring Magical Texts.* [online] Arkeonews. Available at: https://arkeonews.net/love-and-hate-in-ancient-times-exploring-magical-texts/

Bate, R.A. (2020). *Reflections on Druidic Christology | Order of Bards, Ovates & Druids.* [online] Druidry.org. Available at: https://druidry.org/resources/reflections-on-druidic-christology [Accessed 23 May 2024]

Berry, S. (2016). *Trobairitz: The Lady Composers of Medieval France.* [online] Medium. Available at: https://medium.com/@sannieb/trobairitz-the-lady-composers-of-medieval-france-cd2a00a2c6be

David Nez (2015). *The Magician's Tomb.* [online] Tree of Visions. Available at: https://treeofvisions.wordpress.com/2015/10/02/the-magicians-tomb/

Ebrary. (n.d.). *Roman Poetry as Evidence for Ancient Magic.* [online] Available at: https://ebrary.net/67890/religion/roman_poetry_evidence_ancient_magic

Fisher, M. (2022). *Secret Stories of the Ancient Poets.* [online] Martini Fisher. Available at: https://martinifisher.com/2022/01/13/the-secret-stories-of-the-ancient-poets-of-the-celts/

Foundation, P. (2019). *Poetry as Magic by Katy Bohinc.* [online] Poetry Foundation. Available at: https://www.poetryfoundation.org/harriet-books/2019/09/poetry-as-magic

Fraaije, K. (2020). *Magical Verse from Early Medieval England: The Metrical Charms in Context.* [online] Available at: https://discovery.ucl.ac.uk/id/eprint/10132535/7/Karel%20Fraaije%20-%20Magical%20Verse%20from%20Early%20Medieval%20England%20PhD%20Thesis%20Deposited.pdf

Hare, J.B. (n.d.). *The Poems of Sappho: Introduction.* [online] sacred-texts.com. Available at: https://sacred-texts.com/cla/usappho/sph01.htm

Hellenistic History. (2021). *Hellenistic Women II: Nossis – Hellenistic History.* [online] Available at: https://www.hellenistichistory.com/2021/04/08/hellenistic-women-ii-nossis/

Hyland, M. (n.d.). *High Priestess Senshi.* [online] Women of 1000 AD. Available at: https://womenof1000ad.weebly.com/high-priestess-senshi.html

Interesting Literature. (2021). *10 of the Best Poems about Magic and the Supernatural.* [online] Available at: https://interestingliterature.com/2021/04/best-supernatural-poems-about-magic-enchantment

Kelly, J. (2016). *Irish Bards Could Kill Rats with Their Magical Poetry Powers*. [online] Slate. Available at: https://slate.com/human-interest/2016/06/irish-bards-were-rat-killers-according-to-poetry-and-folklore.html

LEFKOVITS, E. (2007). *Deciphering of earliest Semitic text reveals talk of snakes and spells*. [online] The Jerusalem Post | JPost.com. Available at: https://www.jpost.com/jewish-world/jewish-news/deciphering-of-earliest-semitic-text-reveals-talk-of-snakes-and-spells

Literary Hub. (2019). *On the Gleefully Indecent Poems of a Medieval Welsh Feminist Poet*. [online] Available at: https://lithub.com/on-the-gleefully-indecent-poems-of-a-medieval-welsh-feminist-poet/

Magazine, M. (2022). *Prayer and poetry: Enheduanna and the women of Mesopotamia | The Past*. [online] the-past.com. Available at: https://the-past.com/feature/prayer-and-poetry-enheduanna-and-the-women-of-mesopotamia

Mark, J. (2016). *The Magical Lullaby of Ancient Egypt*. [online] World History Encyclopedia. Available at: https://www.worldhistory.org/article/965/the-magical-lullaby-of-ancient-egypt/

Mark, J. (2019). *Twelve Famous Women of the Middle Ages*. [online] World History Encyclopedia. Available at: https://www.worldhistory.org/article/1350/twelve-famous-women-of-the-middle-ages/

Mark, J. (2022). *Hymn to Nisaba*. [online] World History Encyclopedia. Available at: https://www.worldhistory.org/article/2103/hymn-to-nisaba/

Micucci, F. (2021). *Love spells in the Greek Magical Papyri*. [online] Blogs.bl.uk. Available at: https://blogs.bl.uk/digitisedmanuscripts/2021/02/love-spells.html

Newsroom, A. (2021). *Direct evidence of the use of a mediaeval parchment birthing girdle*. [online] Archaeology Wiki. Available at: https://www.archaeology.wiki/blog/2021/03/10/direct-evidence-of-the-use-of-a-medieval-parchment-birthing-girdle/

Nongbri, B. (2023). *A Cursed Figurine.* [online] Variant Readings. Available at: https://brentnongbri.com/2023/01/07/a-cursed-figurine/

Pilkington, D.J. (2019). *Occult Poetics & (Soma)tic Rituals.* [online] Ignota. Available at: https://ignota.org/blogs/news/occult-poetics-somatic-rituals?fbclid=IwAR14_t94VBlLd4-tii-VPf0KlBwVQs9UvuHe-GycMomPY8-gpoh8b9M01qc

Psyche. (n.d.). *How poetry casts a spell through the rhythmic magic of metre | Psyche Ideas.* [online] Available at: https://psyche.co/ideas/how-poetry-casts-a-spell-through-the-rhythmic-magic-of-metre

Rosengren, A. (2017). *Invita Minerva: Going Against a Goddess.* [online] Latinitium. Available at: https://latinitium.com/invita-minerva-going-against-a-goddess/

Scholars, V. (n.d.). *Coptic Magical Papyri.* [online] Coptic Magical Papyri. Available at: https://www.coptic-magic.phil.uni-wuerzburg.de/ Our goal is to advance the study of the corpus of Coptic 'magical texts' – manuscripts written on papyrus, as well as parchment, paper, ostraca and other materials, and attesting to private religious practices designed to cope with the crises of daily life in Egypt.

Seyfzadeh, M. and Schoch, R. (2019). World's First Known Written Word at Göbekli Tepe on T-Shaped Pillar 18 Means God. *Archaeological Discovery*, 07(02), pp.31–53. doi:https://doi.org/10.4236/ad.2019.72003

Teo Eve (2022). *When Words Were Magic: Opening The Ox House.* [online] Nottingham City of Literature. Available at: https://nottinghamcityofliterature.com/blog/when-words-were-magic-opening-the-ox-house/

The Independent. (1997). *Is this Welsh princess the first British woman author?* [online] Available at: https://www.

independent.co.uk/news/is-this-welsh-princess-the-first-british-woman-author-1282555.html

Various Scholars (n.d.). *Ancient Celtic & Irish Magic, Spells and Rituals – Atlas Mythica.* [online] Atlas Mythica. Available at: https://atlasmythica.com/celtic-magic-spells-rituals-charms/

Wikipedia. (2024). *List of female poets.* [online] Available at: https://en.wikipedia.org/wiki/List_of_female_poets

Woodroffe, E.E. and Woodroffe, J.G. (1913). *Hymns to the Goddess / Translated from the Sanskrit by Arthur and Ellen Avalon [pseuds].* [online] Available at: https://iiif.wellcomecollection.org/pdf/b24875107

Videos/ Documentaries

Bettina Joy de Guzman (2022). *Hymn to Hathor: Spell 186. Book of the Dead, Ani Papyrus. Bettina Joy de Guzman. Ancient Egyptian.* [online] YouTube. Available at: https://www.youtube.com/watch?v=2hhVvtQ12r4

Dr Joanna Kujawa Spiritual Detective (2021). *Courtly Love and Cathar Women Dr Joanna Kujawa with Veronique Flayol.* [online] YouTube. Available at: https://www.youtube.com/watch?v=3DnMuvw7IP0&t=617s

Hughes, B. (2023). *Bettany Hughes' Treasures of the World.* [online] Channel4.com. Available at: https://www.channel4.com/programmes/bettany-hughes-treasures-of-the-world

Museum, T.M.L. (2022). *Lecture: She Who Wrote: Enheduanna and Women of Mesopotamia ca. 3400-2000 BC.* [online] www.youtube.com. Available at: https://www.youtube.com/watch?v=DlWewLEWbyM

Penn Museum (2018). *Expedition – Powerful Women of Ur.* [online] YouTube. Available at: https://www.youtube.com/watch?v=4jwxUcoHL5Y&t=13s

Sapphic (2021). *Sappho Love and Life on Lesbos – BBC Documentary 2015.* [online] www.youtube.com. Available at: https://www.youtube.com/watch?v=l0IGg1Bljug

SEIKILO Ancient World Music (2021). *Sappho's Ode to Aphrodite in ancient Greek | Performing*. [online] YouTube. Available at: https://www.youtube.com/watch?v=3onZPLXt_kw&t=126s

SEIKILO Ancient World Music (2022a). *Ancient Lyre – 1st Delphic Hymn by Lina Palera*. [online] YouTube. Available at: https://www.youtube.com/watch?v=jSxfCtHWKCo

SEIKILO Ancient World Music (2022b). *Evoking the Ancient Sicilian Chants – Sicilia Mia with Tita on Vocals*. [online] YouTube. Available at: https://www.youtube.com/watch?v=xZgrGqlfNOk

SEIKILO Ancient World Music (2023). *Ancient Lyre – Hymn to Muse Calliope & Apollo by Lina Palera*. [online] YouTube. Available at: https://www.youtube.com/watch?v=f32DthMNCHE

SEIKILO Ancient World Music (2024a). *Know Thyself (Γνῶθι Σεαυτόν) – The Ancient Philosophy of Self-Transformation #greece #philosophy*. [online] YouTube. Available at: https://www.youtube.com/watch?v=zCS0_G_5abs&t=1s

SEIKILO Ancient World Music (2024b). *Know Thyself (Γνῶθι Σεαυτόν) in the Nature of Our Bodies (e02) #greece #philosophy*. [online] YouTube. Available at: https://www.youtube.com/watch?v=85QuRgMdAWs

TEDx Talks (2023). *Reclaiming the Wisdom of the Feminine | Siobhan MacMahon | TEDxDunLaoghaire*. [online] YouTube. Available at: https://www.youtube.com/watch?v=3qXbWrGmk1E

World History Encyclopedia (2021). *Telesilla of Argos, the Greek Lyric Poetess who defeated Sparta*. [online] YouTube. Available at: https://www.youtube.com/watch?v=X2rotrkPhyA

Podcasts

94.6, R.F. (2023). *Siobhan Mac Mahon Interview – Ciara Lawless 18/07/23 by Ros FM 94.6*. [online] Spotify for Podcasters. Available at: https://podcasters.spotify.com/pod/show/rosfm/episodes/Siobhan-Mac-Mahon-Interview – Ciara-Lawless-180723-e272vf4/a-aa4uas8

Lister, K. (2023a). *Betwixt The Sheets: The History of Sex, Scandal & Society: Ancient Goddesses of Sex and War on Apple Podcasts.* [online] Apple Podcasts. Available at: https://podcasts.apple.com/gb/podcast/ancient-goddesses-of-sex-and-war/id1612090432?i=1000634920262 [Accessed 23 May 2024].

Lister, K. (2023b). *Betwixt The Sheets: The History of Sex, Scandal & Society: Cleopatra to Jane Austen: Perfumes of Powerful Women on Apple Podcasts.* [online] Apple Podcasts. Available at: https://podcasts.apple.com/gb/podcast/cleopatra-to-jane-austen-perfumes-of-powerful-women/id1612090432?i=1000627067460 [Accessed 23 May 2024].

Lister, K. (2024). *Betwixt The Sheets: The History of Sex, Scandal & Society: Kamasutra: The Ancient Playboy Manual on Apple Podcasts.* [online] Apple Podcasts. Available at: https://podcasts.apple.com/gb/podcast/kamasutra-the-ancient-playboy-manual/id1612090432?i=1000641996033

Unconscious, R. (2022). *RU205: KATY BOHINC PRESENTS 'POETRY AS MAGIC' – Rendering Unconscious.* [online] RenderingUnconscious.org. Available at: http://www.renderingunconscious.org/poetry/ru205-katy-bohinc-presents-poetry-as-magic

Biographies

Katie Ness is a knowledgeable writer, budding historian, and yoga instructor specialising in folklore and spirituality, holding a BA Honours in Fine Art from UCLAN, Level 4 certifications in Prehistoric Art and The History of Folklore from Oxford University, and extensive expertise in Yoga history, Vedic philosophy, Sanskrit and the Śākta Traditions from the Oxford Centre for Hindu Studies.

As a yoga instructor and wellness educator specialising in women's spirituality and health, Katie integrates yogic principles with pagan practices, priestess ceremonies and women's circles together with therapeutic arts and folk-crafts, and she also offers instruction on the history and philosophy of yoga, available as a guest teacher for teacher training programs.

She has been a contributing writer for Kindred Spirit Magazine, Femme Occulte, Witches Magazine, Occulture Magazine, Haunted Magazine, The Feminine Macabre, Girl God Books, The C Word Mag, Rebelle Society and You Aligned among a variety of others. Two of her short stories feature in Mulberry Literary and a book collection entitled 'Incurable' published with Running Wild Press. Her poetry is published widely with an array of anthologies and two poetry collections entitled 'Aphrodite Fever Dream' and 'Juggernaut'.

As of 2025, Katie is engaged in learning to play the Lyre Harp with Luthieros Traditional Music Company as well as workshops in corn dolly making and willow basket weaving while preparing to pursue her Master's degree in Occult/ Folklore History, focusing on sacred art and magical crafts.

In her free time she is a passionate globetrotter, she's explored more than 25 countries, backpacked through 5 of them, and even set down temporary roots in Cyprus, Bali, and Australia, all while pilgrimaging to sacred sites on her adventures!

As a devoted Bhakti Yogini of the Shakti tradition and initiated Magdalene Priestess, Katie beautifully weaves together her spiritual practice centred on the sacred feminine with hereditary hedgewitchery and folk magic.

Find her @katie_wild_witch

Siobhan Mac Mahon (MA Creative Writing UCD) is an Irish Poet and 'Word Witch' whose poetry speaks of the return of the Sacred Feminine and of our deep connection to the earth. She has been creating magic, mayhem and mischief with her words for over twenty-five years, collaborating with other artists to combine poetry with music, dance and with film.

Twice awarded Arts Council funding for her work, she has performed her poetry widely in the UK and Ireland. Some highlights include: The Brigid of Faughart Festival, Festival Mná, the Southbank Centre, London, Stanza Poetry Festival, Wicklow Arts Festival, Mountshannon Arts Festival, University of Vienna, Artemis International Festival – Spain, 100 Thousand Poets for Change, Italy. A Hennessey New Irish Writing winner, publications include: The Irish Times, Headstuff.org, Skylight 47, We'Moon and many anthologies including – Hallelujah for 50 Foot Women (Bloodaxe), Bloody Amazing and Washing Windows 4 (Arlen House). IG: @siobhanmacmahonpoet

Contributions:

Thank you to these wonderful women who wanted to be a part of this book and provided a ritual or spell. Since I wrote about goddesses and priestesses, I wanted this to be a sisterhood!

Wendy Rivera created the *'Embracing the Shadow'* and *'Sekhmet Poppet'* rituals

Lizzie Claridge created the *'Animal Protection Jar'* Spell

Johanna Reuter created the *'Soul Door Technique'* ritual
Jade Thorton created the *'Beyond the Veil'* Scrying ritual
Jodie Hansen created the *'Healing with Daisies'* ritual
Ninfa Sferlazzo-Hayes created *'The Hearth of Hestia'* ritual
Joanna Ruminska created *The foraging and tea cleansing* spell

Acknowledgements

I wrote this book and two poetry books plus a plethora of articles on a windows laptop that was falling apart. Held together with duct tape because the screen was coming away from the cracked keyboard, the battery was dying and the memory was struggling, crashing frequently. Thank you to my very tired laptop, who I kept gently saying "hang on a bit longer, just a bit longer". This laptop has journeyed with me to Bali, Australia, Cyprus, Tenerife and Sicily. Uprooted with me from Blackpool to London. We've travelled well together; it was my companion during my recovery from surviving an ectopic pregnancy and it has helped me manifest an abundance of writing projects during my healing. I can let it rest now, I asked so much of it and it kept chugging along with me to the very end. Maybe it's time to treat myself to a new one in celebration of the creation of this book.

I didn't have high tech gear and gadgets. Just this laptop, research books, google docs, a lot of passion and time on my hands whilst going through difficult and delicate health issues and the grief of losing two people very dear to me, I would have loved for them to see a physical copy, I know they'd be proud of me.

I came from nothing but faith, my beginnings quiet and humble, my voice small and only a handful of people who believed in me.

Thank you to Trevor at Moon Books and the Moon Books community for giving me a chance, I'm so happy to be part of the tribe!

Big thank you to Wendy, my Witch sister across the pond, you've been my ear for 12 months listening to snippets of the book, your guidance and ideas were invaluable. Thank you to

Dan Nickson (Dan the Druid) for advice on all things Celtic and Druidic, your wisdom is astounding. Thank you to 'Old Man Mark' Whitaker for gently pushing me and believing in my talents since my days working in Primark with you, cheering me up with your dark humour and sarcasm!

To Claire, for being a true friend, who stuck by me and saw my truth when things were harsh, for the looooooong video calls about nerdy things and for being the best history nerd friend one can ever have.

Despina, you are my muse of art and sacred beauty, thank you for telling me "Katie mou this book is important! You need to write it!", Sarah Steed thank you for your unwavering encouragement and kindness, your soothing voice calmed my imposter syndrome!

Cath thank you for championing me from the moment we met in the gift shop *Athena* and just being so lovely, thank you Sofia for your playful, gentle spirit and your child-like wonder at the world. Cherise my 'mermaid twin' with the biggest heart, thank you for the sharings. Sharada Devi, your beautiful teachings of Vedanta and the goddess paved the way and opened that door to ritualise my life and connect with the energies of Saraswati and Lakshmi within me.

Nicole Mahabir, my teacher of all things Ayu-Yog, thank you for mentoring me with your overflowing wisdom that is often misunderstood or less known in the West.

Diana, Selena, Emily, Lynn, Trystan, Jo, Maddie, Jodie, Joanna, Tracey and others for just being good people who kept my spirits up.

Thank you to Soumyajeet Chattaraji and Ashton August for being the very first editors of online platforms to publish my articles back in 2014. Big thank you to the Femme Occulte team for taking a chance on me and being the first *witchy* magazine to see my potential and knowledge. Thank you to

Occulture, the Feminine Macabre and Witches magazine and others for the further opportunities that opened more doors for me.

Mrs Hesp, my English teacher in high school, when other teachers were giving up on me, she saw my potential and encouraged my writing and I surpassed my peers. Look at me now, I wrote a book!

Phil, no words can express just how much I miss you, you saw my potential back in 2010, took me under your wing and never gave up on me. I wish you were here seeing what you made of me, I hope you're proud.

To Hazel, my heart is broken upon learning of your passing (June 2024). You nurtured the creative and mystical side to me, I feel incredibly blessed to have received your unconditional love and support for 20 years of my life, you would have loved this book as I know you love Moon Books Pagan Portal series. Goodnight and God bless to you both, fly free!

Saving the best until last, Craig, the love of my life, my bestest friend, thank you for all the cuddles, copious amounts of tea, foot massages and listening to me at stupid O'clock reciting poetry and paragraphs out to you, your patience and love makes me feel like a Queen. Your love is the truest magic.

To all those I have not named, thank you for your smiles and the joy you brought to my life. To my readers, thank you for investing in my book, I hope you enjoyed it?

For my ancestors – I hope I've broken some chains. For potential descendants – I hope I've illuminated the way so you can be free in your self-expression, word magic and voices.

For all the women world-wide whose words have been silenced, may you be blessed one day to live, speak and write with freedom.

For all those who consider words sacred. My gratitude is yours.

aim hrīṃ om sarasvatyai namaḥ
om hrīṃ srīṃ paramalakṣmyai namaḥ

"Tiamat uttered wild, piercing cries, She trembled and shook to her very foundations. She recited an incantation, she pronounced her spell."

— ENUMA ELISH: THE EPIC OF CREATION

MOON BOOKS

PAGANISM & SHAMANISM

What is Paganism? A religion, a spirituality, an alternative belief system, nature worship? You can find support for all these definitions (and many more) in dictionaries, encyclopedias, and text books of religion, but subscribe to any one and the truth will evade you. Above all Paganism is a creative pursuit, an encounter with reality, an exploration of meaning and an expression of the soul. Druids, Heathens, Wiccans and others, all contribute their insights and literary riches to the Pagan tradition. Moon Books invites you to begin or to deepen your own encounter, right here, right now.

If you have enjoyed this book, why not tell other readers by posting a review on your preferred book site.

Bestsellers from Moon Books

Keeping Her Keys

An Introduction to Hekate's Modern Witchcraft

Cyndi Brannen

Blending Hekate, witchcraft and personal development together to create a powerful new magickal perspective.

Paperback: 978-1-78904-075-3 ebook 978-1-78904-076-0

Journey to the Dark Goddess

How to Return to Your Soul

Jane Meredith

Discover the powerful secrets of the Dark Goddess and transform your depression, grief and pain into healing and integration.

Paperback: 978-1-84694-677-6 ebook: 978-1-78099-223-5

Shamanic Reiki

Expanded Ways of Working with Universal Life Force Energy

Llyn Roberts, Robert Levy

Shamanism and Reiki are each powerful ways of healing; together, their power multiplies. Shamanic Reiki introduces techniques to help healers and Reiki practitioners tap ancient healing wisdom.

Paperback: 978-1-84694-037-8 ebook: 978-1-84694-650-9

Southern Cunning

Folkloric Witchcraft in the American South

Aaron Oberon

Modern witchcraft with a Southern flair, this book is a journey through the folklore of the American South and a look at the power these stories hold for modern witches.

Paperback: 978-1-78904-196-5 ebook: 978-1-78904-197-2

Bestsellers from Moon Books
Pagan Portals Series

The Morrigan

Meeting the Great Queens

Morgan Daimler

Ancient and enigmatic, the Morrigan reaches out to us. On shadowed wings and in raven's call, meet the ancient Irish goddess of war, battle, prophecy, death, sovereignty, and magic.

Paperback: 978-1-78279-833-0 ebook: 978-1-78279-834-7

The Awen Alone

Walking the Path of the Solitary Druid

Joanna van der Hoeven

An introductory guide for the solitary Druid, The Awen Alone will accompany you as you explore, and seek out your own place within the natural world.

Paperback: 978-1-78279-547-6 ebook: 978-1-78279-546-9

Moon Magic

Rachel Patterson

An introduction to working with the phases of the Moon, what they are and how to live in harmony with the lunar year and to utilise all the magical powers it provides.

Paperback: 978-1-78279-281-9 ebook: 978-1-78279-282-6

Hekate

A Devotional

Vivienne Moss

Hekate, Queen of Witches and the Shadow-Lands, haunts the pages of this devotional bringing magic and enchantment into your lives.

Paperback: 978-1-78535-161-7 ebook: 978-1-78535-162-4

Readers of ebooks can buy or view any of these bestsellers by clicking on the live link in the title. Most titles are published in paperback and as an ebook. Paperbacks are available in traditional bookshops. Both print and ebook formats are available online.

Find more titles and sign up to our readers' newsletter www.collectiveinkbooks.com/paganism

For video content, author interviews and more, please subscribe to our YouTube channel.

MoonBooksPublishing

Follow us on social media for book news, promotions and more:

Facebook: Moon Books

Instagram: @MoonBooksCI

X: @MoonBooksCI

TikTok: @MoonBooksCI